Using Microsoft® InfoPath® 2010 with Microsoft® SharePoint® 2010

Step by Step

Darvish Shadravan
Laura Rogers

Published with the authorization of Microsoft Corporation by:
O'Reilly Media, Inc.
1005 Gravenstein Highway North
Sebastopol, California 95472

ISBN: 978-0-7356-6206-3

Sixth Printing: June 2014

Printed and bound in the United States of America.

Microsoft Press books are available through booksellers and distributors worldwide. If you need support related to this book, email Microsoft Press Book Support at *mspinput@microsoft.com*. Please tell us what you think of this book at *http://www.microsoft.com/learning/booksurvey*.

Microsoft and the trademarks listed at *http://www.microsoft.com/about/legal/en/us/IntellectualProperty/Trademarks/EN-US.aspx* are trademarks of the Microsoft group of companies. All other marks are property of their respective owners.

The example companies, organizations, products, domain names, email addresses, logos, people, places, and events depicted herein are fictitious. No association with any real company, organization, product, domain name, email address, logo, person, place, or event is intended or should be inferred.

This book expresses the authors' views and opinions. The information contained in this book is provided without any express, statutory, or implied warranties. Neither the authors, O'Reilly Media, Inc., Microsoft Corporation, nor its resellers, or distributors will be held liable for any damages caused or alleged to be caused either directly or indirectly by this book.

Acquisitions and Developmental Editor: Kenyon Brown
Production Editor: Adam Zaremba
Editorial Production: Octal Publishing, Inc.
Technical Reviewer: Jonathan Wynn
Copyeditor: Richard Carey
Indexer: Potomac Indexing, LLC
Cover Composition: Karen Montgomery
Illustrator: Robert Romano

This book is dedicated to my parents and my family.
Thank you for your support, love, and assistance during the past few months;
it was much needed...

—Darvish Shadravan

For Charlotte and Kristen: you are the most wonderful daughters in the world,
and you are growing up to be such amazing little ladies.

—Laura Rogers

Contents

What do you think of this book? We want to hear from you!

Microsoft is interested in hearing your feedback so we can continually improve our books and learning resources for you. To participate in a brief online survey, please visit:

microsoft.com/learning/booksurvey

What do you think of this book? We want to hear from you!

Microsoft is interested in hearing your feedback so we can continually improve our books and learning resources for you. To participate in a brief online survey, please visit:

microsoft.com/learning/booksurvey

11 Building an Approval Process   285

12 Managing and Monitoring InfoPath Forms Services   335

13 SharePoint Views and Dashboards   355

Introducing Microsoft InfoPath 2010

Welcome to Microsoft InfoPath 2010, a forms-creation and data-gathering tool that can help you streamline your business processes. InfoPath 2010 is well-suited for almost anyone who needs to design and deploy form solutions—including information workers, IT professionals, and developers. You can use InfoPath 2010 to design sophisticated forms that can quickly and accurately gather information that meet your organizational needs. And its deep integration with the Microsoft SharePoint platform opens up a new world of possibilities for your electronic form requirements.

InfoPath empowers you to design and fill out electronic forms, such as expense reports, event registrations, and customer satisfaction surveys. And you can do this using common form controls that most users are familiar with, such as text boxes, drop-down list boxes, or hyperlinks. When entering data in an InfoPath 2010 form, users are presented with familiar, document-like features. For example, they can change fonts, check spelling, or insert images into certain fields.

If you create your forms as browser-enabled form templates, users who don't have InfoPath installed on their computer can still work with the form in a browser. This lets you share business forms with a variety of users, including employees, customers, and vendors.

You can design forms ranging from simple questionnaires to collect data from a small group to complex surveys that are integral components of a much bigger business process. InfoPath form templates can be used as a standalone tool, or you can design them to work with SharePoint lists, applications, databases, or web services. With this flexibility, designers in your organization can easily integrate the form data into existing business processes. If you utilize SharePoint Server 2010 and SharePoint Designer, InfoPath 2010 forms can be used as part of a fully automated business process. This can include workflows such as routing and notification based on information within the form. And the data that users enter in your InfoPath forms doesn't have to remain sealed inside that form forever; it can be reused in a variety of ways, especially when coupled with the SharePoint platform.

New Features

Microsoft InfoPath 2010 is a major release and has several new features and capabilities compared with the 2003 and 2007 versions. We don't specifically call out all new features in the book, but you will gain experience with most of the new capabilities as you wind your way through the various chapters and exercises. The list below includes some of the new feature highlights that are most relevant for this book:

- The Microsoft Office Fluent Ribbon relieves you of the burden of hunting through menus, submenus, and dialog boxes. This new interface organizes all of the commands that the majority of people use most often, making them quickly accessible from tabs at the top of the InfoPath window.

- If you create your forms as browser-enabled form templates, users who don't have InfoPath installed on their computer can still work with the form in a browser. This lets you share business forms with a variety of users, including employees, customers, and vendors. Improved parity between InfoPath Filler 2010 forms and InfoPath browser forms in SharePoint Server 2010 ensures greater consistency across the spectrum of form users.

- SharePoint Server 2010 offers a robust architecture for managing access to data connections and external systems. InfoPath 2010 has a specific form control—the External Item Picker—that works with Business Connectivity Services (BCS).

- InfoPath 2010 includes a new installation option called InfoPath Filler. Filler presents people who are completing forms with a simple and easy-to-use interface. All of the functionality for designing forms is removed for those who just want to open a form and fill it out.

- In SharePoint Server 2010, it's easy to host your InfoPath forms on SharePoint pages by using the new InfoPath Form Web Part. You can simply add the InfoPath Form Web Part to a SharePoint 2010 Web Part page and point it to your form.

- With InfoPath 2010, you can create forms with a click of a button, based on SharePoint lists. If you have data in SharePoint lists, you can automatically generate a form with all of the SharePoint list column fields, and then customize it with the power of InfoPath.

Let's Get Started!

> *"When at last we are sure, you've been properly pilled, Then a few paper forms, Must be properly filled. So that you and your heirs, May be properly billed."*

> *Dr. Seuss*

Tax forms, school forms, business forms, registration forms, order forms, medical forms—forms of all types and for all purposes. Forms, so ubiquitous, and yet so under appreciated. The decision to take on the challenge of authoring this book was driven in part by our passionate belief that InfoPath and SharePoint 2010 together represent a new opportunity to radically transform the experience of using forms from one of dread and tedium, to a much more positive experience. With this new software platform, the untapped potential for improving people's everyday experience of building and using forms is vast. It was this potential for improvement that led us to share with you our knowledge and our passion for the world's best forms creation and editing tool: InfoPath 2010.

Hardware and Software Requirements

To complete the exercises in this book, you will need a Microsoft Windows–based computer with InfoPath 2010 installed on it (either as part of Microsoft Office Professional or standalone InfoPath installation).

The requirements to install InfoPath 2010 are:

- Processor: 500 MHz or faster processor
- Memory: 256 MB RAM or more
- Hard disk: 2.0 GB available disk space
- Display: 1024 x 768 or higher resolution monitor
- Operating system, Windows XP (must have SP3) (32-bit), Windows 7, Windows Vista with SP1, Windows Server 2003 with SP2 and MSXML 6.0 (32-bit Office only), Windows Server 2008, or later, 32 or 64-bit OS.

For many of the exercises in the book, you will also need access to a SharePoint 2010 Server environment. Some exercises might require the Enterprise features of SharePoint such as InfoPath Forms Services. Ideally, you will have a SharePoint site where you have Site Owner permissions in order to effectively work through the exercises in the book. This will be necessary for creating the required forms libraries, workflows, data connections, and other SharePoint objects.

SharePoint Designer 2010 is also required for some exercises; a free download is available at *http://sharepoint.microsoft.com/en-us/product/related-technologies/pages/sharepoint-designer.aspx*.

Office 365: InfoPath and SharePoint in the Cloud

If you do not have your own SharePoint environment, InfoPath 2010 supports the creation of forms in Microsoft Office 365, which is the online SharePoint service in the cloud. All versions of SharePoint Online have support for basic InfoPath integration, although the more advanced capabilities might require specific versions of Office 365. You can find more information on how to sign up for Office 365 at *http://office365.microsoft.com*. Chapter 2 has more information on how to decide which version of SharePoint best suits your needs.

You might notice some user interface differences in SharePoint Online versus an "on premises" installation of SharePoint in your company's data center. Conceptually, the exercises in this book should work the same with Office 365 in the cloud as they do if you have a SharePoint Server sitting under your desk.

Who This Book Is For

This intended audience for this book is very broad—essentially, it is for any information worker that needs to build and use electronic forms that will be stored in SharePoint. Whether you are an IT professional, an attorney, a sales manager, administrative assistant, or a rocket scientist, this book can teach you the basics of building and using InfoPath 2010 forms in a SharePoint 2010 environment. By the time you finish, you will be fully armed to create a very satisfying form experience for the consumers of your forms.

Because the target audience for InfoPath 2010 (and therefore, this book) is so wide-ranging, we have intentionally set the bar low for required expertise to use this book. If you are a savvy Office and Windows user, that's a great start! For much of the book, some existing knowledge of SharePoint Server will definitely be useful. However, even if you're not a SharePoint guru, most topics in this book should be within your grasp. You might need to become good friends with your SharePoint administrator; their help will be invaluable.

A note to IT professionals and software developers: if you don't have much experience using InfoPath with SharePoint, you will likely find this book valuable. However, we want to be clear that you (the technical software professional) are not the primary reader we had in mind when structuring the content in this book. The mission of this book was not to be a comprehensive administrator or developer guide. That undertaking has already been covered by other excellent InfoPath and SharePoint 2010 books on the market.

How This Book is Organized

This book is organized around the idea of using InfoPath 2010 with SharePoint Server. The book does begin with a few chapters that are primarily focused on understanding Info-Path itself; but by Chapter 4, the focus starts to turn to using InfoPath *with* SharePoint. That was our mantra for much of the book—highlight and focus on the areas of InfoPath that have a strong connection and relationship with SharePoint. Throughout the 14 chapters that comprise this book, you will have an opportunity to design forms that integrate tightly with SharePoint in a variety of ways.

Chapter 1, "Introducing Microsoft InfoPath 2010," explores the InfoPath interface, and helps you learn XML basics and to build a simple form.

Chapter 2, "Form Requirements: Using a Decision Matrix," helps you understand which types of InfoPath forms make sense for your requirements.

Chapter 3, "Form Design Basics: Working with InfoPath Layout, Controls, and Views," shows you how to work with sample forms to help you understand different ways to put the basic form components together.

Chapter 4, "Working with SharePoint List Forms," demonstrates how to use InfoPath to customize SharePoint 2010 list forms.

Chapter 5, "Adding Logic and Rules to Forms," explores the capability of InfoPath to add business logic and data validation to forms, without code.

Chapter 6, "Publishing and Submitting Form Data," helps you to experience the various options for publishing your forms to SharePoint.

Chapter 7, "Receiving Data from SharePoint Lists and Business Connectivity Services," presents information on how to retrieve data in to your forms from SharePoint data sources.

Chapter 8, "Using the InfoPath Form Web Part," leads you through the process of displaying your form in a SharePoint Web Part.

Chapter 9, "Working with the SharePoint User Profile Web Service," teaches you how to integrate information about SharePoint users in to your forms by adding web service data connections.

Chapter 10, "InfoPath Integration with SharePoint Designer Workflows," helps you to understand how SharePoint Designer and InfoPath work together to build custom workflow forms.

Chapter 11, "Building an Approval Process," shows you how to add workflows and routing to your forms.

Chapter 12, "Managing and Monitoring InfoPath Forms Services," leads you through working with a variety of administration tools to manage browser-based forms.

Chapter 13, "SharePoint Views and Dashboards," shows you how to take advantage of SharePoint's power to build customized views and dashboards that contain data from your forms.

Chapter 14, "Advanced Options," explores various tips and tricks for integrating advanced form requirements.

Darvish's Acknowledgments

Contrary to popular belief, an author's primary motivation for writing a book such as this is not always career advancement, money, or fame. In my particular case, my four amazing children have been the underlying motivation for most of the good things I do in my life, and this book is no exception. It is of great importance to me that their eyes are wide open to what's possible in life with enough dedication and hard work. It is my hope that in some small way, seeing their Dad's name on a book will help to expand their mind's boundaries as they grow and explore their own paths. Hannah, Sydney, Devin, and Zoe—thank you for your patience and understanding during the several months that it took Dad to work on this project. I love you all very much. Next summer, we'll stay at the lake a few days longer...

Thanks to the InfoPath and SharePoint team members at Microsoft who supported me in various ways through this effort. During the process of writing this book, I emailed, disturbed, and interrogated many of them quite often. I've had the pleasure of getting to know many team members over the last several years and look forward to continuing to work with them. Particular thanks are extended to the following folks whose contributions, example forms, technical guidance, and support I could not have done without:

- Roberto Taboada
- Peter Allenspach
- Laura Harrington
- Daniel Witriol
- Philip Newman
- Keenan Newton
- Nick Dallett (now with Expedia)

To the local team members with whom I work every day at Microsoft in the North Central District, thank you all for your support and understanding while I undertook this authoring challenge.

Thanks to the editorial teams at O'Reilly Media for their guidance and support throughout the development of this book. A special thanks to our editor Kenyon Brown and copyeditor Richard Carey. It's difficult to imagine two more collaborative, professional, and seasoned professionals. They've been there when I needed support—*and* when I needed a kick in the pants.

Lastly, thank you to my amazing coauthor Laura Rogers. Words can't fully capture what it's like to collaborate so closely with someone like Laura over the course of several months. She's been brilliant, supportive, hard-working, and frankly I just could not have done this project without her. Thank you Laura: you rock!

Darvish Shadravan

Laura's Acknowledgments

For about eight years, InfoPath has been a huge part of my daily work. I thoroughly enjoy working with InfoPath and SharePoint. Thus, writing this book has been an enjoyable and fulfilling experience. It feels great to share the technology with newcomers so that they can create their own custom business solutions, without code.

For my acknowledgments, I'm going all the way back to 1982 in south Louisiana. Thanks to my elementary school teacher, Mrs. Susan Burge. There were seven of us in her gifted class 4 hours of the day, for three years. The class was so special and amazing. That unique learning environment (in a public school) has been a huge advantage. We had to work hard and do spelling and grammar drills every single day, but we also had many frequent field trips to places like nearby New Orleans. It was truly enriching. Now that my children are getting to be that same age, I think about those days, and try to pass some of those learning experiences on to them. I want them to love reading and writing just like their Mommy does.

Charlotte and Kristen, you are the most sweet and beautiful daughters I could ever ask for. Thanks to my husband, Chris, and my girls for being supportive and patient with me when weekend writing was required.

Don't tell him, but I have been a big fan of Darvish Shadravan for several years. I have seen him speak at several conferences, and always took prolific notes in his sessions. When Darvish presented me with this chance to coauthor this book with him, how could I say no? It has been fun and challenging collaborating on this project. We didn't just go off separately and write individual chapters about incongruent topics. A lot of time was spent working on the outline, the order of things, and we made sure to get all of the important points across in the book. We wanted to teach the readers as much as possible.

Also, thank you to Kenyon Brown and the team at O'Reilly Media for all of your hard work and guidance. You have all been extremely knowledgeable and proficient in our collaboration along the way. Thank you for your patience and professionalism.

Laura Rogers

Modifying the Display of the Ribbon

The goal of the Office working environment is to make working with Office documents, including Microsoft Word documents, Microsoft Excel workbooks, Microsoft PowerPoint presentations, Microsoft Outlook email messages, and Microsoft Access database tables, as intuitive as possible. You interact with an Office document and its contents by issuing commands to the program in which the document is open. All Office 2010 programs organize commands on a horizontal bar called the *ribbon*, which appears across the top of each program window, whether or not there is an active document.

Commands are organized on task-specific tabs of the ribbon, and in feature-specific groups on each tab. Commands generally take the form of buttons and lists. Some appear in galleries. Some groups have related dialog boxes or task panes that contain additional commands.

Throughout this book, we discuss the commands and ribbon elements associated with the program feature being discussed. In this topic, we discuss the general appearance of the ribbon, things that affect its appearance, and methods for locating commands that aren't visible on compact views of the ribbon.

Tip Some older commands no longer appear on the ribbon, but they are still available in the program. You can make these commands available by adding them to the Quick Access Toolbar.

Dynamic Ribbon Elements

The ribbon is dynamic, which means that the appearance of commands on the ribbon changes as the width of the ribbon changes. A command might be displayed on the ribbon in the form of a large button, a small button, a small labeled button, or a list entry. As the width of the ribbon decreases, the size, shape, and presence of buttons on the ribbon adapt to the available space.

For example, when sufficient horizontal space is available, the buttons on the Review tab of the Word program window are spread out and you're able to see more of the commands available in each group.

If you decrease the width of the ribbon, small button labels disappear and entire groups of buttons hide under one button that represents the group. Click the group button to display a list of the commands available in that group.

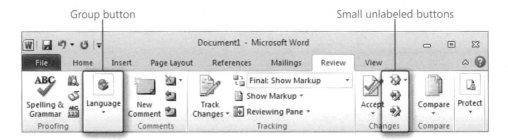

When the window becomes too narrow to display all the groups, a scroll arrow appears at its right end. Click the scroll arrow to display hidden groups.

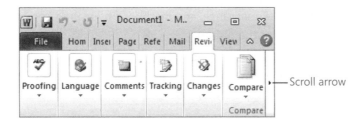

Changing the Width of the Ribbon

The width of the ribbon is dependent on the available horizontal space, which depends on these three factors:

- **The width of the program window**   Maximizing the program window provides the most space for ribbon elements. You can resize the program window by clicking the button in its upper-right corner or by dragging the border of a non-maximized window.

  Tip On a computer running Windows 7, you can maximize the program window by dragging its title bar to the top of the screen.

- **Your screen resolution**   Screen resolution is the size of your screen display expressed as pixels wide × pixels high. The greater the screen resolution, the greater the amount of information that will fit on one screen. Your screen resolution options are dependent on your monitor. At the time of writing, possible screen resolutions range from 800 × 600 to 2048 × 1152. In the case of the ribbon, the greater the number of pixels wide (the first number), the greater the number of buttons that can be shown on the ribbon, and the larger those buttons can be.

  On a computer running Windows 7, you can change your screen resolution in the Screen Resolution window of the Control Panel. You set the resolution by dragging the pointer on the slider.

- **The density of your screen display**   You might not be aware that you can change the magnification of everything that appears on your screen by changing the screen magnification setting in Windows. Setting your screen magnification to 125% makes text and user interface elements larger on screen. This increases the legibility of information, but it also means that less fits onto each screen.

On a computer running Windows 7, you can change the screen magnification in the Display window of the Control Panel. You can choose one of the standard display magnification options or create another by setting a custom text size.

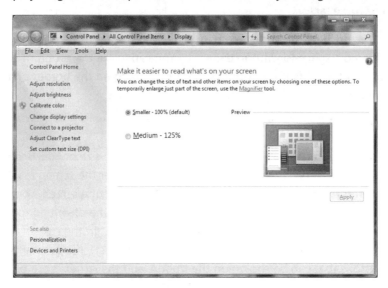

The screen magnification is directly related to the density of the text elements on screen, which is expressed in dots per inch (dpi) or points per inch (ppi). (The terms are interchangeable, and in fact are both used in the Windows dialog box in which you change the setting.) The greater the dpi, the larger the text and user interface elements appear on screen. By default, Windows displays text and screen elements at 96 dpi. Choosing the Medium - 125% display setting changes the dpi of text and screen elements to 120 dpi. You can choose a custom setting of up to 500% magnification, or 480 dpi, in the Custom DPI Setting dialog box. The list allows you to choose a magnification of up to 200%. You can choose a greater magnification by dragging across the ruler from left to right.

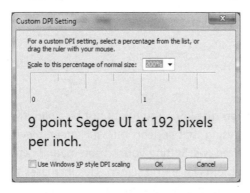

See Also For more information about display settings, refer to *Windows 7 Step by Step* (2009, Microsoft Press), *Windows Vista Step by Step* (2006, Microsoft Press), or *Windows XP Step by Step* (2002, Microsoft Press), by Joan Lambert Preppernau and Joyce Cox.

Adapting Exercise Steps

The screen images shown in the exercises in this book were captured at a screen resolution of 1024 × 768, at 100% magnification, and the default text size (96 dpi). If any of your settings are different, the ribbon on your screen might not look the same as the one depicted in the book. For example, you might see more or fewer buttons in each of the groups, the buttons you see might be represented by larger or smaller icons than those shown, or the group might be represented by a button that you click to display the group's commands.

When we instruct you to give a command from the ribbon in an exercise, we do it in this format:

- On the **Insert** tab, in the **Illustrations** group, click the **Chart** button.
- If the command is in a list, we give the instruction in this format:
- On the **Page Layout** tab, in the **Page Setup** group, click the **Breaks** button, and then in the list, click **Page**.

The first time we instruct you to click a specific button in each exercise, we display an image of the button in the page margin to the left of the exercise step.

If differences between your display settings and ours cause a button on your screen to look different from the one depicted in the book, you can easily adapt the steps to locate the command. First, click the specified tab. Then locate the specified group. If a group has been collapsed into a group list or group button, click the list or button to display the group's commands. Finally, look for a button that features the same icon in a larger or smaller size than that shown in the book. If necessary, point to buttons in the group to display their names in ScreenTips.

If you prefer not to have to adapt the steps, set up your screen to match ours while you read and work through the exercises in the book.

Features and Conventions of This Book

This book has been designed to lead you step by step through all the tasks you're most likely to want to perform in Microsoft InfoPath 2010. If you start at the beginning and work your way through all the exercises, you will gain enough proficiency to be able to create and work with most InfoPath plus SharePoint form scenarios. However, each topic is self-contained. If you have completed all the exercises and later need help remembering how to perform a procedure, the following features of this book will help you locate specific information:

- **Detailed table of contents**   Search the listing of the topics and sidebars within each chapter.

- **Chapter thumb tabs**   You can use these to easily locate the beginning of the chapter you want.

- **Topic-specific running heads**   Within a chapter, quickly locate the topic you want by looking at the running heads at the top of odd-numbered pages.

- **Glossary**   Use this to look up the meaning of a word or the definition of a concept.

- **Keyboard Shortcuts**   If you prefer to work from the keyboard rather than with a mouse, you can find all the shortcuts in one place.

- **Detailed index**   Look up specific tasks and features in the index, which has been carefully crafted with the reader in mind.

You can save time when reading this book by understanding how the *Step by Step* series shows exercise instructions, keys to press, buttons to click, and other information.

Convention	Meaning
SET UP	This paragraph preceding a step-by-step exercise indicates the practice files that you will use when working through the exercise. It also indicates any requirements you should address or actions you should take before beginning the exercise.
CLEAN UP	This paragraph following a step-by-step exercise provides instructions for saving and closing open files or programs before moving on to another topic. It also suggests ways to reverse any changes you made to your computer while working through the exercise.

Convention	Meaning
1. **2.**	Numbered steps guide you through hands-on exercises in each topic, as well as procedures in sidebars and expository text.
See Also	This paragraph directs you to more information about a topic in this book or elsewhere.
Troubleshooting	This paragraph alerts you to a common problem and provides guidance for fixing it.
Tip	This paragraph provides a helpful hint or shortcut that makes working through a task easier.
Important	This paragraph points out information that you need to know to complete a procedure.
Keyboard Shortcut	This paragraph provides information about an available keyboard shortcut for the preceding task.
Ctrl+B	A plus sign (+) between two keys means that you must press those keys at the same time. For example, "Press Ctrl+B" means that you should hold down the Ctrl key while you press the B key.
Page Layout Templates ▾	Pictures of buttons appear in the margin the first time the button is used in a chapter.
Bold	In exercises that begin with SET UP information, bold type displays text that you should type; the names of program elements, such as buttons, commands, windows, and dialog boxes; and files, folders, or text that you interact with in the steps.

Downloading the Practice Files and eBook

Before you can complete the exercises in this book, you need to copy the book's practice files to your computer. These practice files, and other information, can be downloaded from here:

http://go.microsoft.com/FWLink/?Linkid=230437

Display the detail page in your web browser and follow the instructions for downloading the files.

Important The Microsoft InfoPath 2010 program is not available from this website. You should purchase and install that program before using this book.

The following table lists the practice files for this book.

Chapter	File
Chapter 3, Form Design Basics: Working with InfoPath Layout, Controls, and Views	Raw Flight Delay Form.xsn
	Flight Delay Form Post Exercise 1.xsn
	Flight Delay Form Post Exercise 2.xsn
	Flight Delay Form Post Exercise 3.xsn
	Flight Delay Form Post Exercise 4.xsn
	Blue Yonder Header.bmp
Chapter 5, Adding Logic and Rules to Forms	No rules procurement.xsn
	Completed Procurement.xsn
	Blue Yonder Records Management SharePoint Site Request Form.xsn
	Completed - Blue Yonder Records Management SharePoint Site Request Form.xsn
Chapter 7, Receiving Data from SharePoint Lists and Business Connectivity Services	Flight Delay Form.xsn
	UDC Form.xsn
	External Item Picker Example.xsn
Chapter 11, Building an Approval Process	ContosoReimbursementForm.xsn
	ContosoReimbursementFinal.xsn
Chapter 13, SharePoint Views and Dashboards	Helpdesk Requests.XSN
	NewFormButton.png
Chapter 14, Advanced Options	Translate example.xsn

Your Companion eBook

The eBook edition of this book allows you to:

- Search the full text
- Print
- Copy and paste

To download your eBook, please see the instruction page at the back of this book.

Getting Support and Giving Feedback

Errata

We've made every effort to ensure the accuracy of this book and its companion content. Any errors that have been reported since this book was published are listed on our Microsoft Press site at oreilly.com:

http://go.microsoft.com/FWLink/?Linkid=230438

If you find an error that is not already listed, you can report it to us through the same page.

If you need additional support, email Microsoft Press Book Support at *mspinput@ microsoft.com*.

Please note that product support for Microsoft software is not offered through the addresses above.

Getting Help with Microsoft InfoPath 2010

If your question is about Microsoft InfoPath, and not about the content of this Microsoft Press book, your first recourse is the Microsoft InfoPath Help system. You can find general or specific Help information in a couple of ways:

- In the Microsoft InfoPath window, you can click the Help button (labeled with a question mark) located in the upper-right corner of the window to display the Microsoft InfoPath Help window.
- On the ribbon, you can click the File tab to access the Help button.

If your question is about Microsoft InfoPath or another Microsoft software product and you cannot find the answer in the product's Help system, please search the appropriate product solution center or the Microsoft Knowledge Base at:

http://support.microsoft.com

In the United States, Microsoft software product support issues not covered by the Microsoft Knowledge Base are addressed by Microsoft Product Support Services. Location-specific software support options are available from:

http://support.microsoft.com/gp/selfoverview

We Want to Hear from You

At Microsoft Press, your satisfaction is our top priority, and your feedback our most valuable asset. Please tell us what you think of this book at:

http://www.microsoft.com/learning/booksurvey

The survey is short, and we read *every one* of your comments and ideas. Thanks in advance for your input!

Stay in Touch

Let's keep the conversation going! We're on Twitter:

http://twitter.com/MicrosoftPress

Chapter at a Glance

Learn about Office Backstage in InfoPath, **page 9**

Understand how to create a simple XML file, **page 16**

Create an InfoPath form, **page 13**

Add data connections to a form, **page 19**

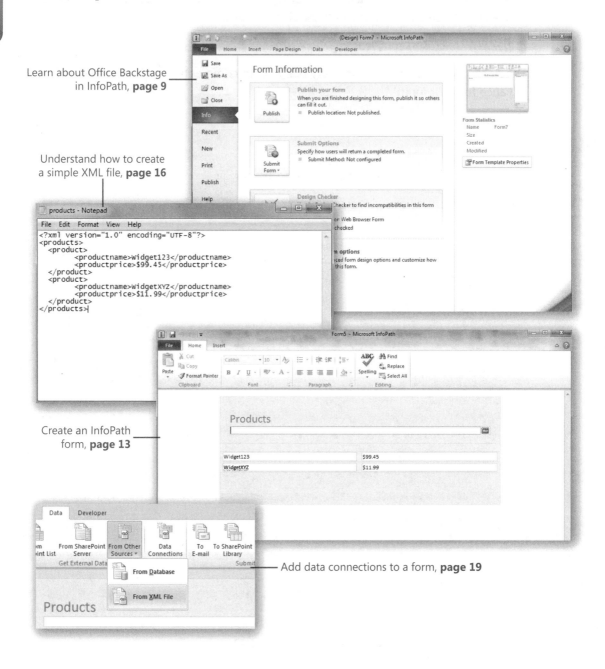

1 Introducing Microsoft InfoPath 2010

In this chapter, you will learn how to:

✔ Enumerate the benefits of using InfoPath 2010 forms with Microsoft SharePoint 2010

✔ Use the Microsoft Office Backstage functions to create a new InfoPath form

✔ Navigate the InfoPath interface

✔ Create a basic XML file and integrate it into an InfoPath form

When speaking about Microsoft InfoPath at technology conferences, I often open the discussion by posing the following question to the audience: who or what is it that "runs the show" here on planet Earth? The responses include many entertaining and thoughtful comments, such as "money," "The Illuminati," "the military," and my personal favorite, "Bill Gates." While I acknowledge all of these as good guesses, the premise I submit to the audience is that *forms* run the world. Imagine modern life without forms, both paper and digital—it's not possible! Everything that is known and recorded about you, from your birth city to your magazine subscriptions, to your preference of aisle or window seats—yes, all this information was entered in a form at some point in time. Forms of all sizes, shapes, colors, and styles have positively flourished!

We have become so accustomed to consuming information in modern life that the experience of creating and *capturing* that information is often overlooked. Forms now permeate daily life so deeply that we often don't consciously realize the extent to which they have proliferated, and the extent to which we have come to rely on them. And let's be honest: most of these forms could be improved to make them more user friendly, more efficient, and more capable of providing long-term business value with all that data that's being collected.

If you are reading this book, we can safely assume that you have a mission of building, deploying, and using digital forms on the SharePoint 2010 platform. Accordingly, the mission of this book is to help you understand how to create business forms that provide a pleasant, reliable, and intuitive experience for your users and customers.

And just how exactly shall you endeavor to accomplish this lofty objective? This is where Microsoft InfoPath 2010 will assist with your mission. While it is true that e-forms have been around for a couple decades, it is only now that we are seeing a complete platform capable of truly revolutionizing the way data is captured, stored, reported, and utilized for collaboration. Armed with this book, we will take you, the business forms designer, on a journey of understanding so that you can make the most of this amazing set of software tools now at your finger tips.

> **Practice Files** No practice files are required to complete the exercises in this chapter.

Benefits of Using InfoPath 2010 with SharePoint 2010

InfoPath is now in its third major version and has matured into a product capable of designing forms for business, schools, and government agencies of all sizes. It is suitable for scenarios as simple as a small business that needs basic information tracking, all the way up to enterprises with many thousands of users entering data simultaneously worldwide. Many of the core concepts of InfoPath have not changed over the years. It's still a flexible, powerful, easy-to-use, XML-based forms editor. But what *has* changed is the level of integration InfoPath 2010 has with the Microsoft SharePoint 2010 platform.

SharePoint 2010 is a perfect companion application server platform on which to host InfoPath forms because of the complementary set of features SharePoint offers. SharePoint 2010 has a broad set of capabilities for businesses, including collaboration, search, content management, reporting, workflows, and forms. Almost all of the major functionality areas in SharePoint 2010 can be integrated with InfoPath forms and the data contained therein. While you can bring *so many* value-added solutions to your users with InfoPath, it is important to use your imagination and think beyond "just a form." This book will help spur your thinking as you complete the comprehensive exercises and form-building scenarios.

SharePoint *libraries*, specifically *form libraries*, are well suited for storing and managing InfoPath forms. And because form libraries are fundamentally just another type of SharePoint list, you have an abundance of SharePoint capabilities such as workflow, columns, and user-defined views to enhance the interface and functionality of your form solutions. We will review publishing InfoPath to SharePoint form libraries in depth later in the book.

SharePoint 2010 also offers a very robust workflow platform that your forms can easily use. The possibilities are limited only by your imagination—approvals, routing, and almost every business process require some level of workflow, and fortunately, SharePoint 2010 has a very capable workflow framework. Several of the examples in this book will contain workflow integration. Chapter 11, "Building an Approval Process," focuses primarily on understanding how to integrate a common business workflow scenario with InfoPath forms.

Reporting and Business Intelligence capabilities in SharePoint 2010 help you extract the data from your forms and present it to business users in a format from which they can immediately derive value. The InfoPath data can be "promoted" to populate SharePoint columns, and thus numerous opportunities exist to reuse the information, including Key Performance Indicators (KPIs), Business Intelligence dashboards/reports, and more. We will take a deeper look at integration of form data into reports and dashboards in Chapter 13, "SharePoint Views and Dashboards."

Often, forms are not islands of data by themselves; they need integration of data from other systems to be used in drop-down fields, text fields, and other controls. With SharePoint 2010, we have multiple ways to meet this requirement. InfoPath itself supports *data connections* to many data source types, including web services, XML files, and databases. This will be covered in depth in Chapter 7, "Receiving Data from SharePoint Lists and Business Connectivity Services," and Chapter 9, "Working with the SharePoint User Profile Web Service." We now also have *Business Connectivity Services* (BCS) in SharePoint 2010 with which you can easily create *External lists* of data in SharePoint that can be used in your forms. These External lists of business data can provide access to a wide variety of information that is stored in your existing systems (for example, CRM, product databases, Human Resources). The underlying concept of the BCS in SharePoint is a powerful one: easily make connections to business data. This will help you build InfoPath forms that do not require the creation of redundant data sets for use in common form controls such as drop-down menus. Imagine a standard form that allows your users to order widgets that they will use during the course of their daily work. Does it make sense to re-key this product data in a drop-down field in the order form, or does it make more sense to connect InfoPath to your existing product/ordering database?

The list of capabilities that your forms can take advantage of in SharePoint 2010 goes on and on: enterprise search, a variety of useful Web Parts, portal pages, extranets, enterprise content management, and much more.

This book is unique in that its focus is the use of InfoPath 2010 in a SharePoint environment. While InfoPath 2010 can be published to a variety of locations, including email, network shares, or your desktop, this book is primarily focused on forms that are designed for use in conjunction with SharePoint 2010.

New Features of InfoPath 2010

For those of you upgrading from previous versions of InfoPath, you will immediately notice many significant improvements in this version. The first thing that might strike you is that InfoPath 2010 is the first version of InfoPath to receive the new Microsoft Office Fluent interface. This new user interface includes the ribbon and the Backstage view. These are major advancements toward improving the usability of InfoPath and providing productivity gains for both the designers and the form users.

The Office ribbon provides a series of tabs that are "intelligent" in the respect that they are context sensitive. In other words, they present buttons to you organized by activity and particular tasks. For example, when you create a new form, choose the Insert tab on the ribbon, and then click Custom Table, you are automatically taken to the Table Layout tab so that you can refine your table.

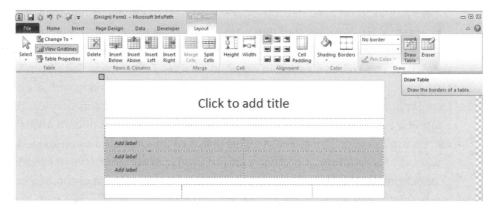

In the 2007 version of InfoPath, users would consume forms in two primary ways: either in InfoPath on their desktops or in a browser if the form had been published to SharePoint Form Services. With InfoPath 2010, you have a third option. The InfoPath desktop client now consists of two parts: InfoPath Designer, which provides the full design experience, and InfoPath Filler. Filler is a new InfoPath desktop installation option for users who need to fill in and submit forms but do not need to modify or create new form templates. Chapter 2, "Form Requirements: Using a Decision Matrix," has in-depth descriptions of the three options and the particular use-cases that are most appropriate for each one.

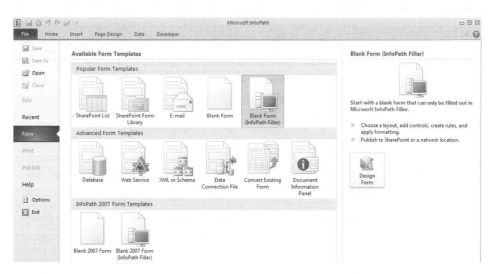

One very common request in the past from SharePoint customers was for an easier way to customize the default input form for a SharePoint list. In previous versions of SharePoint, customizing a list form required significant expertise and was not a straight-forward process. But now, with InfoPath 2010, you can create attractive input forms on SharePoint lists with the click of a button. If you have existing data in SharePoint lists, you can quickly generate a new input form with all of the SharePoint column data. We have exercises that will cover this capability in depth in Chapter 4, "Working with SharePoint List Forms."

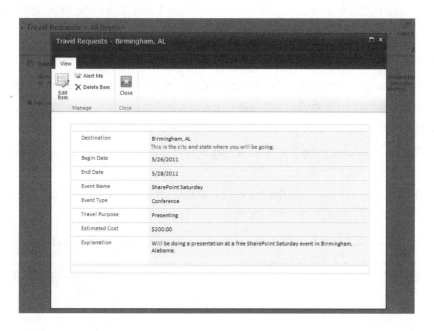

If you decide to utilize SharePoint Form Services to deliver your forms for consumption in web browsers, InfoPath 2010 includes enhanced support for browser-based forms. Web browser forms in 2010 provide a more consistent and richer, user experience, nearly matching the experience of using the InfoPath client application. Controls and functionality now supported in browser forms include the following:

- Date and time controls for adding rich date and time fields
- Bulleted, numbered, and plain lists
- Multiple selection list box, which is a control with which users can select multiple items within a single field
- Combo boxes for when you need to let users either type in their own text or choose from a list of pre-populated items in a drop-down field
- Hyperlink capabilities
- Choice of group and section; users can decide whether or not they need that particular section of the form
- Person/Group pickers for adding a control to your forms with which users can select user names from a SharePoint user list
- Filtering data that is displayed in controls that can now be filtered in web browser forms, limiting the number of items displayed to a user in list boxes, drop-down list boxes, combo boxes, repeating tables, and repeating sections
- Picture buttons for when you prefer a button that is an image of your choice.

One of the primary tools for adding logic and formatting to a form is via the use of rules. Common examples of the types of things you can use rules for are as follows:

- Automatically updating the contents of a field based on a selection or choice a user made somewhere else in the form
- Hiding controls/fields until a user takes some specific action in the form
- Dynamically changing the formatting of text based on input or selections the user has made in the form
- Showing a pop-up message based on actions the user has taken or in accordance with specific data they have input

InfoPath 2010 has a much easier way to work with rules, validation, and conditional formatting: it's called the Rules task pane.

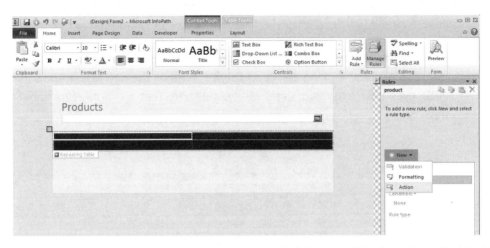

Along with the Rules pane, we have the very helpful new Add Rules (also called Quick Rules) button on the ribbon, with which you can very quickly add common, pre-built logic and validation rules to your form without code. The new rules features make it so easy to add data validation and conditional formatting that you will have no problem designing forms that easily guide your users through the process of filling them out! Rules will be covered in depth in Chapter 5, "Adding Logic and Rules to Forms."

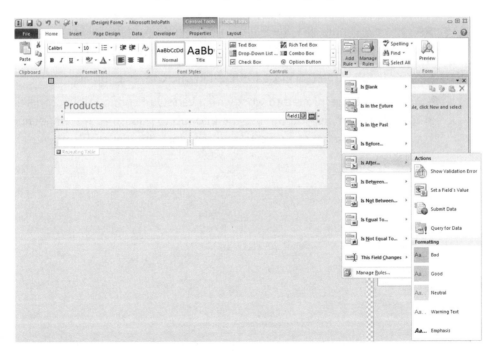

InfoPath 2010 makes laying out an attractive and visually pleasing form easier than ever. You can insert one of the pre-built page layouts from the Page Design tab on the ribbon to give your form structure. And then you can easily apply a theme to provide your form professional-looking colors and styles. With all the new layout tools in InfoPath 2010, even novice InfoPath users can create forms that are highly functional and visually pleasing.

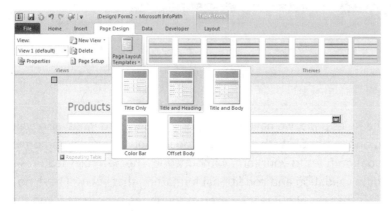

The Backstage view is a major enhancement in the way you perform common tasks with your forms, such as printing, publishing, and setting form options. To access the Backstage view, simply click the File tab on the ribbon. In Backstage view, you will find a variety of very useful features and tools all in one place, including the following:

- You can save, open, or close forms all in one convenient place.

- You can use the Info tab to work with a variety of configurable properties of your form. For example, you can use the Info tab to publish your form, define how it will be submitted by your users, and scan for potential problems with the Design Checker.

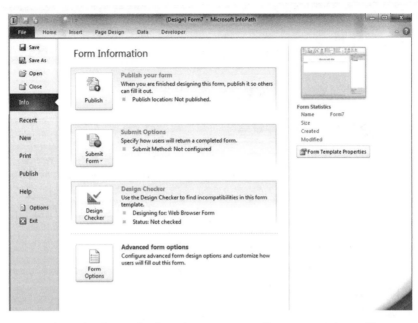

- You can use the Form Options button to configure a number of important settings for your form, including offline support, compatibility of your form with browsers, and versioning.

- You can use the Recent tab to see a list of forms that you have worked with recently.

- On the New tab, you can initiate the creation of a variety of form templates, including the primary templates we are concerned with in this book—the SharePoint form library and list templates.

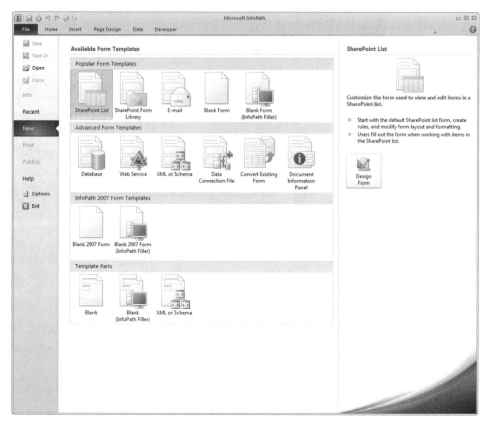

- Using the Print tab, you can handle all printing tasks, including the ability to determine which printer you want to print your finished form to. It also provides a very handy print preview feature so that you can see just what your form will look like when it is on paper. With this WYSIWYG ("what you see is what you get") print preview, there are no more excuses for wasted printer paper.

- The Publish tab is the area in the Backstage view where you decide the location in which to publish your form template. This will determine where your users will access and save their copies of the form later. While you have a variety of options for where to publish your form templates, the primary focus of this book is on SharePoint.

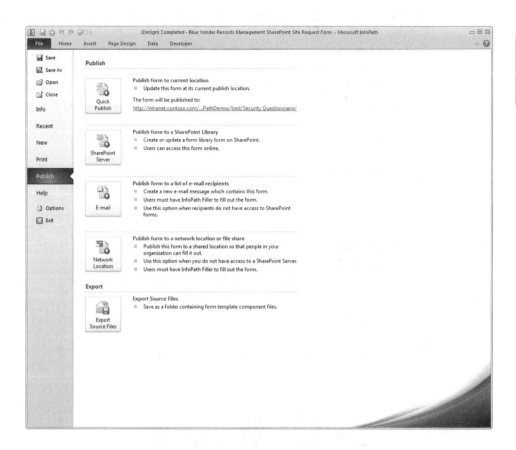

How InfoPath Works

InfoPath is unique in its ability to provide forms design capabilities that include sophisticated logic rules, conditional formatting, and data validation to information workers who might not be programmers. To benefit from these capabilities previously would have required a great deal of technical expertise. A large part of the power of InfoPath is that the file format of the forms is eXtensible Markup Language, or XML, which provides many inherent benefits in terms of flexibility, power, and standardization. However, as the forms designer, you are not required to know *too* much about XML, XSD, XSLT, and all the other technical details behind the scenes. Of course, we'd still encourage you to gain as much knowledge as possible; it will increase your skills and confidence with InfoPath.

The user interface of InfoPath is very similar to the other Microsoft Office 2010 products. If you are familiar with Microsoft Word, Microsoft Excel, or Microsoft Access, you will feel right at home in InfoPath 2010. It is a hybrid tool that combines the best of a traditional document editing experience with the structured data-capture capabilities of a forms package, thus providing end users with the ability to create valid XML documents. Below is a sample InfoPath form that is used for a procurement application. We'll revisit this form later in the book.

InfoPath is available either by itself or as part of the Office 2010 suite. The forms can be published to a variety of locations, including email, file shares, and SharePoint. One very powerful InfoPath capability is the ability to publish the forms in such a way that the form consumer can either use InfoPath on her desktop or via her browser, using InfoPath Forms Services. This will enable you to target different types of forms to different types of use-case scenarios based on your specific requirements. We will cover these options in great detail in Chapter 2 and provide all the necessary detail for you to make an informed decision.

When you create a new form, you are actually creating an InfoPath *template*. The template is saved with the .xsn file extension. After you publish your template to a location that is accessible by your users, they can create forms that are based on your template, but each *instance* they create and save will be saved with an .xml file extension. So to recap, you use InfoPath in Design mode to create .xsn templates, which are published to locations where your users can generate new form instances (.xml files), based on your template. You will learn more about designing forms in later chapters. For now, it is important you understand a bit about XML and then the difference between a form template and a form instance.

Quick Tour of the Backstage View in InfoPath 2010

In the following exercise, you will work with the InfoPath Designer and become familiar with the ribbon, controls, themes, and the Backstage view.

 SET UP Open your Windows Start menu.

1. Open the InfoPath Designer.

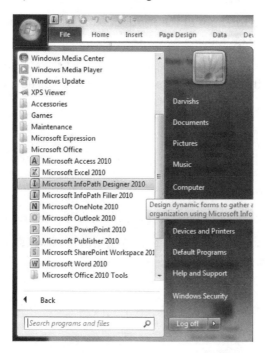

Blank Form

2. In the Backstage view, on the **New** tab, double-click **Blank Form** in the **Popular Templates** section.

3. At the top of the form, click **Click to add title**.

4. Type in **Products**.

5. On the ribbon, click the **Page Design** tab.

6. In the **Themes** area, click the drop-down arrow.

7. Select **Industrial - Graham** from the **Industrial** themes.

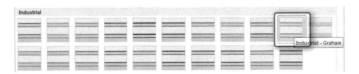

8. On the ribbon, click the **Home** tab.

9. Place your cursor just to the right of the **Products** title, and then press **Enter** so that your cursor is active on the line below the title.

10. From the **Controls** area on the ribbon, select the **Date Picker**. A single click should add it to your form in the location where your cursor was positioned.

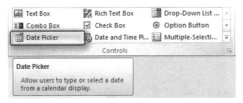

11. Still on the **Home** tab of the ribbon, select the **Preview** button on the far right.

12. After your preview opens up, select a date from the date picker so that you can see how this control works.

13. Click **Close Preview**.

14. On the ribbon, click the **File** tab.

15. Click **Save As**, and then name the form **Products**. Save it in your **Documents** folder on your local computer.

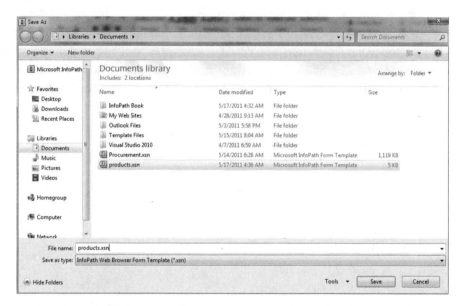

After you've completed the preceding steps, you can leave the form open because you will use it in the next exercise.

 CLEAN UP Leave InfoPath Designer open if you are continuing to the next section of this chapter. Otherwise, close it.

XML 101

XML is perhaps the single most powerful method of storing and sharing structured data to come along since the advent of digital computing. And fortunately, the native tongue of InfoPath is XML. The fact that the file format InfoPath uses to store and manage data is XML provides an amazing amount of power in an easy-to-use tool. InfoPath does an exceptional job of providing everyday business users of Microsoft Office with the ability to take advantage of the plentiful benefits of XML, while hiding much of the complexity. You do not need to become an expert in XML to create powerful forms, but to have a basic understanding of what XML is and how it works seems a reasonable goal if you want to take full advantage of InfoPath's power.

InfoPath uses XML as its primary file/output format. Behind the scenes, when a user creates an InfoPath form, they are actually creating an XML Document and an associated XML Schema. In addition, InfoPath can use XML data files and XML web services as "data connections" in your forms. So if your business already has other XML data sources, rest assured that you can take advantage of that data in InfoPath. For example, as shown in the following illustration, you could use a simple XML file containing product information to populate a field in your InfoPath form, such as a table or drop-down menu. In fact, you will create this XML file later in this chapter and build a simple form with a table based on the data in it.

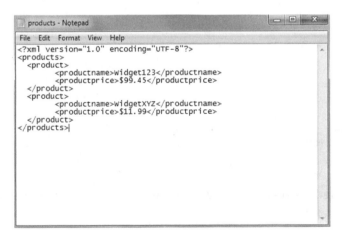

You'll notice in the preceding screenshot that although the structure might appear strange to you, the data in the XML file is "human readable." This is one of the many great benefits of XML. In this regard, XML is similar to HTML, with a key difference being that XML has a much more defined structure. And as you can see, if you need to open and work with the raw data in the XML file, you can use simple tools such as Microsoft Notepad.

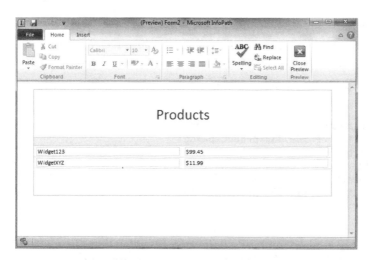

A user who edits an InfoPath form is actually editing an XML document, although the InfoPath interface strips away the complexity. InfoPath also takes advantage of another industry standard technology when editing a form: Extensible Style Sheet Language (XSLT). XSLT style sheets "sit in front of" the underlying XML and transform it into the rich and easy-to-use forms that InfoPath can produce.

InfoPath uses XML standards to provide end users with a flexible yet structured XML editing software tool for data gathering. It provides similar levels of power and flexibility as more traditional forms created by programmers with complex tools, but InfoPath provides the ease of use of the family of Office products.

Creating the Products.xml File

In the following exercise, you will create a small XML data file.

 SET UP Open your Windows Start Menu, and then click Accessories.

1. From **Accessories**, open Notepad.

2. Type the following code into Notepad *exactly* as it appears here:

   Note If you prefer, you can skip this step and download the Products.xml file from the book's companion website.

   ```xml
   <?xml version="1.0" encoding="UTF-8"?>
   <products>
    <product>
       <productname>widget123</productname>
       <productprice>$99.45</productprice>
    </product>
    <product>
       <productname>widgetXYZ</productname>
       <productprice>$11.99</productprice>
    </product>
   </products>
   ```

3. Save the file to your **Documents** folder with the file name **Products.xml**. It is important to add the .xml extension; otherwise, Notepad will save it as a .txt file.

 **CLEAN UP** Close Notepad.

Adding Products.xml to the Form as a Data Connection

In the following exercise, you will add the products.xml file as a resource file data connection to the Products form you created earlier in the chapter.

SET UP Open InfoPath Designer.

1. In InfoPath Designer, ensure that you still have the **Products** form open that you created earlier in the chapter. (You might need to open it from the location where you saved it on your desktop.)

2. On the ribbon, click the **Data** tab.

3. Select **From Other Sources**, and then select **From XML File**.

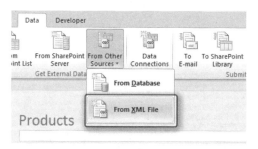

4. Browse to your **Documents** folder, and then click the **Products.xml** file you created in the first part of this exercise.

5. Click **Next**, click **Next** again, and then click **Finish**, leaving all pages in the wizard set at their defaults. Nothing obvious will change on your form yet, but you have added the **Products.xml** file as a data connection.

6. From the **Fields task pane** on the right side of your screen, click the drop-down arrow, and then choose **Products (secondary)**.

    This represents the data connection to the XML file you just added. Your form now has two data connections: the default Main and your products connection.

    Tip If you don't see the **Fields** task pane, you can open it by clicking the **Show Fields** button on the **Data** tab on the ribbon.

7. Ensure that your cursor is positioned below the dashed line on your form in the design surface.

8. In the **Fields** pane, right-click **product** in the **products** data connection, and then in the shortcut menu that appears, select **Repeating Table**.

   This action adds the data from your **Products.xml** file to the form design surface as an **InfoPath Repeating Table** control.

9. On the ribbon, click the **Home**, and then click **Preview**. Voilà! You have a form displaying data from the XML file that you created in the last step.

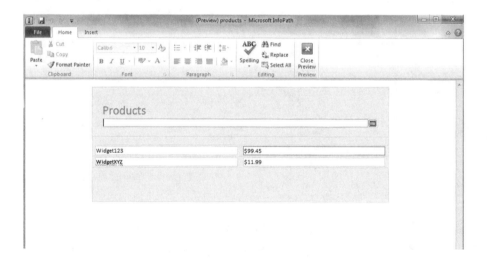

Keep in mind that it's generally not necessary to create an XML data connection file. InfoPath will do that work for you in most cases. We went through that process simply to give you a taste for what XML really looks like and to illustrate the ability InfoPath has to easily work with external data connection sources.

 CLEAN UP Close the preview, and then save your form template.

Using the Template to Create a Form Instance

In the following exercise, you will use the Products form template to create and save an instance of the form. This will help you distinguish the difference between a template and an .xml form instance that is based on the template.

SET UP Ensure that InfoPath Designer is closed. Open your Documents folder where you saved the products.xsn form template.

1. Double-click the **products.xsn** file.

   An instance of your form opens, but you're not in design mode. You're in data input Filler mode, using the template you created.

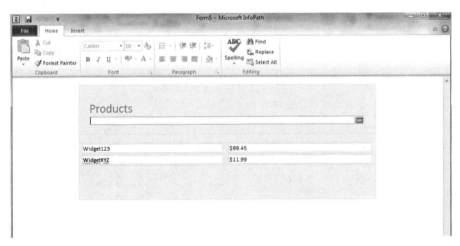

2. Select a date from the date picker, and then click the **Save** button.

3. Save the form to your **Documents** folder with the default file name.

   Notice the default file format is .xml. You have now filled out and saved a new form *instance* based on your *template*. Cool!

 CLEAN UP Close out of this instance of the form, and then exit InfoPath Filler.

Exporting the Template

In the following exercise, you will export the template into its component files so that you can see what's under the covers of an InfoPath .xsn template.

 SET UP Open InfoPath Designer.

1. Find the **products.xsn** template in your **Documents** folder, right-click it, and then in the shortcut menu, choose **Design**.

2. On the ribbon, click the **File** tab, and then click **Publish**.

3. Click **Export Source Files**.

4. Click **Make New Folder**.

5. Create a folder called export files, and then click **OK**.

6. Open your **Documents** folder, and navigate to the **export files** folder you just created.

Inside the export files folder you should see several files. Included among them are all the component files that InfoPath uses to give us a form template (.xsn). Notice that our Products.xml file is contained inside the .xsn template along with several critical .xsd and .xsl files that help define the layout and behavior of the actual form. For the purposes of this book, it is *not* important that you understand the details of how these foundational technologies work, but if you're curious, an Internet search for "xsd" or "xsl" will turn up everything you need.

 CLEAN UP Close InfoPath Designer.

Key Points

- The InfoPath 2010 user interface received a significant update to put it on par with the other Office applications.

- InfoPath 2010 allows non-programmers to build powerful forms that are based on the XML standard.

- InfoPath 2010 has two desktop components: the Designer and the Filler.

- InfoPath can consume data from external data sources such as XML files.

- InfoPath can take advantage of many of the SharePoint 2010 capabilities, such as workflows, lists, and reporting.

- InfoPath .xsn files are "packages" of individual components that comprise a functional form template.

Chapter at a Glance

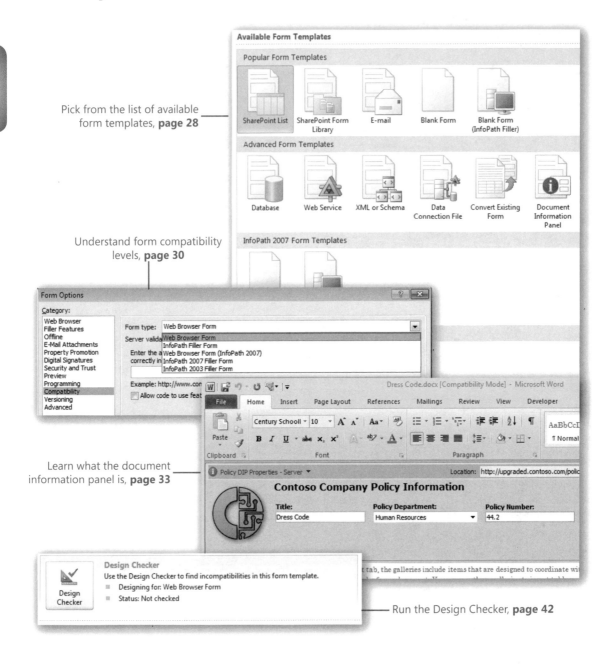

Pick from the list of available form templates, **page 28**

Understand form compatibility levels, **page 30**

Learn what the document information panel is, **page 33**

Run the Design Checker, **page 42**

2 Form Requirements: Using a Decision Matrix

In this chapter, you will learn how to:

✔ Pick from the available form templates

✔ Gather requirements for form creation

✔ Work with all the form choices

✔ Decide which type of form needs to be created

For each new form that you create, you need to make several decisions before the form creation process even starts. When you are aware of the factors to consider, you can save a lot of time and effort from the beginning. You will need to make key decisions based on form requirements, and some of them are easier to make than others.

In this chapter, you will learn the most important factors to consider before creating an InfoPath form so that your form development process can be as efficient as possible. All the decisions will be discussed, and then you will learn all the factors involved. Each factor affects the final decision. First, all of the available templates will be described. Then you will learn how to determine the best choice for each form. Most of the concepts that are mentioned in this chapter will be covered more extensively in future chapters. This chapter's purpose is to provide a reference when you start to develop your own forms.

> **Practice Files** No practice files are required to complete the exercises in this chapter.

Form Templates

When InfoPath Designer 2010 is started, the initial interface is a set of choices, which comprises a list of the available form templates. To create a new InfoPath form, one of these templates must be selected. At first, it might appear that you can create sixteen different types of forms, but that's not really the case because a few of these templates are redundant. Each template will be described in this section, and the "what" and "why" will follow later, when you are guided through your form decisions.

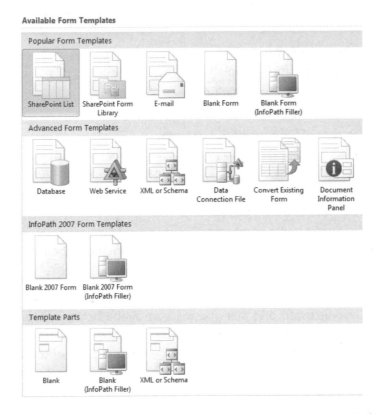

One common theme to notice among the template names is the word *Filler*. This leads us to the topic of filler forms (client-based) versus browser-based forms. It's important to understand these concepts before being overwhelmed by all of the template choices.

InfoPath Forms Services was first introduced in Microsoft Office SharePoint Server 2007. InfoPath Forms Services provided the ability to create browser-based forms in InfoPath. In InfoPath and SharePoint 2003, before Forms Services was introduced, forms could be created and published to SharePoint but everyone filling out the forms was required to have the InfoPath software on their computers. This was a show-stopper in many larger organizations because it simply was not feasible to deploy InfoPath and ensure that every client computer (possibly thousands) had the correct version of Microsoft Office. When InfoPath Forms Services with new browser-based forms were introduced, this opened up many more possibilities for form development. With a browser-based form, no special software is required when filling out forms; all you need is a web browser such as Internet Explorer. Thus, the two implementations of InfoPath can be summarized as follows:

- **Client-Based Library Form**   The InfoPath client software is part of the Office 2010 suite of products (in Office Professional Plus). When a form is created as an Info-Path Filler form, anyone filling out the form needs to have the InfoPath software installed. For organizations that have systematically deployed InfoPath to all of the computers, this option is feasible.

- **Browser-Based Library Form**   Forms that are browser-based can be filled out in Internet Explorer and in some other web browsers. When a form is browser-compatible, InfoPath software is *not* required, and virtually anyone can fill out a form, from anywhere. The only person who needs the InfoPath software is you, the form creator. As of the time of this writing, the compatible browsers are Internet Explorer, Mozilla Firefox, and Apple Safari.

One reason for the long list of available forms is that many of them are simply providing you a choice between a filler form and a browser-based form (compatibility). After you have selected a template, a compatibility setting is associated with that template in InfoPath. This setting can be changed at any time.

Another common thread is that some of these templates are named after types of data connections. Data connections will be covered extensively in Chapter 7, "Receiving Data from SharePoint Lists and Business Connectivity Services." Basically, creating connections is how you define where the data in the form will go after the form is filled out as well as what lists or databases the data will come from if it needs to be used in the form (such as in a drop-down list).

Form compatibility settings are important to understand when prompted with a list of templates. The client-based (filler) and browser-based settings can be changed after a form has been created. The compatibility can be changed at any time during the form design process by clicking File and then clicking Form Options. Take a look at the Compatibility section in the following screenshot.

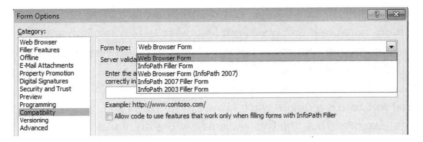

The following forms are available:

- **Web Browser Form**   Fill out forms in the browser in SharePoint 2010
- **InfoPath Filler Form**   Fill out forms by using the 2010 Filler
- **Web Browser Form**   Fill out forms in the browser in SharePoint 2007
- **InfoPath 2007 Filler Form**   Fill out forms by using the InfoPath client in Office 2007
- **InfoPath 2003 Filler Form**   Fill out forms by using the InfoPath client in Office 2003

Important Unlike the other templates, a SharePoint list form cannot be changed to a form library form and vice versa. A SharePoint list form is browser-based only.

Following is a list of the templates and their descriptions:

- **SharePoint List**   Introduced in the SharePoint 2010 Enterprise version, InfoPath can now be used as the form interface to SharePoint lists. Instead of the .aspx pages for filling out forms, the form can be completely designed and customized by using InfoPath. Many of your organization's simpler forms can be created as SharePoint lists and customized by using InfoPath. Using this method, the broadest audience of users can create forms. The interface is simplified, which means that end users will require a minimal amount of training to get up to speed in creating basic forms. Read more about SharePoint list forms in Chapter 4, "Working with SharePoint List Forms."

- **SharePoint Form Library**   This is the most frequently used template. With this template, a browser-based form is created with some layout tables on it to give you a head start in form design. The following image shows an example of a form library template.

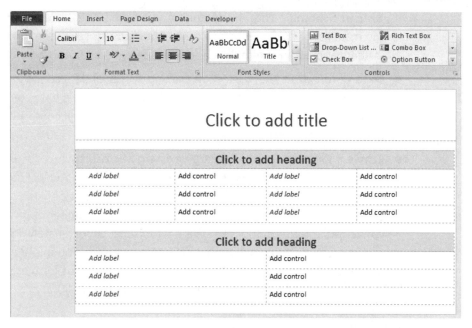

- **E-mail** This is a template that is intended for use in conjunction with a data connection that submits information directly in an email. You can pick the SharePoint Form Library template instead of this one and simply add an email data connection by using the form's Data tab.

- **Blank Form** This is an empty browser-based form. It is the same as the form library template, except that it does not contain the formatted table layout.

- **Blank Form (InfoPath Filler)** This template is the same as the blank form. The difference is that the compatibility setting is for an InfoPath filler form. This is also a form library.

- **Database** This template allows for the selection of any Microsoft Access or SQL database. The forms fields would be directly connected to tables in the database. This type of template is not compatible with browser-based forms. This template can become a bit tricky when authenticating to the back-end database.

- **Web Service** This template is a type of data connection where a form can be created and data can be received and/or submitted through a web service. With this template, the web service fields will automatically be populated in the form's main list of fields. This is also a form library.

- **XML or Schema**   With this template, an existing XML file can be used to create the main list of fields in the new form. Alternatively, select the form library template instead, and add this template as a secondary data connection.

- **Data Connection File**   Select an existing universal data connection that is based on a web service. This connection will be selected from a data connection library in SharePoint. All of the fields in the data connection will comprise the main list of fields in the new form. This is also a form library.

- **Convert Existing Form**   Select an existing Microsoft Word document or Microsoft Excel spreadsheet to convert into a new InfoPath form. You will have options to select certain attributes in the file and select what types of fields or cells will be converted to InfoPath fields. In cases where a large number of forms need to be converted, this useful tool can save a bit of time. Unfortunately, in many cases, the end result is not the most aesthetically pleasing form. You might end up spending just as much time fixing the formatting on the converted form as you would have in creating a new form from scratch. This is also a form library.

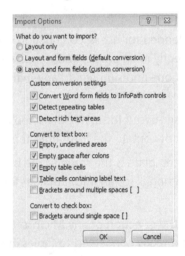

- **Document Information Panel**   The document information panel is seen at the top of Office files that are stored in SharePoint document libraries. Interact with the file's metadata in this panel. The term *metadata* refers to all the columns in the library. The following image shows a document information panel before it has been customized using InfoPath.

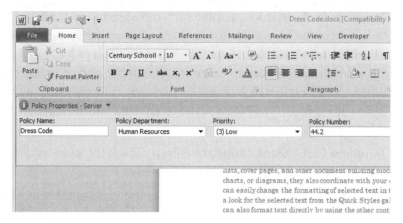

Tip Instead of using this standard panel for all files, use InfoPath to create a custom one. With a custom document information panel, use company colors and logos to add a professional look.

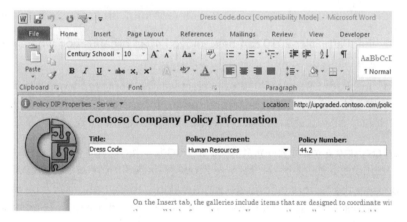

- **InfoPath 2007 - Blank 2007 Form** This is a blank form. It is the same as the blank form template with the exception that the compatibility setting is Web Browser Form (InfoPath 2007).

- **InfoPath 2007 - Blank 2007 Form (InfoPath Filler)** This is a blank form. It is the same as the blank form template with the exception that the compatibility setting is InfoPath 2007 Filler Form.

- **Template Part - Blank** An InfoPath template part is a modular template that can be reused inside of multiple forms. These are commonly used when a standard set of data is to be collected such as the requestor data at the top of a form. This would include a name field, department, phone number, and other commonly used fields. When the template part is saved, all the fields, controls, and data connections are stored along with it. This file is saved as an XTP2 file and can be inserted into other InfoPath forms as a custom control.

- **Template Part - Blank (InfoPath Filler)** This is the same as the template part, with the compatibility setting as InfoPath Filler Form.

- **Template Part - XML or Schema** This is the same as the template part, with the additional functionality of selecting an existing XML file to base it on.

InfoPath Filler

In the Office suite of products, two different InfoPath products are available:

- InfoPath Filler 2010 can be deployed in an organization where people might be filling out client-based InfoPath forms.

- InfoPath Designer 2010 can selectively be deployed to only those people who need the ability to create and design forms.

When creating a form, you first need to decide which type you want it to be. There are three options: a client-based form, a browser-based form, or a SharePoint list form. As we go over the factors in form decision-making, these options will be represented by circles. A solid circle indicates that the factor applies to the option; an open circle means the factor does not apply to the option.

Client Based	Browser Based	SharePoint List
●	●	●

Where's the Data?

Another important requirement is to learn about the data. Where is it coming from, and where is it going?

- **Submit To** When someone fills out a form and submits it, where would you like this form data to go? The typical answer is "to SharePoint."

- **Receive From** Where is the data coming from? Sometimes information will be received in the form from external sources. This data can be presented in drop-down lists and other such lookups. It is important to find out about these external data sources because of authentication considerations. For example, if the list of information for a drop-down list exists in a table inside of a SQL database, some sort of logon authentication will be required for gaining access to that data.

Not every form is going to receive data, but most forms will be submitted to a location. When form data is submitted to SharePoint, much can be done with that information. Custom views, reporting, filtering, and workflows can be used. If the first requirement is that all forms should be submitted to a database, it is important to ask yourself *why*. The simplest way to gather form data is in a library. As long as you understand that users can easily discern what is needed from submitted data, you often have no need to get a database involved. As we go through the next factors, the data will be a consideration in several cases.

Note In Chapter 13, "SharePoint Views and Dashboards," you will learn about reporting and how to make the most of the data that has been gathered in forms and submitted to SharePoint.

Your SharePoint Version

Depending on which version of SharePoint you have—whether it is SharePoint Online with Office 365, SharePoint Server 2010, or SharePoint Foundation—you are going to have limitations:

- **Office 365 plans E3 and E4** These plans provide InfoPath Forms Services, which means that browser-based forms can be created.

- **Other Office 365 plans** The E1, E2, and other Office 365 plans do not include InfoPath Forms Services, which means that browser-based forms are not sup-ported. A person filling out the form would need the InfoPath Filler software on his computer.

- **SharePoint Server 2010 Enterprise** With SharePoint Server Enterprise, there are no limitations. Every type of form can be created. However, just because there are no compatibility hindrances doesn't mean that form decisions are any easier. With no limits and all options available, it is even more difficult to know what direction to go each time you create a new form.

- **SharePoint Foundation and Standard** These versions of SharePoint do not offer forms services, which means no browser-based forms. A person filling out the form would need the InfoPath Filler software on his computer.

In this chapter, as we go over the factors in form decision-making, the following options will be represented by circles:

- **Enterprise**   SharePoint Server 2010 Enterprise
- **Non-Enterprise**   SharePoint Standard, SharePoint Foundation, and Office 365 plans other than E3 and E4
- **Office 365**   Plans E3 and E4

Factors to Consider

Before creating an InfoPath form, it is important that the requirements have been gathered and that you have a clear vision of what the form, layout, rules, and possible workflow might look like. What is different about these types of form templates, and why is the compatibility level important? Specific controls and functions are used in each form, and some of these can be used only with certain versions of SharePoint and the client. Don't worry: if you try to do something like insert a control that is not compatible, InfoPath's Design Checker will let you know. For each factor that is listed, in the box on the left, find your SharePoint version, and the box on the right will let you know which types of form template or compatibility can be used.

Repeating Tables

Will the form need to have repeating tables? What is a repeating table? An example is an expense report form. A form is filled out for each trip you take, but each trip has multiple expenses to enter. This type of list uses controls called *repeating tables* and *repeating sections*, which can allow multiple list items inside of a single form. This is called a *hierarchical information structure*, and it is not available in SharePoint list forms.

Note   For more information about repeating tables, see Chapter 3, "Form Design Basics: Working with InfoPath Layout, Controls, and Views."

Large Number of Fields

How many fields will there be in the form? When a client-based or browser-based form library form is created, you can pick and choose which fields are promoted to become columns in the library. When a SharePoint list form is created, each field is equivalent to a column in SharePoint. As a general rule, if a form is going to have more than 50 or 60 fields, it is a better idea to use a form library form.

User Roles

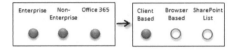

This feature allows you to define a set of Active Directory users and their roles in the form. For each set of user names or group names, roles can be assigned. Conditions in the rules of the form can look at what the current user's role is and perform actions accordingly. Following are some caveats when working with user roles:

- They do not work with SharePoint groups.

- Only Active Directory groups or individual logon names can be used. In general, it is not a good practice to put individual names in a form. When there is attrition in the company, it is hard for form developers to keep track of which forms need to be modified.

- User roles are available only with client-based (filler) forms, but that's okay. You have several ways to achieve the same functionality without it. For example, there is a user profile service, which is discussed in Chapter 9, "Working with the SharePoint User Profile Web Service."

When we can tap into all of the profile information about any user, such as her department or manager's name, the form's rules can be tailored by basing conditions on the values in those fields.

Spelling Checker, AutoComplete, Placeholder Text

Text box controls have settings on the display tab of their properties, which lets you select check boxes to enable AutoComplete and the spelling checker. Placeholder text is the gray text that appears in a field before it is filled in. These settings will be visible, but the functionality will not exist when the form is filled out in a browser.

Tip With browser-based forms, the browser's inherent AutoComplete settings will be used, which are independent of the InfoPath setting.

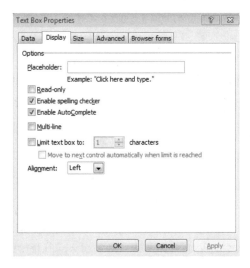

Tip Instead of using placeholder text, go to the Advanced tab and fill in the ScreenTip box. This text will display as a ToolTip and is compatible with browser-based forms.

Submit to a Database

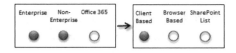

One of the templates you can choose creates a form based on a database. Even if this template is not initially selected, there is also a type of data connection that can be created for submitting data directly to a database. Third-party tools can be purchased to accomplish this. In many cases, companies use in-house developers to write web services to communicate with their proprietary systems.

Form Parameters

New in SharePoint 2010 are form input and output parameters. During a form's publishing process, a dialog box opens in which you can select form fields to use as input, output, or input/output parameters. With parameters, you can use the InfoPath Form Web Part on Web Part pages. Parameters can be passed to the form from other Web Parts, and vice versa.

Note Learn more about the InfoPath Form Web Part and parameters in Chapter 8, "Using the InfoPath Form Web Part."

Offline Forms

Does the form need to be filled out when the client computer is offline, not connected to the network? A setting in the form's options allows users to fill out the form if data is unavailable. Before making the initial form decision, you'll need to understand the following factors:

- A form cannot be filled in offline in the browser. This means that although a form can be configured with browser-based compatibility, some client software will be required for those users who will be filling out the form offline.

- If the form is a SharePoint list form, it can be filled out offline by using SharePoint Workspace 2010.

- For form library forms, the InfoPath Filler software must be installed on the client. Also, caching data from secondary data sources occurs only when the form is filled out on the client.

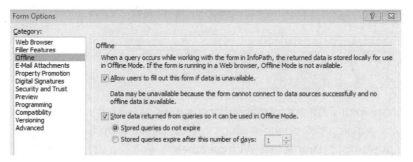

Note The offline setting and how it is used will be covered in Chapter 14, "Advanced Options."

Other Controls

A set of more obscure form controls are available only in client-based forms. These controls are vertical labels, ink pictures, signature lines, scrolling regions, horizontal regions,
repeating recursive sections, horizontal repeating tables, master/detail, and repeating
choice groups. If any of these are used on the form, it cannot be published as a browser-
based form.

Administrator-Approved Template

An administrator-approved template is an XSN file that is created and uploaded in Central
Administration in the Enterprise version of SharePoint Server. This can be done in cases
where a form needs to be deployed globally, to multiple site collections. In some cases,
the form must be created as an administrator-approved template and cannot simply be
published to a form library. The following are some major factors:

- **Custom code**   In some cases, the built-in functionalities in InfoPath are not sufficient, and custom code is added to the form. When custom code is involved, the
  form's compatibility settings must be browser-based and it must be published as an
  administrator-approved template.

- **Data sources across site collections**   When data sources receive data from or submit data to a site collection other than the one where the form is being filled out, the form must be created as an administrator-approved template. Otherwise, when the form is opened and queries the data, the user is presented with an error.

- **Full-trust or restricted security level**   There are some security settings in the form's options. When the full-trust security level is selected, the form must be published as an administrator-approved template. Furthermore, it must be digitally signed with a trusted root certificate.

When an administrator-approved template is required, it will be obvious during the form publishing process.

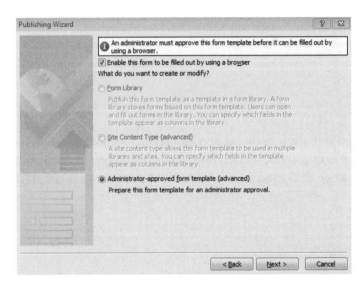

Note Learn more about publishing and submitting forms in Chapter 6, "Publishing and Submitting Form Data," and learn more about InfoPath Forms Services in Chapter 12, "Managing and Monitoring InfoPath Forms Services."

Custom Code in SharePoint Online with Office 365

Programmers can add managed code to their forms by using Visual Studio Tools for Applications (VSTA), which is a setup component when installing InfoPath 2010. If the Microsoft SharePoint Foundation Sandboxed Code Service is running on the site collection, administrators can publish form templates (that have code) to form libraries as sandboxed solutions. If the form designer is also the site collection administrator, she can publish forms without requiring SharePoint Online Administrator approval. The sandboxed solutions will run in an environment that has access to a subset of the server object model. Forms with the "full trust" security setting are not supported in SharePoint Online.

Note Read more about sandboxed solutions in the SharePoint Online for Office 365 Developer Guide at *http://msdn.microsoft.com/en-us/library/hh147180.aspx*.

The Design Checker

When overwhelmed with form decisions and compatibility considerations, InfoPath's Design Checker can help you out. When compatibility issues occur, InfoPath will let you know. In InfoPath, when designing a form, click the File menu to see the Design Checker button.

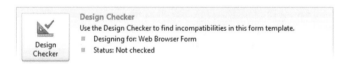

In the following exercise, you will create a new blank form and then test it by using the Design Checker. When controls that are not supported in the current compatibility setting are added to a form, the Design Checker will show an error. Chapter 3 will cover form layouts and controls in detail; in this exercise, you will be testing compatibility settings only.

SET UP Open InfoPath Designer 2010.

Design
Form

1. In the Backstage view, select **New**. Click **SharePoint Form Library** from the list of templates, and then click **Design Form** on the right.

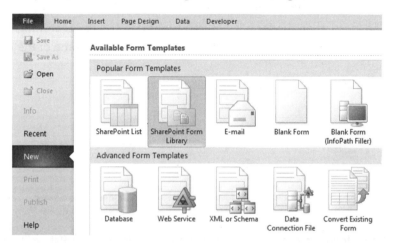

2. By default when this form library template is selected, the form is browser-compatible. Take a quick look at the list of controls that are available. On the ribbon, click the **Home** tab, and then click the arrow at the bottom right of the **Controls** section.

3. Scroll through the list of controls in the pane on the right, and take a quick look at the control names.

4. Click **File**, and then select **Form Options.**

Form
Options

5. In the **Category** section, select **Compatibility**, and then in the **Form type** field, change the selection to **InfoPath Filler Form**. Click **OK**.

A non–browser-compatible control will be inserted on the form. Now that the form has been converted to a Filler form, you will add a control from the **Containers** section.

 Scrolling Region   **6.** Click the **Scrolling Region** control to add it to the form.

The location on the form is not important because this is a simple test. The following screenshot shows the empty scrolling region and some of the controls on the right.

Some features and settings are not compatible, and InfoPath is intelligent enough to indicate this with an error. InfoPath will not allow the form to be published until the errors are resolved. Other incompatible settings will give a warning but will not prevent the form from being published. One such example is the placeholder text.

7. From the list of controls on the right, insert a text box on the form. Again, because this is a test, it is not important where this text box is placed.

8. Double-click the new text box, and then on the **Properties** tab, click the **Control Properties** button.

9. On the **Data** tab, for the **Field Name**, type **FirstName**. On the **Display** tab, in the **Placeholder** box, type **Type your first name here**, and then click **OK**.

10. On the **Home** tab, click the **Preview** button to see what the placeholder looks like.

Notice that as soon as you start to type in the text box, the placeholder text disappears.

11. Click the **Close Preview** button.

12. To demonstrate the Design Checker's compatibility errors and warnings, the form will change back to a browser-based form. Click **File**, and then select **Form Options** again. In the compatibility section, set the form type to **Web Browser Form**, and then click **OK**.

Notice that the horizontal region on the form has a red error on it now, alerting you that this control is not supported. A message about the placeholder text will also be displayed on the text box that was inserted. It's time to run the Design Checker.

13. Click the **File** menu, and then select **Design Checker**.

All of the errors on the form will be displayed in the Design Checker pane. When you go through the form and remove incompatibilities such as the placeholder text and scrolling region, click the Refresh button at the bottom of the pane to refresh the list of errors.

 CLEAN UP Close InfoPath Designer, and then when prompted to save changes, click Don't Save.

Note For a full list of all InfoPath features that are not compatible with browser-based forms, see the following web page: *http://office.microsoft.com/en-us/infopath-help/infopath-2010-features-unavailable-in-web-browser-forms-HA101732796.aspx*.

Form Library Settings

In a form library's advanced settings, there is an option that enables documents to open in the browser. For the non-enterprise clients, this setting is irrelevant because the forms will never open in the browser.

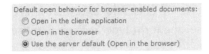

By default, when forms are opened, they use the server default option, which is to open in the browser. However, you can select the Open In The Client Application setting if you want to force the form to open in InfoPath Filler. If you want to make sure that the form is always opened in the browser, whether the client has the filler installed or not, select Open In The Browser.

Combine Client-Based and Browser-Based Controls

Are there some controls or features that need to be included in your form that are not browser-compatible but that a certain subset of users need access to? There's a setting for that!

Note Chapter 3 provides detailed information about the concept of views in a form.

The compatibility settings can be changed per view in a single form. On the Page Design tab in InfoPath, when a view is selected, the Properties button can be used to modify the settings for each view.

To add browser-incompatible controls to this view, select the Design view for InfoPath Filler Only check box. With this option enabled, only clients who are filling out the form with the InfoPath client software can use this view.

Using the Decision Matrix

This chapter has presented an overview of design considerations when starting to build a form. Each time a new form is created, this quick list of factors can be used for deciding which type of form can or should be created. Again, before deciding what type of form or template to create, form requirements should be gathered. Now we'll go through some examples of the decision-making process:

- **The Simple "New Employee" Form**   The new employee form has 20 fields that need to be filled out for each new hire in the company. The fields are all text boxes and drop-down boxes. The form contains no repeating tables, and no other complex requirements are needed.

  - If you have SharePoint Server 2010 Enterprise or Office 365, this form can be created from the SharePoint List template.

  - If you have a non-enterprise version of SharePoint or Office 365, this form will be created from the Blank Form (InfoPath Filler) template and published to a form library.

- **The Expense Report**   Each time an employee travels, he needs to fill in this form. It will contain multiple lines in a table, representing a row for each receipt from the trip. Because the form will need a repeating table, it cannot be created as a SharePoint list form. No special controls are needed, but the form might need to be filled out offline.

  - For all versions of SharePoint, this form is created as a form library form, and the SharePoint Form Library template can be used. For non-Enterprise customers, the compatibility level will need to be changed to InfoPath Filler Form.

  - Clients who will be filling out the form offline need to install the InfoPath Filler client on their computers.

- **The Vacation Request**   This form needs to be deployed to multiple site collections and have a data connection that receives data from a SharePoint list in another site collection.

  - For Enterprise versions, this form can be published as an administrator-approved template and can be uploaded to the list of form templates in Central Administration. The data connection can be converted to a universal data connection and uploaded to the list of data connections in forms services in Central Administration.

○ For non-Enterprise versions and Office 365, it is not possible to deploy a single form to multiple site collections at once. It could be published as a content type, but this could be done only for one site collection at a time. The data connection to another site collection would not be supported.

Key Points

- When a new form is created in InfoPath Designer, a form template must be selected.
- Browser-based forms do not require any specific client software, but filler forms require that InfoPath Filler is installed on client computers.
- There are five compatibility settings; these settings can be changed at any point.
- Newly introduced in SharePoint 2010, SharePoint list forms can be customized by using InfoPath.
- Existing Word documents or Excel spreadsheets can be converted to InfoPath forms.
- The location of the data is important to know because a form's complexity can be increased if it needs to be received from or submitted to a database, rather than SharePoint.
- It is important to become familiarized with the organization's current version of SharePoint or Office 365 because it is a big factor in the form decision-making process.
- With each of the list of factors, to determine which type of template should be used, consider the current version of SharePoint and the priority of the requirement.
- When custom code is included in the form, the form can be deployed in only a limited number of scenarios.
- The Design Checker can compare the current compatibility settings to the currently used controls and functionalities and subsequently list any errors and warnings.

Chapter at a Glance

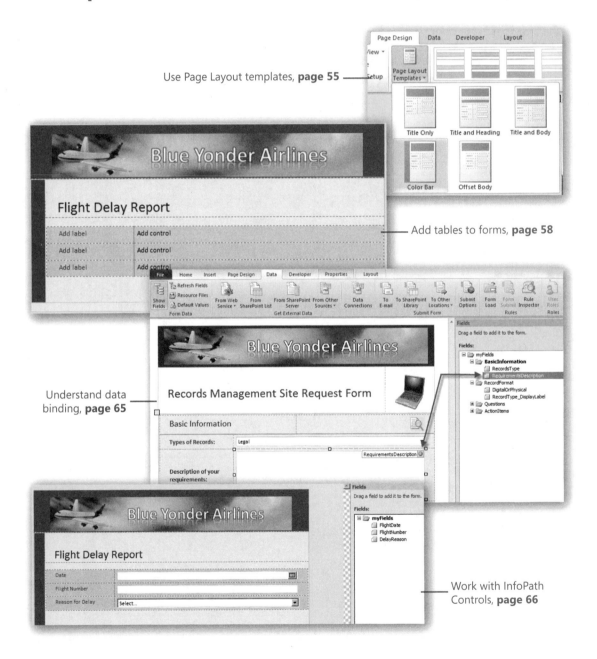

Use Page Layout templates, **page 55**

Add tables to forms, **page 58**

Understand data binding, **page 65**

Work with InfoPath Controls, **page 66**

3 Form Design Basics: Working with InfoPath Layout, Controls, and Views

In this chapter, you will learn how to:

✔ Use InfoPath's layout tools to build visually appealing forms

✔ Work with the InfoPath Table tools

✔ Add fields and controls to your forms

✔ Use sections and containers to organize the controls in your form

✔ Add multiple views to a form

Most Microsoft InfoPath forms you create will have several basic design concepts in common. The form design process typically begins with the following two tasks:

● Building the visual aspects of the form by using tables, themes, and page designs.

● Adding the necessary controls to provide the functionality and data fields that your form requires.

Depending on the complexity of the form, you might need to do much more than this, but typically the creation of most InfoPath forms starts with layout and controls. In this chapter, you will learn how to build a form from scratch with visual layouts, themes, controls, and views.

In Chapter 1, "Introducing Microsoft InfoPath 2010," you learned that InfoPath uses XML for storing data and managing the schema of the form for you. Most of the tools you will use to build the form have a direct correlation to the underlying XML. However, InfoPath removes the need for you to interact with all of the XML "plumbing" behind the scenes. For example, when you add a simple text control, InfoPath automatically generates an XML leaf node (the XML equivalent of an InfoPath field) in the underlying XML schema. Once again, it is not necessary to be an XML guru to use InfoPath, but it is important to understand that when you create an InfoPath form, InfoPath is generating a "well-formed" XML document for you.

> **Practice Files** Before you can complete the exercises in this chapter, you need to copy the book's practice files to your computer. The practice files you'll use to complete the exercises in this chapter are in the Chapter 3 practice file folder. A complete list of practice files is provided in "Downloading the Practice Files and eBook," on page xxvi.

Form Layout

Depending on which template you choose when you first generate a new form in InfoPath Designer, you will find yourself with a relatively clean slate on which to work. Essentially, the Blank Form template has nothing on it other than a simple design surface. The SharePoint Form Library template shown in the following illustration has slightly more structure, including predefined tables and locations for controls.

Notice in the preceding illustration that the InfoPath Designer displays gridlines along the borders of the tables. These gridlines are to assist you in designing and formatting a new template. They are not displayed when the form is actually being filled out by a user. They are purely a "design-time" feature. InfoPath has several design-time visuals to assist you when you are in design mode.

It is important that we clarify a couple terms that will be used in this chapter—when you are in Designer building a form, you are in *design time,* working with the *design surface.* When you preview the form or actually fill out a form instance, you are in *run time.* Run time is the experience your users will have when they fill out your forms.

Tip When you are in Designer, you can press the F5 key to quickly preview a form in run time mode. This functionality is also available on the Home tab on the ribbon by clicking the Preview button.

The design time visual layout tools that you will use most often can be found on the ribbon. The following tabs on the ribbon are relevant to form layout:

- **The Home tab**   This is where you can find the basic text editing tools that you would find in a word processor. The functionality available on the Home tab is for controlling fonts size, color, and so forth. These tools are fairly standard and work just like the other Microsoft Office products.

- **The Insert tab**   This is where you can find the pre-built table styles. These tables can give your forms a consistent and professional layout.

- **The Page Design tab**   The Page Design tab contains InfoPath's predefined page layouts and color themes to quickly give your form a professional look and feel. The color themes are the same ones that are in Microsoft SharePoint 2010, so it's easy to make your forms blend in nicely on a SharePoint site. Also, on the Page Design tab you can work with Views and add headers and footers if necessary.

- **The Layout tab**   Also known as the Table Tools tab, the tools on this tab are used for modifying properties of the tables in your forms. Tables are the primary structural tool for organizing controls, labels, and images in your forms. This is also the location where you can use the Table Drawing tool if you don't want to use any of the provided table styles.

There are two schools of thought regarding how to build a new form:

- Use one of the built-in page layouts, adding some tables and a color theme, and then adding data controls.

- Start by adding all the data fields you need (in the Fields pane), and then worry about design and layout later.

The second, more idealistic approach can be a good choice if you already know what data fields, data types, and controls you need to support the functionality in your form. Both approaches have their benefits, but the reality is that most of the time you might not have all the information you need to accurately create all your data structures. You will need to modify the form as it comes to life, probably altering it a number of times before it's actually finished.

Therefore, the first approach—starting with a built-in layout and then adding controls—is the one we'll use for the exercises in this chapter because it more closely matches what InfoPath designers often do in the real world. The good news is that InfoPath's design tools and data controls are flexible enough that you can easily add or change your design later as requirements dictate.

Adding a Layout and Table

 SET UP Ensure that you have downloaded to your desktop the **Blue Yonder header. bmp** image file from the Practice Files to your desktop. You will use this image on your form.

In the following exercise, you will create a new blank form and add all the necessary design components such as tables, an image, and a theme. This will be a Flight Delay form that employees of the fictitious Blue Yonder Airlines company use to file reports on reasons why a plane was late in arriving at its destination.

Blank Form

1. On your desktop, click the **Start** button, and then open InfoPath Designer. Double-click **Blank Form**.

2. Place your cursor in the top table row where it says **Click to add title**. The placeholder text should go away.

3. On the ribbon, click the **Insert** tab, and then select **Picture**. Browse to the location on your desktop where you saved the **Blue Yonder** header image file.

4. Double-click the image to insert into the table.

5. Click the image to ensure that it's selected, and then on the **Home** tab, click the **Center Text** button to center the image in the table. Your form should now look like the screenshot that follows.

6. On the ribbon, click the **Page Design** tab. Ensure that your cursor is active in the bottom table row, and then select the **Color Bar** option from the **Page Layout Templates** drop-down list.

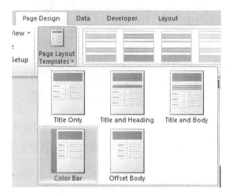

Your form should now have a color bar and an additional row.

7. To give the form a professional color scheme, apply a theme. Select the entire design surface area by clicking the selection button at the upper-left corner of the design surface.

Tip You might need to click inside the top table row to activate the selection button.

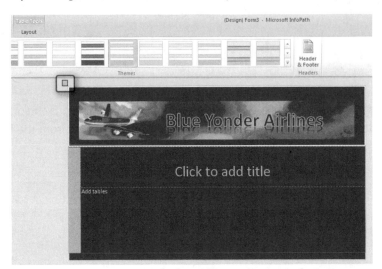

8. With the entire design surface selected, on the ribbon, in the **Themes** area, click the drop-down arrow. Select the **Industrial Vantage** theme to apply this theme.

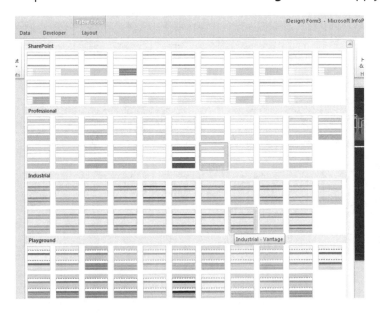

With the theme applied, let's add shading to the top row of the table (the one with the image inside it).

9. Position your cursor in the top row of the table by clicking anywhere within it. On the ribbon, click the **Layout** tab, and then click the drop-down arrow at the bottom of the **Shading** button to show all the colors from the theme that you can apply as shading.

10. Select the blue color **Accent 5, Darker 25%**.

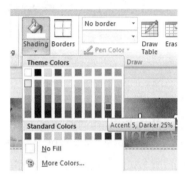

Your form should now appear as below. You're off to a great start on the visual aspect of the Flight Delay Form!

11. Position your cursor in the row with the **Click to add title** text, and then change the title to **Flight Delay Report**.

12. Place your cursor in the bottom row of the form by clicking in the area labeled **Add tables**. On the **Insert** tab, click the **More** button to open the drop-down list for the tables so that you can see all the different options. From the **Two Column** section of tables, choose the **Two Column Offset with Emphasis 4 No Heading** table.

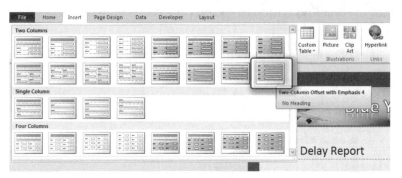

13. Click the **Layout** tab, click the **Cell Padding** button, and then set the top to **16 px** so that there isn't so much excessive empty space above the image.

The cell padding properties are useful for controlling and managing the spaces inside your table cells.

The form should appear similar to that shown in the following illustration. Your form is now ready to have controls added, which you will do in the next exercise, after you learn about InfoPath controls.

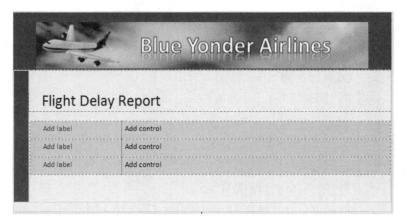

CLEAN UP You will use this template in the next exercise, so be sure to save it; close out of InfoPath Designer if you are not going to continue on to the next exercise right away.

InfoPath Controls

Apart from creating the visual layout, the most common task that you will perform when designing a new form is adding controls. The controls in InfoPath cover a wide range of functionality that you will need in your form. In this section, we will discuss the most commonly used InfoPath controls and provide a brief overview of what each one does.

Tip For the purposes of this book, assume that your forms need to be browser-compatible so that they can work with SharePoint Forms Services. Therefore, we will focus on the controls that are enabled when you create browser-compatible forms. Additional controls are available if your forms will be used only with InfoPath Filler. You can view those additional controls by changing the compatibility of your form from browser to InfoPath Filler. This is performed by going into Form Options in the Info section of the Backstage view. (You can access the Backstage view by clicking the File tab on the ribbon.)

The controls are separated into three different categories when you view them in the Controls pane: Input, Objects, and Containers.

- The functionality of most input controls is fairly self-evident; they capture different types of data from users. (See the table below for a description of the input controls.)

- Object controls are for adding objects that your users will interact with in the form, such as attaching a file or clicking a button.

- Container controls are for grouping controls or adding repeating controls in the forms—for example, a repeating table such as the one you used in Chapter 1 for the Products form.

Input Control Name	Description	Data Type
Text Box	Probably the most common control, which is why it's at the top of the list. Text Box is used for adding text fields that will have standard, unformatted text, such as names, sentences, and numbers.	Text (String)
Rich Text Box	Use this control when you need formatted text, including bold and italic, varying font styles, colors, and sizes.	Rich Text (XHTML)
Drop-Down List Box	Use this control to present users with a list of choices in a drop-down box. The data that populates the list of choices can come from a list that you create manually or from values that come from a data connection to an XML file, database, web service, or a SharePoint list.	Text (String)
Combo Box	This control presents users with a list of choices in a box from which they can either select an item or type their own. The data that populates the list of choices can come from a list that you create manually or from values that come from a data connection to an XML file, database, web service, or a SharePoint list.	Text (String)
Check Box	This control provides the ability to set yes/no or true/false by selecting a check box.	True/False (Boolean)
Option Button	Presents the user with a mutually exclusive choice. When one of the option buttons in a group is selected, the other option buttons are cleared.	Text (String)
Date Picker	Gives the user the ability to type a date or use a calendar button to select a date.	Date
Date and Time Picker	Same as Date Picker but adds time.	Date and Time
List Box	Presents users with a list of choices in a box from which they select the desired item. The data that populates the list of choices can come from a list that you create manually or from values that come from a data connection to an XML file, database, web service, or a SharePoint list.	Text (String)

Input Control Name	Description	Data Type
Bulleted List	Used to add or delete bulleted list items in the form.	Text (String)
Numbered List	Used to add or delete numbered list items in the form.	Text (String)
Plain List	Used to add or delete plain list items in the form.	Text (String)
Person/Group Picker	Use this to select users and groups from the list of members in a SharePoint site. Usually, this means the same list of names that are in your Active Directory and Outlook address list.	String
External Item Picker	Use this control for scenarios in which a user needs to pick an external item from a SharePoint list. External, in this case, means that the data originated from a system outside of SharePoint.	String

Object Controls (described in the following table) are different from Input controls in a couple of important ways. First, Object controls don't necessarily add a field to the underlying XML; some of them are purely for design surface purposes. For example, the Button control creates no fields in the schema but is still one of the most useful InfoPath controls. The other difference with Object controls is that they can be added to the form at design time, and some of them, such as the Hyperlink and Picture controls, can also be added by the user at run time.

Object Control Name	Description	Data Type
Button	Use this control for tasks, such as submitting the form, querying a data source, and much more. The button can have rules associated with it as well, making it a very flexible tool.	n/a
Picture Button	Similar to the Button control in functionality but also allows for the use of an image rather than the standard button look and feel. Another key capability is that the Picture Button control can display a different image when the pointer hovers over it, thus creating a very dynamic experience.	n/a
Calculated Value	Useful for when you want to display read-only text, display the value of another control on the form, or display values based on formulas. This control does not actually store data; it references other data and displays a value.	Variable
File Attachment	Used for attaching a file to the form. If you are creating a SharePoint List form, the file attachment will be stored as part of the SharePoint list rather than in the form itself.	Picture or File Attachment
Picture	Used for attaching images (or a link to the image).	Picture or File Attachment
Hyperlink	Allows users to insert a hyperlink in a form.	Text (String)

As defined in the following table, Container Controls are designed to group other controls together for the purposes of organizing (for example, the Section control) or providing repeating and optional data structures (for example, the Repeating Table control). The structure of container controls is different than the other controls in that container controls do not directly contain data themselves. When you add a container control, it appears in the Fields pane as a folder with fields (also called *leaf nodes*) underneath it. Although the containers do not directly contain data, they are extremely useful for organizing data because they represent a group node in the underlying XML schema. This is a key difference between container controls and tables. While tables are excellent for visual layout, they do not connect to the data source and therefore can't have properties and rules applied to them in the same way container controls can. Therefore, the best practice is to use tables and controls inside a Section control (or other type of container) when you need to manage controls together as a group.

Containers

- Section
- Optional Section
- Repeating Section
- Repeating Table
- Choice Group
- Choice Section

Container Control Name	Description
Section	Container for other controls. A Section control can include any of the other controls (including other Section controls). When you add a Section control, an XML group is added in the schema. This means that you can apply validation and formatting rules to the Section, and thus to all the controls contained within it (more on rules in Chapter 5, "Adding Logic and Rules to Forms").
Optional Section	Same as a Section control except that users are given the choice at run time as to whether or not they want to add that particular section to the form.
Repeating Section	Same as Section control except that users are given the ability to add additional instances of the Section, either above or below it.
Repeating Table	Used for adding tables that display information in a tabular structure and allow the user to add or delete rows. As with Section containers, repeating tables can contain other controls.
Choice Group	A unique control that contains two or more Choice Sections. The form users can replace one Choice Section with another at run time. When filling out a form with a Choice Group, users can replace the default Choice Section with a different Choice Section.
Choice Section	Like a regular Section control, this is a control that contains other controls. But Choice Sections are used inside Choice Groups. Choice Sections are useful when you need to add more choices to an existing Choice Group. They can be used only inside a Choice Group or repeating Choice Group (Filler-only control). If you try to add a Choice Section outside of a Choice Group, InfoPath automatically adds the Choice Group for you.

Control Properties Ribbon

When working with controls, many properties can be set. However, the specific properties that you can set vary, based on the type of control. Fortunately, the ribbon has a Properties tab that becomes active when you select a control in a form. This is a convenient central location in which you can work with nearly all the options available to you for a particular control.

Following are the main control-related tasks that you can carry out on the control Properties tab:

● You can change the name of a control. As a best practice, you should always rename your controls to something that is meaningful to you.

● For certain controls, you can change the data type and data format on the fly.

● You can set default values so that the form will have pre-populated values in fields where it makes sense.

● You can use the Change Binding button to change the binding of the control to a different field in the schema.

● You can set the field to be read-only if you don't want users modifying data in that particular field, or conversely, you can set the field to require data input by selecting the Cannot Be Blank check box.

● If you've added the control as the wrong type, you can change it (for example, changing Text Box to Rich Text Box).

● All of the aesthetic properties of the control can be modified here, including height, shading, and borders.

● And last but definitely not least, you can add and manage logic rules on your control (more on this in Chapter 5).

Understanding the Basics of Data Binding

When you add a control to the form design surface, InfoPath automatically creates a field in the underlying InfoPath document that corresponds to the correct data type for your field. (For example, a Text Box is a string data type.) This process of tying the control to the field in the underlying XML is called *data binding*. You can easily tell which field a control is bound to simply by selecting the control on the design surface; InfoPath then automatically selects and highlights the bound field in the Fields pane. You can also create your own fields in the Fields pane if you need to, but to keep things simple, it's generally best to let InfoPath generate the fields for you when possible. There are obvious exceptions, such as when you need a hidden field that will be used to store some data or variable but won't actually be displayed on the form. The following screenshot shows the correlation between a control on the design surface and its corresponding entry in the Fields pane.

Tip It is always a best practice to rename your fields to something useful that you can understand. By default, InfoPath uses field1, field2, and so on.

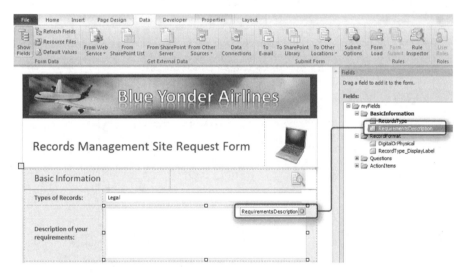

When you add a control on to the design surface, InfoPath automatically adds the corresponding field or group to the Main data source. As you saw in Chapter 1, it is possible to have multiple data sources for your form if you need to integrate data that is coming from other sources, such as databases, XML files, or web services.

Tip Because fields are automatically generated in the data source when you add a control, a common point of confusion for beginning InfoPath users arises from the false assumption that the fields are also automatically deleted if the control is removed from the design surface. To remove the field from the data source, in the Fields pane, right-click the field, and then choose Delete.

Most controls will automatically create a field in the data source that they are bound to, but not all. For example, the Button control is purely a visual design tool, and by default, it's not bound to anything. Basically, your controls will be bound to two types of structures: fields and groups. Fields are equivalent to XML leaf nodes, which means that they are used for holding and working with data (for example, text fields). Groups are equivalent to XML container nodes; they are for holding and organizing other fields. Section controls are probably the most common group objects. The following screenshot shows a section on the design surface that has multiple controls associated with it. Notice how it correlates to a folder (group) in the Fields pane.

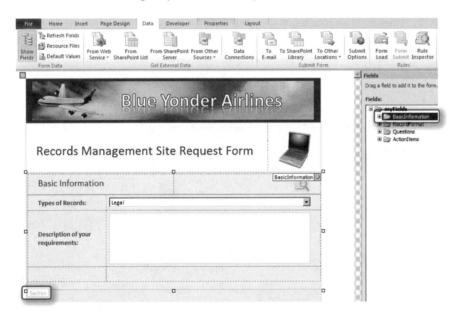

Adding Controls to the Flight Delay Form

 SET UP Open InfoPath Designer and the **Flight Delay** form you created in the first exercise of this chapter. Alternatively, you can download the practice file named **Flight Delay Post exercise 1.xsn**. Remember, you can right-click the .xsn template file, and then choose Design.

In the following exercise, you will continue building the Flight Delay Form. Your job now is to add the controls that will provide the needed functionality. The data you need to capture includes the items listed in the following table.

Data Needed	Control You Will Use
Date	Date Picker
Flight number	Text Box
Reason for flight delay	Drop-Down List Box
Follow-up ticket awards	Repeating Table with 3 columns (Customer Name, Half-Price Ticket, Free Ticket)
Pilots report	Choice Group (File Attachment or Hyperlink)
Submit button	Button

1. In the top row of the table on the form, position your cursor in the label field, and then type **Date**.

2. Tab into or click in the first row of the right column. On the ribbon, click the **Date Picker** control. Remove the label that InfoPath automatically inserted.

   There are two ways by which you can add controls to a form. One is to position your cursor on the design surface so that it's active in the location where you want the control added. Then, click the desired control on the ribbon or the **Controls** pane to add it at that location on the form. The second method is to drag a control from the **Controls** pane. To open the **Controls** pane, click the expansion arrow at the bottom of the **Controls** area on the ribbon, as shown here:

   In the following screenshot, you can see the fully expanded **Controls** pane.

Tip By default, InfoPath automatically creates a field in the **Fields** pane when you add the data control. (You can turn this off by clearing the check box at the very bottom of the **Controls** pane.) If you accidentally delete your control from the design surface, you can add it back to the form by dragging it from the **Fields** pane. Remember, deleting the visual occurrence of the control from the design surface does not remove it from the schema in the **Fields** pane. Likewise, if you accidentally add a control that you don't want, you can right-click and delete the field from the **Fields** pane. If you do this, the control will still appear on the design surface but it will have a blue warning icon that indicates it is unbound, as shown in the following screenshot. Unbound controls are those that have lost their connection to fields in the underlying schema. You want to remove unbound controls because they will not function.

3. On the ribbon, click the **Control Tools/Properties** tab set, and then rename the **Date Picker** field that you just added to **FlightDate**.

This will alter the name of the field in the **Fields** pane so that later you can remember the purpose of this field. This is much better than **Field1**. (Remember, you need to select the control that you want to modify in order to activate the **Control Tools** tab on the ribbon.)

The next thing you need to do for the **Date** field is to add a default value. Default values are extremely helpful when you want a control to be pre-populated with a value for the user. The user can still optionally select or enter a different value, but in a case such as a date, it often makes sense to just populate the control with a default value so that the user doesn't need to enter anything.

4. Verify that your date control is the active selection, and then on the **Control Tools** tab, click the **Default Value** button

5. Click the formula button on the default values field.

6. Click the **Insert Function** button, find the **Date** category, and then select **today**.

This sets the default value of the **Date Picker** control to be equal to the current day. This makes sense because users will most likely be entering flight delay information on the same day it happens.

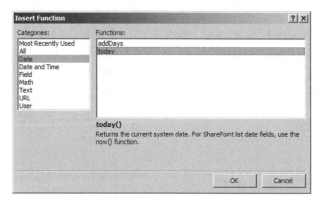

7. Click **OK** three times to return to the design surface. Preview your form by pressing **F5** to confirm the date field populates with the current date.

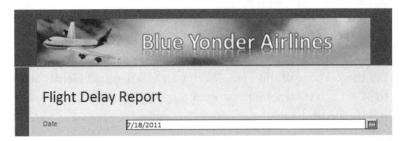

8. On the second row, add a label that says **Flight Number**, and then add a **Text Box** control. Remove the auto-generated label, and then rename the field to **FlightNumber** by using the **Control Tools** tab.

   Tip If you prefer, you can also right-click a field in the **Fields** pane, and then change the name of the field by using the **Properties** option.

9. On the third row of the table, enter **Reason for Delay** in the **label** column, and then add a **Drop-Down List Box** control in the right column. Rename the field to **DelayReason**.

   Your form should now look like the following screenshot.

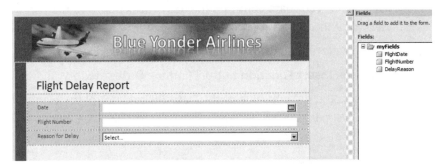

10. Ensure that the **Drop-Down List Box** control is the active selection, and then on the ribbon click the **Properties** tab. Click the **Edit Choices** button. Click the **Add** button, enter **National Aviation System** into the **Value** field, and then click **OK**.

11. Add three more choices: **Weather**, **Late-Arriving Aircraft**, and **Security**. Click **OK**.

    You can preview the form **(F5)** at this point to ensure that your drop-down list is working.

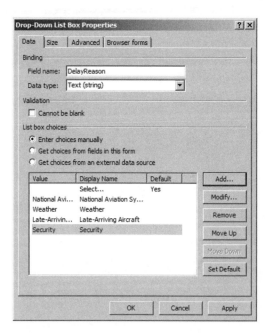

The next control you need is a **Repeating Table**, in which the form users can enter a list of customers that need to be awarded a free or half-priced flight as a result of the flight delay.

12. Position your cursor below the table on the design surface, press **Enter** a couple times to give yourself some space between tables, and then insert a **Repeating Table** control. Set it for 3 columns.

13. The top row of the new repeating table is for labels. In the left column, enter **Customer Name**; in the middle column, enter **Half Price Ticket**; and in the right column, enter **Free Ticket**.

14. Using either the **Fields** pane or the **Properties** tab, rename the three fields to **CustomerName**, **HalfPriceTicket**, and **FreeTicket**, respectively.

15. With the **HalfPriceTicket Text Box** control active on the design surface, use the ribbon to change the control from **Text Box** to a **Check Box**. Do the same thing to the **FreeTicket** control.

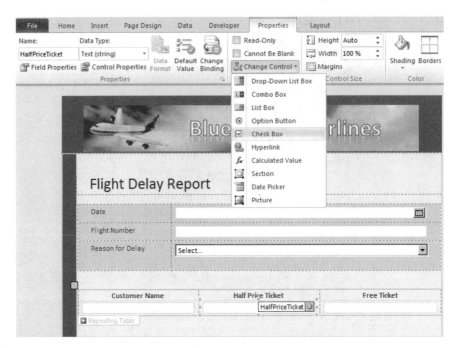

16. Select the **Check Box** controls. On the **Home** tab, in the **Format Text** area click the **Center** button to center the controls in the column. Preview the form, and verify that it looks like the following screenshot. Enter a name or two; use the **Insert item** arrow to add more rows to your repeating table.

17. Add a **Choice Group** control in the **Container** controls by positioning your cursor beneath the repeating table and then pressing the **Enter** key twice (to allow a little space). On the ribbon or in the **Controls** pane, add a **Choice Group** control.

18. Rename the two fields that were added (they are actually Choice Sections) to **ReportHyperlink** and **ReportFileAttachment**.

19. Inside the **ReportHyperLink** section, add a **Hyperlink** control, and then rename it to **PilotHyperlink**.

20. Inside the **ReportFileAttachment** sections, add a **File Attachment** control and rename it to **PilotFileAttachment**.

The reason why you are adding this **Choice Group** control is because the pilots are required to submit a report in the event of a flight delay. They can either post it on a SharePoint site or email the file. So use a **Choice Group** control to allow the form user to either directly add a file attachment or provide a hyperlink to the report on a SharePoint site. The form should now appear as shown in the following illustration (in Design mode).

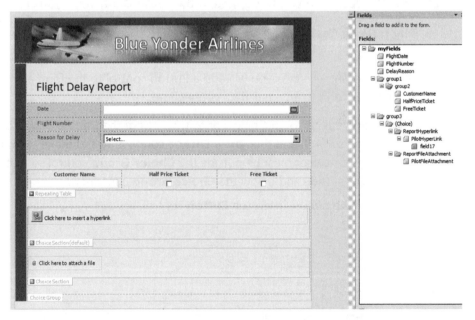

If you preview the form now, you will see a button pop up when you hover over the **Hyperlink** control in the **Choice Group** control. You can click this button to switch between a **Hyperlink** control and a **File Attachment** control.

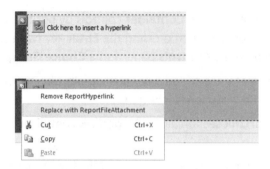

 CLEAN UP Be sure to save your form template. You will add more functionality to the **Flight Delay** form in the next exercise.

Adding a Submit Button with a Rule to the Flight Delay Form

SET UP Open InfoPath Designer and the **Flight Delay** form you created in the last exercise of this chapter. Alternatively, you can download the practice file named **Flight Delay Post exercise 2.xsn**. Remember, you can right-click the .xsn template file, and then choose Design.

In the following exercise, you will add a Button control to the form along with a rule that submits the form to an email data connection.

1. Insert your cursor just below or to the right of the **Choice Group** control on the design surface, and then press **Enter** a couple times to make room to insert a button. Your cursor must be outside the **Choice Group** control so that you have open space (outside and below the **Choice Group** container).

2. From the ribbon, insert the **Button** control.

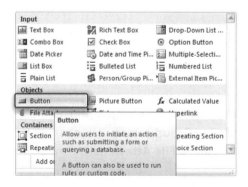

3. On the ribbon, click the **Home** tab, and then in the **Format Text** section, use the center function to position the button in the center of the form.

4. On the **Control Tools** tab, in the **Label** box, change the button's name from **Button** to Submit Form.

5. While still on the **Control Tools** tab, click the **Add Rule** button, and then click **Submit Data** to add a rule that sends the data when a user clicks the button

6. When the **Rule** details window opens, click **Add**.

   When using a rule to submit a form, it is necessary to provide a data connection to instruct InfoPath about how to handle the submission. When the **Data Connection Wizard** opens, it defaults to submit data. Click **Next**.

7. Select **As an e-mail message**.

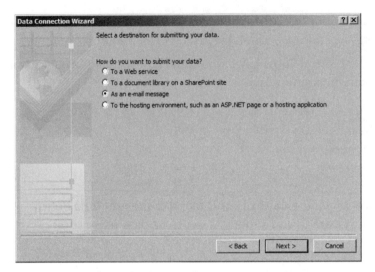

8. On the next wizard page, enter your own email address in the **To:** text box, enter **Flight Delay Report** in the **Subject** text box, and then click **Next**.

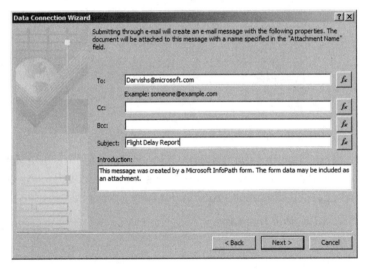

9. Leave the default setting to send as an attachment. Click **Next** again, and then click **Finish**. Click **OK** in the **Rule Details** window so that you're back in the form.

   The **Rules** pane automatically opens for you on the right side of the Designer.

Now you have an email data connection with a submit rule attached to your button so that when users fill out the form and click submit, the form will be emailed to you as an attachment. (You'll find more information about rules in Chapter 5.)

 CLEAN UP Be sure to save your form template if you want to keep your changes, and then close out of InfoPath Designer. You will continue to add more functionality to the form in the next exercise.

Views

Your forms often will have too many controls to fit cleanly on a single page. One of the worst mistakes novice forms designers can make is putting everything on one page and forcing the user to scroll through an unnecessarily long and complex form—or even worse, creating multiple forms for users to fill out when having one consolidated form is far more efficient and manageable. InfoPath views can help alleviate these problems and solve a few other challenges, as well.

A view in InfoPath is simply another way to display data from the same data source, but in a different way. It is perhaps easiest to think of a view simply as another page in the same form. If you create a second view, additional or different fields might be displayed, or even a completely different visual layout, but underneath the covers, all the views in a form use the same data source(s) and schema. The beauty of this approach is that you can manage all the properties of your form—such as security, fields, data connections, and workflows—in one place and still have the power and flexibility of presenting the right view of data to the right people, at the right time.

Following are six common situations for which using InfoPath views make a lot of sense:

- Taking a lengthy or unwieldy form and breaking it into more manageable pieces.
- Building a wizard-like or survey-like interface. Because you can use buttons with rules to switch views, views provide an easy way to build a form with multiple pages through which a user progresses. Chapter 5 has a robust example of a wizard-like form.
- Presenting different views to different users based on role. Using InfoPath Roles, you can define which views a user can see depending on which security groups she is in. For example, your form might need to have an extra page of data that only members of the "Managers in Finance" group can see.

  Note Roles are an InfoPath Filler-only feature.

- Adding a read-only "confirmation" view that displays when the user has finished entering data.
- Providing a summary or roll-up view. Some forms need a dashboard that consolidates data from multiple other views into one place. Also, some forms might need a very different visual layout than the input views of the form.
- Providing a print view. Similar to the summary view, a print view can be useful when you want to give users a page to print out data from your form, consolidated in one special view just for printing.

Adding a Second View to the Flight Delay Form

 SET UP Open InfoPath Designer and the **Flight Delay** form that you created in the last exercise of this chapter. Alternatively, you can download the practice file named **Flight Delay Post exercise 3.xsn**. Remember, you can right-click the .xsn template file, and then choose Design.

In the following exercise, you will add a confirmation view to the Flight Delay form. And you will add another rule to the submit button that moves the user from the Default view (View 1) to the confirmation view.

1. On the ribbon, click the **Page Design** tab.

    The **Page Design** tab is the primary location used for creating and managing views.

2. Click **New View**, and then name it **Confirmation**.

3. On the **Page Design** tab, use the **View** drop-down list to switch back to **View 1**, and then copy the **Blue Yonder Graphic**. Switch back to the **Confirmation** view, and then paste it at the top of the table. From the **Insert** tab, add the **Two-Column with Emphasis 3** table.

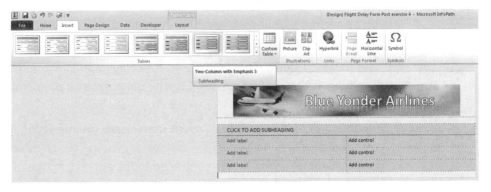

4. In the text area provided for a subheading, type **Confirmation – your submission for the following flight delay has been processed**.

5. In the first label of the table, type **Flight Date**. In the control cell on the same row, insert a **Calculated Value** control from the **Objects** category. Click the function button to edit the formula.

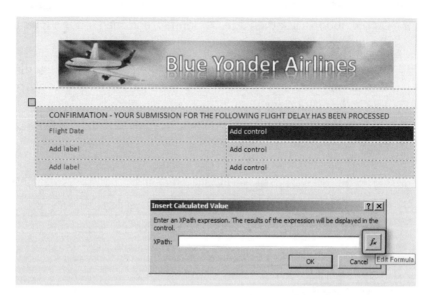

6. Click **Insert Field or Group**, and then select the **FlightDate** field. Click **OK** three times to return to the design surface.

   This adds the value from the **FlightDate** field in **View 1** as a read-only control on the **Confirmation** view.

7. Perform the same steps on the next row for the **Flight Number**. Once again, use the **Calculated Value** control.

8. In the third row of the table, add one more **Calculated Value** control with a label of **Delay Reason**. Your form should now look like the following screenshot.

9. On the ribbon, click the **Page Design** tab, and then in the **Views** area, click the **Properties** button.

Notice all the properties that can be set for the view, including the option to set it as read-only. You don't need to set any properties for the **Confirmation** view right now, so just click **Cancel**.

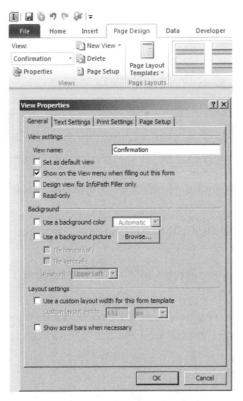

10. On the **Page Design** tab, use the **View** drop-down list to switch back to **View 1**.

11. Make the **Submit** button the active selection, and then on the ribbon, click the **Control Tools** tab. Click the **Add Rule** button, and then select **Switch Views**. Set it to switch to the **Confirmation** view; this rule will automatically redirect a user to the confirmation view when he clicks **Submit**.

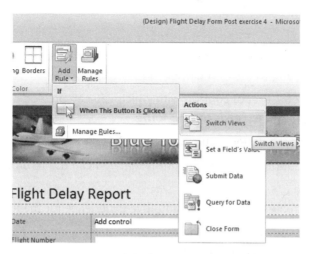

12. Preview your form, and fill out the information as if you were a user. After you've added a flight number, a reason, and so on, click the submit button.

The rules you added on the submit button should perform two actions: first, Info-Path will attempt to email you a copy of the form using your default email program; second, it will automatically switch you to the Confirmation view. Your Confirmation view should now look like the following screenshot.

Congratulations! You now have a functional Flight Delay form that not only collects data but also has a button to submit the form via email and a rule that switches your users to a second view of the form. One last real-world feature that you'd probably want to consider adding is a button on the Confirmation view that makes it easy for the user to close the form. Again, you can do this easily via a Close Form rule on the button. As a best practice, you never want to leave a user guessing what to do with the form when they are done inputting data. A nice, big Close Form button is always a good idea.

 CLEAN UP Be sure to save your form template if you want to keep your changes, and then close out of InfoPath Designer.

Key Points

- InfoPath provides page layout tools and templates that make it easy to build professional-looking forms with tables.
- InfoPath has a robust set of controls with which you can provide different types of input depending on the needs of your form.
- InfoPath controls are bound to the underlying XML schema.
- Containers are data-bound group controls that you can use to organize other controls.
- Default values create an easier, more intuitive experience for the form user.
- You can use InfoPath views to organize your form into multiple pages, which makes the form easier to fill out, or for providing a special print, summary, or confirmation view of the form data.

Chapter at a Glance

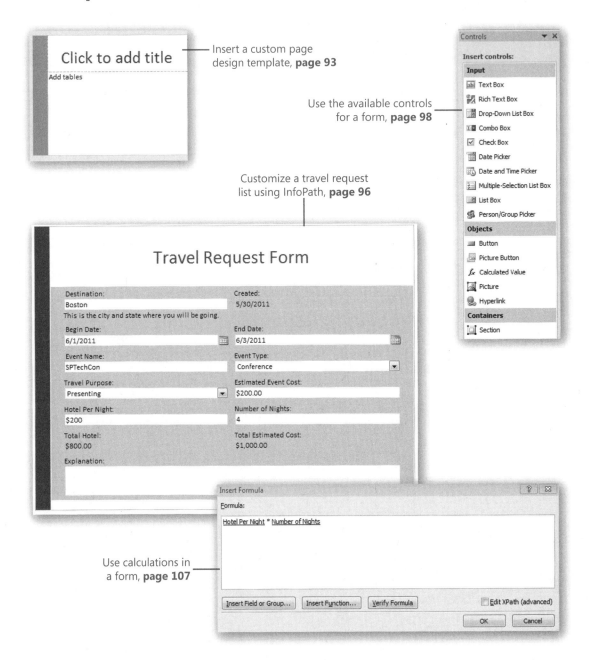

Insert a custom page design template, **page 93**

Use the available controls for a form, **page 98**

Customize a travel request list using InfoPath, **page 96**

Use calculations in a form, **page 107**

4 Working with SharePoint List Forms

In this chapter, you will learn how to:

- ✔ Convert a SharePoint list form to InfoPath
- ✔ Work with fields and controls
- ✔ Modify the list form layout
- ✔ Understand the limitations of list forms

In Microsoft SharePoint 2010 and SharePoint Online, SharePoint list forms can be customized by using Microsoft InfoPath 2010. By default, when SharePoint lists are created, such as tasks, contacts, and other custom lists, the forms that we fill out are .ASPX web pages. The problem with these types of web page forms is that customizing them is not an easy task and usually entails custom development and code modification.

With the ability to quickly and easily customize SharePoint list forms without the need for code or developers, professional-looking business forms can be created efficiently. What is gained by converting a list form to InfoPath? Reasons can range from simply modifying the colors to have a standard corporate look and feel to using advanced concepts such as rules to hide and show controls based on certain conditions.

> **Practice Files** No practice files are required to complete the exercises in this chapter.

Basics of a SharePoint List

A SharePoint list is a simple list of items made up of one or more columns. It can be compared to a spreadsheet or a table in a database. In its simplest form, a SharePoint list consists of a single column called Title; this basic list is called a custom list. When a SharePoint list is first created, the custom list template can be selected and any needed columns can be added and modified to create a business solution. Besides a simple custom list, there are several other templates that you can start with instead, such as the contacts template if you are creating a list of people. A SharePoint list consists of some of the following fundamental components:

- **Columns**   Also referred to as *fields*, columns are the attributes of all of the items that will be entered in the list. For example, for a contacts list, included columns might be First Name, Last Name, Email Address, and Job Title. Each column has a column type that is selected when the column is created. The most common column types are Single Line Of Text, Multiple Lines Of Text, Choice, Number, Currency, Date And Time, Lookup, Yes/No Check Box, Person Or Group, Hyperlink Or Picture, Calculated, External Data, and Managed Metadata.

- **Views**   Views are simply another way of looking at the same list of data. They are also considered to be a very simple reporting method. For each different view that exists in a list, different columns, sorting, grouping, and filtering can be set up. You also have a few more options in view settings, such as inline editing, styles, and totals.

- **Items**   Also referred to as *records*, items are the data that exist in the list. In the example of a list of contacts, each item would be a different person.

- **Versioning**   On each list and library in SharePoint, versioning is a setting that can be turned on. When versioning is used, each time someone saves changes to an item, it is saved as a new version. This gives a nice detailed version history that can be explored, which lists not only who made the change and when, but what fields were changed. Older versions can be viewed and even restored.

- **Alerts**   Each user who visits a SharePoint site has the ability to create alerts on lists or items about which they want to stay informed. An *alert* is an email alert or text message that is sent each time data in the list changes, and several different settings can be configured for each alert. Choose from settings such as whether you would like to be notified when only new items are added, when existing items are changed, and if the notification should come immediately or on a daily or weekly basis.

- **Forms** When entering items into a list, the form is the page with the text boxes, drop-down boxes, and other controls that are filled out with data about that individual item. The transition between the different forms is seamless to the end user, but each list contains three basic forms by default, which will be covered a little later in the chapter.

As you can see, SharePoint lists alone contain a rich set of functionality, even before forms are customized. Concepts such as views and alerts are great as basic methods for reporting and workflows. All of this exists before InfoPath is brought into the picture.

What does InfoPath 2010 give you when it comes to customizing a SharePoint list? Before SharePoint 2010, if list forms needed to be customized, it was done by modifying the code behind the form, using SharePoint Designer or Microsoft Visual Studio. In some cases, it could be done by using a data view Web Part for simple changes, but for more complex functionality, it required some programming knowledge. With InfoPath 2010 and SharePoint 2010, these browser-based forms can be customized so that they are not only visually enhanced but you can also take advantage of the robust features such as conditional formatting. This can all be done with zero programming knowledge, just a little understanding of basic logic.

Note Even though we will use the InfoPath Designer 2010 client to create these forms, the client computers will simply use the browser to fill out forms, so no special software is needed on the end-user computers.

In the following exercise, you will create a travel request as a SharePoint list and customize the list's form using InfoPath.

 SET UP In the web browser, open your SharePoint site so that a new list can be created.

More Options...
Create other types of pages, lists, libraries, and sites.

1. Click **Site Actions**, choose **More Options**, and then choose **Custom List** as the template. Type **Travel Requests** as the list name, and then click **Create**.

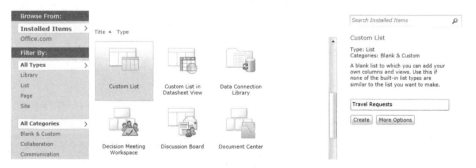

Now that the list has been created, you need to create all of the columns needed for a travel request.

List
Settings

2. On the ribbon, click the **List** tab, and then click the **List Settings** button.

3. Scroll down to the **Columns** section, click the name of the **Title** column, and then rename it **Destination**. Click **OK**.

4. Click the **Created By** column, rename it **Requestor**, and then click **OK**. Every list and library in SharePoint has this **Created By** field, and it can always be renamed.

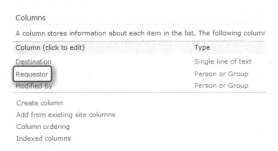

5. Click **Create column**, and create several more columns, as itemized in the following table.

Column Name	Data Type	Other Settings
Begin Date	Date and time	
End Date	Date and time	
Event Name	Single line of text	
Event Type	Choice	**Drop-down menu**: Conference, Meeting
Travel Purpose	Choice	**Radio buttons**: Presenting, Learning, Marketing
Estimated Cost	Currency	**Number of decimal places**: 2
Explanation	Multiple lines of text	**Specify the type of text to allow**: Plain text

Columns

A column stores information about each item in the list. The following column

Column (click to edit)	Type
Destination	Single line of text
Begin Date	Date and Time
End Date	Date and Time
Event Name	Single line of text
Event Type	Choice
Travel Purpose	Choice
Estimated Cost	Currency
Explanation	Multiple lines of text
Requestor	Person or Group
Modified By	Person or Group

6. While still on the **List Settings** page, click **Advanced Settings**. For the attachments setting, change it to **Disabled**, click **OK** at the bottom of the **Advanced Settings** page, and then click **OK** to dismiss the pop-up warning.

Note In this travel request list, it has been determined that attachments will never be necessary when people fill out these requests. The best action to take in this case is to disable the use of attachments. Avoid presenting users with features and buttons that are not needed.

7. Now it's time to create a travel request before converting the list form to InfoPath. In the breadcrumb trail at the top, click the name of the **Travel Requests** list to open the default view of the list.

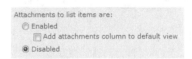

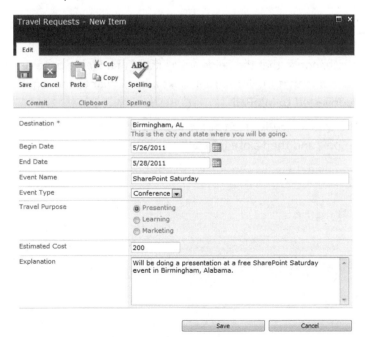 **8.** Click the **Add new item** link next to the green plus symbol, and then fill out a new travel request.

Save

9. Click **Save** after all the information has been filled in.

10. Now that the first list item has been submitted to the list, notice that one row (record) of data appears in the list. Click the name of the new item (**Birmingham, AL**) to display it.

11. Now the form can be customized by using InfoPath Designer 2010. In the **Travel Requests** list, on the ribbon, click the **List** tab, and then click the **Customize Form** button.

Customize Form

> **Tip** A best practice is to create all of the form fields first and then start customizing the form as a last step so that the layout of the fields on the form has to be done only once.

> In InfoPath, notice that the fields are all listed in a **Fields** pane on the right side of the screen and that the form itself looks a bit similar to the regular list form before it was converted to InfoPath.

12. Click the **Quick Publish** icon at the upper-left corner, click **OK** on the confirmation pop-up box, and then close InfoPath.

> **Tip** If you do not see the **Quick Publish** button, click **File**, and then click **Quick Publish**.

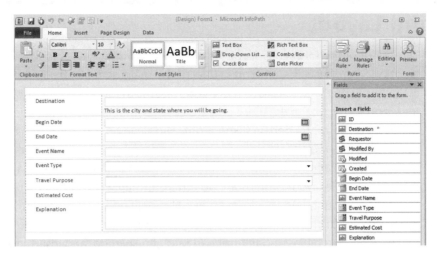

13. With the **Travel Requests** list still open in the browser, it's time to take a look at the form again. Click the name of the previously created list item (**Birmingham, AL**) to view it.

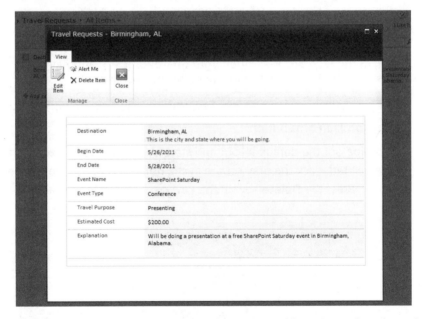

Finally, a simple list has been created and customized by using InfoPath, and the differences between the two types of forms are visible. We will further explore these differences and how they impact your form design decisions.

 CLEAN UP Leave InfoPath Designer and the browser open if you are continuing to the next section of this chapter. Otherwise, close InfoPath Designer and the browser.

List Form Layout

The layout of the form consists of the way it looks visually, its colors, and the arrangement of controls (such as in tables). One of the main benefits of converting a SharePoint list to InfoPath is that you have more control over the way the form looks. It is important to design forms that make sense and are easy to understand. Think about the form from the perspective of the person filling it out, and develop the form so that it will be easy to use. The layout, look, feel, and overall structure are important concepts in making a form that is polished and functional. When it comes to modifying a form's layout, the page design and table layout options are no different than when working in an InfoPath form that has been published to a form library. Not only do you have a plethora of table layout templates to choose from, you have many creative possibilities, including the ability to create custom tables, modify cell padding and shading, and insert images. It can seem a bit overwhelming at times, getting the form to look just right. The exercises in this chapter will give you the confidence to create some well-built, easy to use forms.

In the following exercise, you will customize the layout of the InfoPath form to make it more professional-looking. With the 2010 layout and table features, you will be on your way to creating some great forms.

 SET UP In the web browser, open your SharePoint site and navigate to the **Travel Requests** list that was created in the previous exercise.

1. On the ribbon at the top of the **Travel Requests** list, on the **List** tab, click the **Customize Form** button.

2. To wipe out the default layout and start from scratch, the existing layout needs to be deleted. Click the gray square at the upper-left of the table to select the whole table. Press the **Delete** key on the keyboard to delete this table.

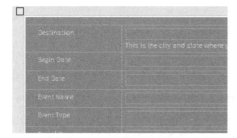

On the now completely blank form, notice that in the **Fields** pane on the right, all of the fields are still there. They are simply not used anywhere on the form yet.

Page Layout
Templates ▾

3. On the ribbon, click the **Page Design** tab, click the **Page Layout Templates** button, and then click to select the layout called **Color Bar**.

Click to add title

Add tables

4. In the field labeled **Click to add title**, type **Travel Request Form**.

5. Put the cursor where it says **Add Tables**, and then on the ribbon, click the **Insert** tab. In the section that has table templates, insert the table template called **Two Column With Emphasis 4**.

Dragging Controls into Tables

Each time a control is dragged over from the list of fields into a table that has more than one column, you have two different ways to place the control into the table.

Label Left of Text Box

While dragging the control into the table, when both the left and right cell appear to be dark (selected) at the same time, release the control.

Label Above Text Box

While dragging the control into the table, when the cursor mouse arrow appears in a single cell and no cells appear to be dark (selected), release the control.

---

6. You can now change the color scheme to reflect the company colors or just your favorite color. On the ribbon, click the **Page Design** tab to see all of the choices for themes. Select the theme called **Professional - Summer**.

Notice that the left column says **Add label** and the right column says **Add control**. With the goal of efficiency and not wasting space on the form, this travel request is going to be configured with each label above each control, instead of in parallel columns. We just need to modify a bit of formatting.

Select

7. Put the cursor in the left column. In the **Layout** tab, click the **Select** button, and then click **Column**.

8. With the left column selected, click the **Home** tab, and then select the **Normal** style.

In addition to switching the style, notice that the bold button is currently toggled on.

9. Click the **Bold** button in the format text section on the ribbon to remove the bold formatting.

10. Two more rows need to be added at the bottom of the table. With the cursor in the last cell, click the **Insert Below** button in the **Layout** tab, twice.

11. From the **Fields** list on the right, drag the following fields into the table:

Table Cell	Field
Row 1, Left	**Destination**
Row 1, Right	**Created**
Row 2, Left	**Begin Date**
Row 2, Right	**End Date**
Row 3, Left	**Event Name**
Row 3, Right	**Event Type**
Row 4, Left	**Travel Purpose**
Row 4, Right	**Estimated Cost**
Row 5, Left	**Explanation**

12. Select both cells in the row that **Explanation** is in, and then on the ribbon, on the **Layout** tab, click **Merge Cells**.

The **Created** field is a built-in date that exists in every list and library in SharePoint, and along with the **Created By (person)** field, it is automatically captured each time a new item is added to the list. Because a date will not exist in the **Created** field until the form has been submitted for the first time, a default value can be displayed so that today's date can be shown while the form is being filled out.

 Created **13.** Double-click the **Created** field in the **Fields** pane on the right.

 14. Click the **fx** button next to the **Value** field.

> **Note** Functions are similar to math formulas and are discussed in Chapter 5, "Adding Logic and Rules to Forms."

Insert Function… **15.** On the **Insert Formula** page, click the **Insert Function** button.

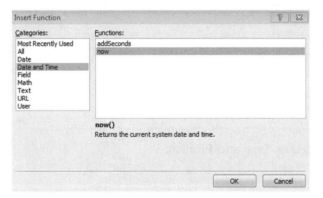

16. In the **Insert Function** dialog, under **Categories**, select **Date and Time**, click **now**, click **OK**, and then click **OK** again.

17. On the **Field or Group Properties** page, clear the **Refresh value when formula is recalculated** check box. Click **OK**.

It should be made obvious when filling out the form that the **Created** date is not something that can be changed. A couple of small cosmetic modifications can change the way this field looks.

18. Delete the second box, which is the time portion of the date. Right-click the date picker box, click **Change Control**, and then click **Text Box**.

19. On the ribbon, on the **Properties** tab, click the **Shading** box, and then choose **No Fill**.

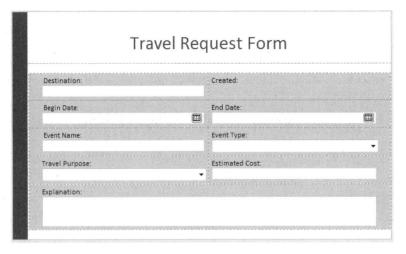

20. Close the window by clicking the **X** at the upper-right corner of the InfoPath window. At the prompt, click **Save and Publish**.

The form has now been customized by using InfoPath, and it can be filled out. Examine your new creation by filling out and saving a new form. The form is much more visually appealing with just a few changes. We've turned an ordinary SharePoint list into an aesthetically pleasing form that is easy to fill out and makes sense.

 CLEAN UP Leave InfoPath Designer and the browser open if you are continuing to the next section of this chapter. Otherwise, close InfoPath Designer and the browser.

List Form Fields

With a SharePoint list form that has been customized with InfoPath, there is a one-to-one ratio of columns that exist in the list settings to the list in the Fields pane in InfoPath. When it comes to this list of fields, not only is there an interface difference between list forms and form library forms but there is a major functional difference, as well. List forms inherently have a flat structure; thus, they cannot have a hierarchical information structure the way form library forms can.

What does this mean to you? It means that there can be no repeating tables in the form or any kind of lists inside of the form. An example of a great use of a repeating table is an expense report. At the top of the form, the information about the trip is entered, such as the destination and department name. In a table inside of the form, all of the rows of data are entered regarding each expense that was incurred. This list could range from one item to as many as necessary. The type of control that is typically used for this in InfoPath is a Repeating Table or Repeating Section. If your form needs a list like this, a SharePoint list is not the best option, and a SharePoint form library would be needed.

Sixteen different types of controls can be used in a SharePoint list, and they are indicated by unique icons. The Home tab on InfoPath's ribbon provides an expandable list of controls.

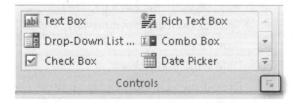

Click the small gray arrow at the lower-right of the Controls section to see the full panel of controls.

Note Chapter 3, "Form Design Basics: Working with InfoPath Layout, Controls, and Views," has more details about all of the types form controls and what each one is used for.

The names of the column types in the lists settings do not match the names of the input controls in InfoPath. The following table displays a mapping of column data types in SharePoint with InfoPath controls.

SharePoint List Data	InfoPath Control Name
Single line of text	Text Box
Multiple lines of text	Rich Text Box or Text Box
Choice	Drop-Down List Box, Option Button, Combo Box, Multiple-Selection List Box, List Box
Number	Text Box (formatted as a number)
Currency	Text Box (formatted as currency)
Date and Time (Date Only)	Date Picker
Date and Time (Date & Time)	Date and Time Picker
Lookup	Drop-Down List Box, Option Button, Combo Box, Multiple-Selection List Box, List Box
Yes/No	Check Box
Person or Group	Person/Group Picker

SharePoint List Data	InfoPath Control Name
Hyperlink or Picture	Hyperlink
Calculated	Calculated Value
External Data	Not supported in InfoPath
Managed Metadata	Not supported in InfoPath

Note Objects and Containers can be placed on a form and utilized, without the necessity of creating new fields in the form. Input fields need to be bound to list columns.

In the form that was created in the example earlier in this chapter, fields were dragged from the Fields pane and placed in an organized table structure. There are three different ways to modify, add to, or remove columns from the list of fields.

Field-Naming Best Practices

When naming fields in InfoPath, it is a best practice to give the fields accurate names as they are created. When controls are added to a form, their default names are Field1, Field2, and so on. Be sure to rename all fields so that they will make sense.

- **From InfoPath** From the list of available input controls (not to be confused with the list of fields that have already been created), drag a new control into the form. The first time this is done, the field will be called field1; the number increments for each new field that is created this way. After a field has been created in this manner, it is important that it be given an accurate name.

- **From List Settings** In the browser, on the list's List Settings page, click Create Column at the bottom of the Columns section. If this is done after the form has been customized by using InfoPath, the field must be manually added to the form's design surface. The same applies for deleted fields. They must be manually deleted from the form.

- **From SharePoint Designer** When the SharePoint site is opened in SharePoint Designer from the Lists And Libraries button on the left, any list can be modified and its columns can also be modified. The impact on the form is the same as if the columns had been changed from the List Settings page.

Note Learn more about InfoPath and SharePoint Designer integration in Chapter 10, "InfoPath Integration with SharePoint Designer Workflows."

After fields have been added and are seen in the Fields pane on the right in InfoPath Designer, by default they are displayed in a simple list, with each field represented by an icon that shows its field type. This is referred to as the basic view of fields and is seen in step 11 in the preceding exercise. At the bottom of the Fields pane, when Advanced View is selected, you can see the fields in the same manner in which they are seen in form library forms. There is also a drop-down box that contains other data connections. Select any other data connection to see its fields listed.

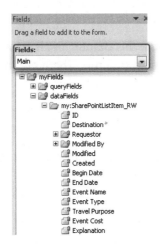

Receive Data—Data Connections

A data connection is a dynamic link that is configured to receive or submit data from your form to another location like SharePoint, Web Services, or a SQL database. When working with a form that has multiple data connections, especially multiple connections that receive data from other sources such as SharePoint lists, it is often beneficial to see the data that is retrieved in that source. In the Fields pane on the right side in InfoPath Designer, click Advanced View. Click the Main drop-down box, and then choose another source. The folder icon that contains all of the dataFields for that source can be dragged right onto the form's surface as a repeating table. When the form is previewed, this is a good way to get a sneak peek at what the contents are.

Note For more information about data connections, take a look at Chapter 7, "Receiving Data from SharePoint Lists and Business Connectivity Services."

In the following exercise, you will add new fields to the form, using different methods.

 SET UP In the web browser, open your SharePoint site and navigate to the **Travel Requests** list that was created previously in this chapter.

Create Column

1. On the ribbon at the top of the **Travel Requests** list, on the **List** tab, click the **Create Column** button.

2. Create a new Currency column called **Hotel Per Night**, and then click **OK**.

You can now see the **Hotel Per Night** column in the default view of the list. However, when any new columns are added from SharePoint, they will *not* be dynamically added to an already customized form.

3. In the **Travel Requests** list, on the **List** tab, click **Customize Form**.

   The following dialog box opens, stating **One or more fields in the SharePoint list have changed. Do you want InfoPath to update the set of available fields? You may need to modify your form view to add or remove the updated fields.** Take a quick look at the list of fields on the right, and notice that the new field is not yet listed.

4. Click **Yes**. The **Hotel Per Night** field now appears in the **Fields** pane.

5. Put the cursor in the **Travel Purpose** cell so that a new row can be inserted below it. In the **Layout** tab, click **Insert Below**.

 Insert Below

6. Drag the **Hotel Per Night** field from the list of fields to the left cell of the new row.

   The next new field will be added from InfoPath instead of from the **List Settings** dialog, which is how all of the other fields have been created so far in this chapter.

7. Put the cursor in the blank cell next to the **Hotel Per Night** field. On the ribbon, click the **Home** tab, and then in the **Controls** list, click the **Text Box** control.

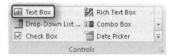

8. By default, the newly created field is called **field1** and is formatted as a single line of text. Double-click to select this new text box, and then on the ribbon, take a look at the **Control Tools Properties** tab. Change the Name to **Number of Nights**, and change the **Data Type** value to **Number**.

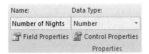

9. Put the cursor to the left of the new text box, and then type **Number of Nights** in the form.

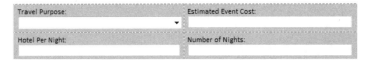

10. Close InfoPath. When prompted, click **Save and Publish**.

11. In the **Travel Requests** list in the browser, click **Add new item** to add a new travel request, and then save it.

    Notice that the two new columns now have the information that you filled in about the hotel and nights.

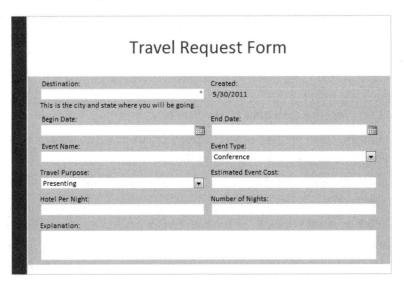

✖ **CLEAN UP** Leave InfoPath Designer and the browser open if you are continuing to the next section of this chapter. Otherwise, close InfoPath Designer and the browser.

Calculated Fields

Calculated fields have always existed as a column type in SharePoint. This concept has not changed, but it is important to understand how these columns behave in a form. What are the differences between a calculated column in a SharePoint list and a calculated value control in InfoPath?

When a calculated column is created in a SharePoint list, the following behaviors can be expected:

- The result of the calculation is a column that can be displayed in any view in the SharePoint list.
- The result of the calculation is a read-only value.
- When the form is filled out for the first time or edited, the result of the calculation does not dynamically change on the form as the values of the other fields change.
- The new result of a changed calculation is not updated until the form changes are saved.

Alternatively, when a calculation is created on an InfoPath form, the following behaviors can be expected:

- The calculation result is displayed dynamically on the form, which means that it changes immediately as other column values change.
- The calculation can be added to a form whether or not there is a calculated column in the SharePoint list.
- If the calculated value is added to the form independently of a list calculated column, there will not be a column in the SharePoint list to display the result of the formula.
- The list of functions available for calculations in the form is drastically different than the calculations available in the SharePoint list column.

In the following exercise, you will add two new calculated columns to the Travel Request form. Now that new fields have been added to the Travel Request form, the next type of field needed would be a calculation that multiplies the hotel cost-per-day by the number of nights. In doing this, the differences between types of calculation fields will be explored.

SET UP In the web browser, open your SharePoint site and navigate to the **Travel Requests** list that was created previously in this chapter.

1. On the ribbon, on the **List** tab, click **List Settings**.

2. In the **Columns** section, create a new column called **Total Hotel**. Fill in the new column information according to the following table, and then click **OK**.

Column Data	Value
Column name	Total Hotel
Column type	Calculated
Description	Hotel per night multiplied by the number of nights
Formula	[Hotel Per Night]*[Number of Nights]
Data type	Currency

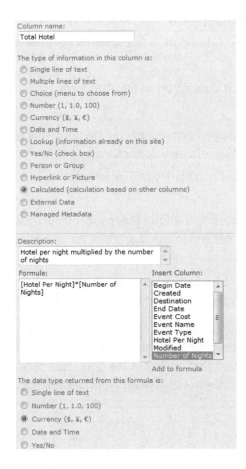

Customize
Form

3. Create a new travel request in the list, ensuring that the **Hotel Per Night** and **Number of Nights** fields are filled in.

Notice that the new **Total Hotel** field does not exist in the form yet, but after the new item is saved, the calculation is apparent as a column in the list.

4. On the ribbon, on the **List** tab, click **Customize Form**. Click **Yes** to the prompt to update the fields.

Insert
Below

5. Right-click in the **Number of Nights** table cell, click **Insert**, and then choose **Rows Below** to add a new row to the table.

6. Type **Total Hotel:** in the left cell of the new row, and then drag the **Total Hotel** field from the **Fields** pane to the table; position it immediately after the text that was just typed.

7. With the **Total Hotel** control selected, press **Alt+Enter** to open the **Control Properties** screen. In the **Format as** drop-down box, click **Decimal**.

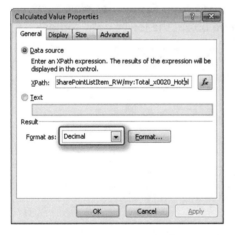

8. Click the **Format** button. Select the format of **Currency symbol**, and then in the **Other Options** section, select **2** in the **Decimal places** drop-down box.

Format...

9. Close InfoPath. When prompted, click **Save and Publish**.

10. Open an existing form, and notice that the calculation now appears on the form. Create a new travel request. Notice that as the number of nights and hotel cost-per-night are entered in the form, the **Total Hotel** field does not show any data. The calculated value will not show in the form until after it has been saved. On the ribbon, click **Customize Form** again.

11. In the **Fields** pane on the right, double-click the **Total Hotel** field.

12. On the **Data** tab of the **Field or Group Properties** dialog box, click the **fx** button adjacent to the **Default Value** box at the lower-right corner.

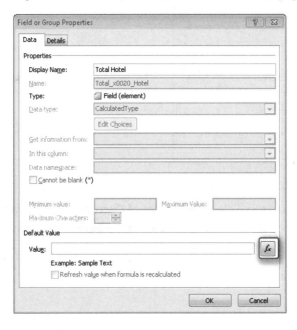

13. Click the **Insert Field or Group** button to select **Hotel Per Night**. Type the multiplication symbol (asterisk) with a space on each side of it, and then insert the **Number of Nights** field. Click **OK**.

    Note It is important that there is a space on either side of the asterisk, or errors will occur when **OK** is clicked.

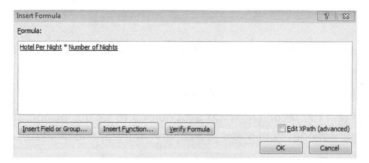

14. To give this control dynamic functionality, on the **Field or Group Properties** page, ensure that the **Refresh value when formula is recalculated** check box is selected. Click **OK**.

    Now that a SharePoint list calculated column has been added to the form, an Info-Path calculated value control can be added so that the difference between the two will be obvious.

15. Put the cursor in the empty cell to the right of **Total Hotel**. Type Total Estimated Cost:.

fx Calculated Value 16. On the ribbon, click the **Home** tab, and then in the **Controls** section, click **Calculated Value** to add a new calculation to the form.

17. Click the **fx** button next to the empty box.

18. Using the same method that fields were added to the formula box in step 12 of this exercise, create a calculation that adds **Event Cost** to **Total Hotel**, and then click **OK**. (Start by clicking **Insert Field or Group**.)

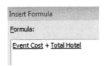

19. Format the new calculation as currency by repeating steps 7 and 8 for the **Total Estimated Cost** field.

20. Close InfoPath, and then click **Save and Publish**.

    Notice that this second field was a lot quicker to set up, includes the dynamic functionality, but does not appear as a column in the SharePoint list.

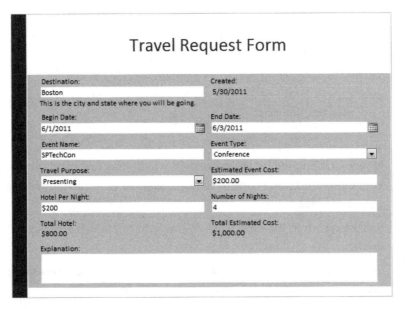

After completing the preceding exercise, you'll notice that the second method of creating a calculated field is great for displaying in the form, but because it is not a column in the list, it will not be available for filtering and sorting in the list of travel requests. Both methods of creating calculated fields have now been covered, so you can see that different behavior is apparent, depending on the way the column is created.

 CLEAN UP Leave InfoPath Designer and the browser open if you are continuing to the next section of this chapter. Otherwise, close InfoPath Designer and the browser.

List Form Pages

SharePoint 2010 provides a new Web Part called the InfoPath Form Web Part. (Chapter 8, "Using the InfoPath Form Web Part," describes this Web Part in detail.) This Web Part is fundamental to how the forms are displayed in a list. When forms are opened in SharePoint 2010, they are presented in a modal pop-up box. This is the default behavior, and each form is inherently alone on its own Web Part page. As you can see, with modal pop-ups, time is saved by eliminating the time the browser takes to navigate to a new web page. The form simply comes up in front of the current page.

Modal Pop-Ups

What is a modal pop-up dialog box? Newly introduced in SharePoint 2010, these dialog boxes are used when opening forms in SharePoint. Instead of navigating to a different page when opening a form to edit or view it, the modal pop-up displays on top of the existing page. The current page changes to a dark gray color with the pop-up as an overlay on top of it. You must close the pop-up to get back to the list of items. If undesired, modal pop-ups can be turned off per list or library, in the advanced settings. Change the Launch Forms In A Dialog setting to No.

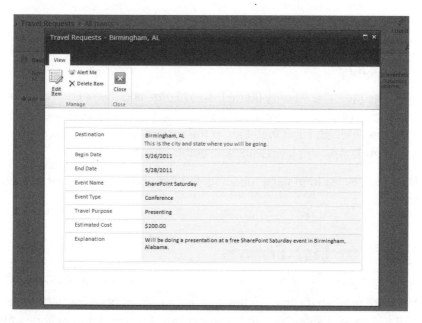

Tip When a SharePoint list has been customized by using InfoPath, the changes can be reverted at any time. On the list settings page, click Form Settings, and you can change the setting back to Use The Default SharePoint Form.

Before digging into the form's design, it's important to understand how the form pages work.

- On the ribbon, on the List tab, you can click the Form Web Parts button to open any of the form Web Part pages in Edit mode. By default, a custom list has three different form pages:

  - **New Form**   The name of the default file is NewForm.aspx. This is the form that is filled out only when creating a new item in the list.

  - **Edit Form**   The name of the default file is EditForm.aspx. This is the form that is filled out when the list item already exists and is being modified from its original version. By default, this form looks the same as the New Form.

  - **Display Form**   The name of the default file is DispForm.aspx. When the name of an item in a list is clicked to view the item, the display form is the form that is used and shows the values in all of the fields in a read-only interface.

- The Default New Form, Default Display Form, and Default Edit form are the Microsoft ASP.NET Web Forms that existed before the SharePoint list was customized with InfoPath.

- The (Item) New Form, (Item) Display Form, and (Item) Edit Form are specific to the Item content type and are Web Part pages. Each of these Web Part pages contains one InfoPath Form Web Part of the current form. The actual file names of these are newifs.aspx, displayifs.aspx, and editifs.aspx.

Now that the list form page fundamentals have been covered, we can delve into the form's design.

Limitations of List Forms

When a SharePoint list is customized as an InfoPath form, there are several nuances to be aware of when it comes to the difference in form behavior between a SharePoint ASP.NET page, a SharePoint list as an InfoPath form, and a form library form. Chapter 2, "Form Requirements: Using a Decision Matrix," included a decision matrix with details about gathering form requirements and deciding which direction to take in InfoPath.

This section covers several examples of inconsistencies to look out for when working with a SharePoint list as an InfoPath form.

● **Field Descriptions**   In the SharePoint list settings, each time a new column (field) is created, a description box is provided so that you can type a description of the data that should be entered in that field. For example, in the travel request form that we've created in this chapter, for the Destination text box, a description was entered in the column settings. If the description were to be changed at any point from the list's settings, the default ASP.NET form would immediately reflect the change in the existing forms. When the form was converted to InfoPath, the description was still seen in the form. Unfortunately, when we wiped out the whole form to start from scratch with a new layout, the description did not come back when the Destination field was added back to the form.

● **Data Connections**   In form library forms, there are no data connections at first, and each one must be created by using a wizard. However, a SharePoint list form inherently has a "submit" data connection that saves data to the current SharePoint list. This data connection cannot be removed or modified. Also, for each "choice" or lookup field that exists in the form, a "receive" data connection exists. These are also locked down and cannot be deleted or modified. However, new connections can always be added, with full functionality.

● **Views**   With a SharePoint list form, multiple views can be created as with a form library form, but the behavior is slightly different.

● **Option Buttons**   These are not listed in the insert controls but can still be used in the form. Right-click a control, and in the Change Control To list, the option button is there.

● **No Developer Tab**   There is no Developer tab on the ribbon, which means that custom code cannot be added to these types of forms.

The Travel Purpose field was created as a radio button choice, but when the form was converted to InfoPath, the control changed to a drop-down box. Also, the Destination box had descriptive text underneath it, which is now gone. Another thing to notice is that when the dates are being filled out, although the Begin Date should be before the End Date, any dates can be entered.

In the following exercise, you will add the descriptive text back to the field and then explore the results when the description is changed from the list's settings.

SET UP In the web browser, open your SharePoint site and navigate to the **Travel Requests** list from the previous exercise.

1. On the ribbon at the top of the **Travel Requests** list, on the **List** tab, click the **Customize Form** button.

2. Put the cursor after the white text box under **Destination**, and then press the **Enter** key to add a new line. Type **This is the city and state where you will be going**.

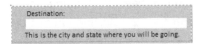

3. Close InfoPath. When prompted, click **Save and Publish**.

List
Settings

4. In the browser, on the **List** tab, click **List Settings**.

5. In the **Columns** section, click the name of the **Destination** column. Change the description to **This is the city and state**, and then click **OK**.

6. Now click **Travel Requests** in the breadcrumb trail at the top of the page. Click **Add new item** to fill out a new form. Notice that the description has not changed.

The point of the preceding exercise was to show that when a form has been customized by using InfoPath, the description that is typed into the list settings cannot be expected to dynamically change in the form. Therefore, any descriptions that are needed should be typed directly on the form itself, as we did in step 2 of the exercise.

✖ **CLEAN UP** Leave InfoPath Designer and the browser open if you are continuing to the next section of this chapter. Otherwise, close InfoPath Designer and the browser

Form Options

In a SharePoint list that has been customized to use an InfoPath form, the form options screen looks a bit different from a form library form. To take a look at the form options for any form, click the File menu to display the Backstage view, click the Info tab, and then select Form Options.

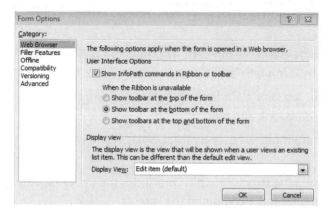

The form options consist of several tabs down the left side of the dialog box. Many of these options also exist in form library forms. The following items are significantly different in SharePoint list forms:

- **Web Browser**   Optionally clear the Show InfoPath Commands In Ribbon Or Toolbar check box. This removes the ribbon from the form. When the form is opened, it displays no button for a user to click to edit the data in the form. Additionally, when this check box is cleared, the three options under When The Ribbon Is Unavailable are disabled.

- **Filler Features**   The settings on this dialog box have no impact on SharePoint list forms.

- **Offline**   Determines whether this form data should be available offline and whether queried data expires.

  Note Learn more about offline capabilities in Chapter 14, "Advanced Options."

- **Compatibility**   All options on this tab are grayed-out (disabled) because they are not configurable in a SharePoint list form.

- **Versioning**   Each time the form is modified, a new version number is automatically created. These settings are usually used as a reference to see the current revision number.

- **Advanced**   This tab contains the Enable Form Merging option, which is not applicable to list forms.

Key Points

- It is important to understand the inherent fundamentals of SharePoint lists before customizing them by using InfoPath.

- SharePoint list forms are very plain-looking before they are customized, and they all have the same standard look and feel.

- There are three different forms for every list: Display Form, Edit Form, and New Form.

- SharePoint lists have a flat structure, which precludes the use of repeating tables, and every field in the form is a column in the list.

- Descriptions typed in SharePoint columns are not dynamically updated in the form after it has been customized by using InfoPath.

- Calculations can be done in the InfoPath form, but there is a difference between a calculated field in SharePoint and a calculation control in InfoPath. There is also a big difference in the functions available using the two different methods.

- There are many different layout table templates and color schemes to choose from when customizing the way a form looks.

- With InfoPath and SharePoint lists, all of the required data connections already exist, and other customized connections can be added manually.

- There are several ways that columns can be added to a SharePoint list that has been customized by using InfoPath, including SharePoint, SharePoint Designer, and InfoPath.

- There are some limitations when working with SharePoint lists compared to form library forms—for example, there are fewer form options, and the default data connections are not editable.

Chapter at a Glance

Work with the InfoPath Rules Task Pane, **page 123**

Add conditions to Rules, **page 130**

User Rules with Picture Buttons, **page 133**

Create Forms with Wizard-Style Interfaces, **page 140**

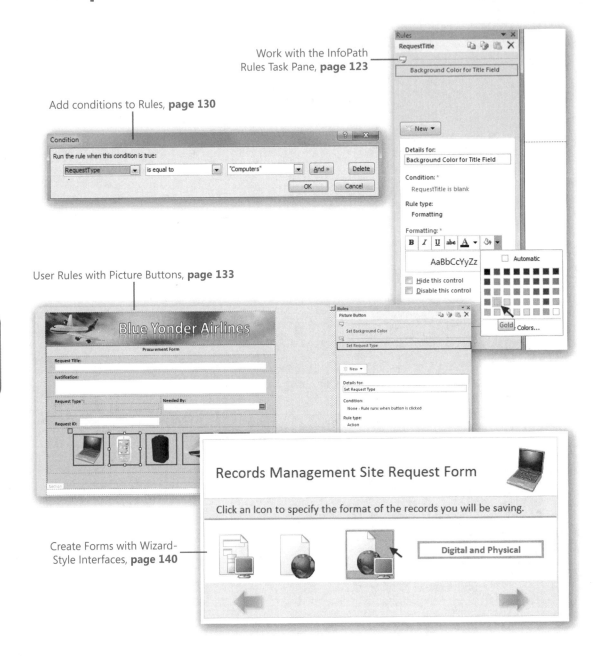

5 Adding Logic and Rules to Forms

In this chapter, you will learn how to:

- ✔ Use logic and validation in your forms without writing code
- ✔ Work with the Rules task pane
- ✔ Add conditional formatting to your forms
- ✔ Implement data validation
- ✔ Work with more advanced rules using formulas and functions
- ✔ Create intuitive user interfaces by using rules with views

---

The core purpose of most forms is to gather useful data. To help facilitate this in an efficient, accurate, and intuitive manner, InfoPath has several built-in mechanisms for adding logic and formatting to your forms. In the past, if a digital form required sophisticated data validation, logic, or conditional formatting, it almost always required extensive involvement from a programmer who understood how to build the logic in computer programming code. InfoPath simplifies much of the complexity of adding logic to forms but still retains the power to support the complex requirements you might have for adding logic and validation to your forms.

Part of the appeal of digital forms versus paper is the ability that software-based forms have to *dynamically adapt* to user input. For example, imagine that you have a form field that asks a simple yes/no question. If the user's answer is "yes," perhaps he is presented with further required input fields, or perhaps he is automatically presented with an entirely new section of the form that was previously hidden. However, if the answer to the question is "no," perhaps he is automatically redirected to an entirely different page (view) of the same form. This ability to adapt and respond in real time to user input is a major part of the InfoPath logic engine. The most common method you will use to add this type of logic to your forms is by using rules in InfoPath, of which there are three types: validation, actions, and formatting. We will briefly describe each of these rule types in the next section.

> **Practice Files** Before you can complete the exercises in this chapter, you need to copy the book's practice files to your computer. The practice files you'll use to complete the exercises in this chapter are in the Chapter 5 practice file folder. A complete list of practice files is provided in "Downloading the Practice Files and eBook," on page xxvi.

Primary Types of Form Logic in InfoPath

Data validation rules help to ensure that users enter data into your forms in an accurate and consistent manner, in exactly the format you intended. A common example is the use of data validation to ensure that a user types a Social Security number in a specific format (for example, 999-99-9999). This validation rule uses the *matches pattern* condition. You can use data validation to present the user with ScreenTips and error messages that help guide her to enter the data correctly. Other examples of data validation rules within forms could be ensuring that a user has entered an email address or phone number as you intended. The following screenshot shows how most of the InfoPath data validation logic conditions are self-explanatory. These rules make adding validation logic to forms easy, even for the non-programmer.

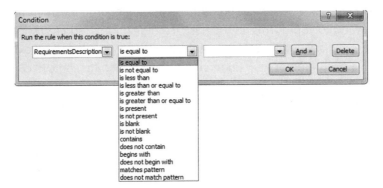

Another type of rule that you can add to your forms is called an *action rule*. Actions can be triggered in your forms in a variety of ways; they are often initiated by user-driven events such as a button click. An example of an action would be setting the value displayed in a field based on a selection the user makes in a drop-down control in another part of the form. You can add multiple actions to a rule, making action rules extremely powerful tools. The primary types of action rules are briefly described in the following:

- Switch views
- Set a field's value
- Query for data
- Submit data
- Close the form
- Send data to Web Part

- **Switch Views**   An action typically applied to a button or image that switches the user to another view in the form.

- **Set A Field's Value**   Use this when you want the value in one field to be automatically determined by the value from another field.

- **Query For Data**   You can use this when you need to run a query against a data source to submit or receive data.

- **Submit Data**   Most forms need this for publishing the form to SharePoint or some other location.

- **Close The Form**   This action is often useful when you want your form to be automatically closed on the user's computer after the necessary input has been provided.

- **Send Data To Web Part**   This is a new Microsoft SharePoint 2010 Web Part, specifically designed for hosting InfoPath forms. This helps you send data between InfoPath and other Web Parts. We'll cover this action in more depth in a later chapter.

A third type of rule is called *conditional formatting*. This is a very useful type of form logic with which you can manipulate the appearance of the form as the user fills it out. An example would be hiding an entire section of the form unless the user selects "yes" on a check box control. If he selects "no," the section remains hidden. Formatting rules allow you to create forms with dynamic interfaces that display only the relevant fields/sections. The primary types of conditional formatting rules are as follows:

- Font formatting (bold, color, and so on)
- Background color
- Hiding a control (including an entire section)
- Disabling a control

In addition to rules, InfoPath also supports formulas and functions for situations in which you need to have more power and flexibility than the pre-defined rules allow for. InfoPath has functions that support a broad array of capabilities, such as date and time, math, and text manipulation.

Inserting a formula can be very powerful. The Formulas input box allows you to add fields or groups, functions, and operators that are used to calculate and display other values. As a quick example to illustrate this concept, the following two screenshots are from a simple form with just two fields: *DueDate* and *ShipDate*. In this case, what you want to do is have the user select a date from the DueDate field, which is a date picker control. Then the formula calculates the value of the ShipDate field by using the addDays function to automatically add seven days. You can see how the InfoPath formula builder was used to easily build this logic.

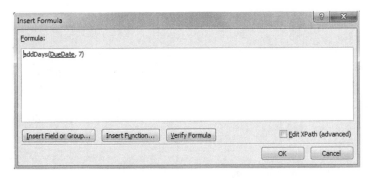

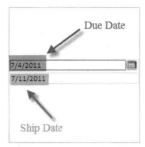

InfoPath functions are not unlike those you might have worked with in Microsoft Excel or SharePoint. Functions typically return a value that is derived from the results of a calculation. Each function has values called arguments.

Functions generally fall into one of the following categories:

- Date and time functions
- Field functions
- Math functions
- Text functions
- URL functions
- User functions

Functions consist of three parts:

- **Name**   Usually gives a hint as to the type of action that the function performs (for example, min, max)
- **Return value**   The actual result of the function
- **Arguments**   The specific values used by the function to perform a calculation

InfoPath functions can be used with default values and rules. You will have an opportunity to apply a few simple date and text functions in this chapter and then work with more complex scenarios in Chapter 14, "Advanced Options."

Working with Validation and Formatting

The first sample form you'll be using for this chapter is a procurement form that the fictitious Blue Yonder Airlines company provides its employees for purchasing items they need to do their jobs. The form gathers basic information from the user that's necessary to place an order, such as name, date, and product details.

In this first exercise, you will add a validation and formatting rule for the *Request Title* field. The validation will ensure that the field cannot be blank and also will give the user a visual cue by using a background color formatting rule.

 SET UP Open the **no rules Procurement** form template that is provided in the practice files. Open the form in Design mode (right-click the file), and then choose Design.

1. In the form template, right-click the **Request Title** field, and then choose **Text Box Properties**. Under the **Validation** section, select **Cannot be blank**, and then click **OK**.

   This designates the field as required; the user must always provide a title. If she does not, she will not be allowed to complete the form.

Tip The following figure shows that you can also accomplish this validation task on the **Control** tab on the ribbon.

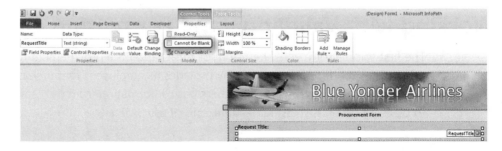

Manage Rules

2. On the ribbon, click the **Manage Rules** button to open the **Rules Task** pane (on the right side of the InfoPath Designer).

3. Ensure that you have selected the **Request Title** text box in the form design area. A single left-click will make it the active selection.

   Tip When working with fields and rules, you can select either the control on the design surface or the appropriate field in the **Fields** pane. Either selection will make that field active in the **Rules** pane.

4. In the **Rules** pane, select **New**, and then select **Formatting**. Give your rule a descriptive name, such as **Background Color for Title Field**.

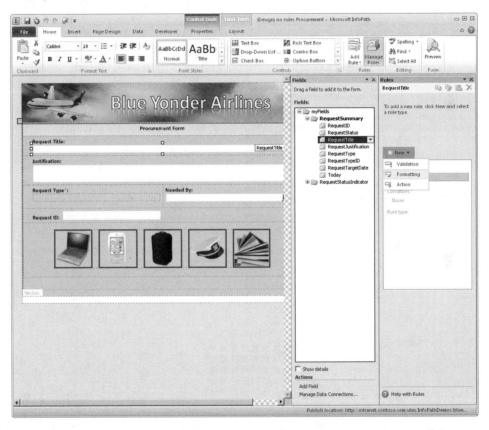

5. In the **Rules** pane, in the **Condition** section, click **None** to open the **Condition** dialog box. Select the middle drop-down list, pick **is blank**, and then click **OK**.

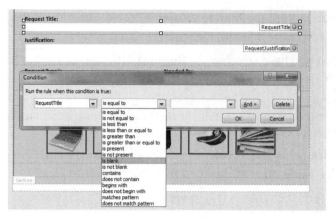

6. In the **Rules** pane, in the **Formatting** section, click the arrow to the right of the **Shading Color** tool (the bucket), and then select **Gold**.

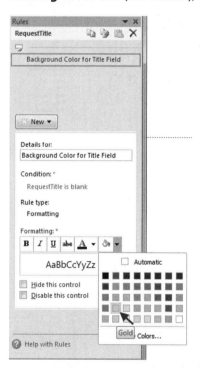

7. On the ribbon click **Preview**.

Notice that your **Request Title** field has a red asterisk in it and also shows a Screen-Tip that says **Cannot be blank** when you hover over the field. This is InfoPath's way of visually indicating to the user that the field requires data input. You took it one step further and added a formatting rule that forces the **Title** field to remain gold as long as it is equal to "is blank." Notice that if you type something in the field and then tab to the next field, the color reverts back to white. This is your rule doing exactly what it is supposed to—congratulations!

Tip Remember that F5 is the shortcut key for previewing your form. You will be previewing a lot in this chapter.

Tip As the following figures illustrate, you could have quickly accomplished this same task by using the **Add Rule** button on the ribbon. The "quick rules" button is applicable to many of the exercises in this chapter if you want to use it rather than the **Rules** pane.

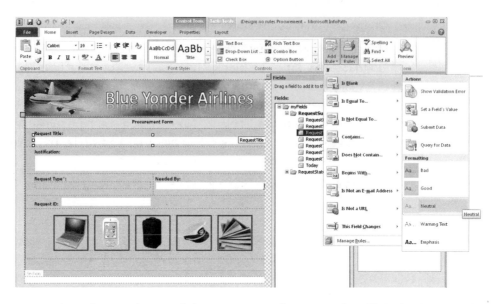

 CLEAN UP Close the preview, and then save your form template if desired. Leave the procurement form template open in InfoPath Designer if you plan to continue on to the next exercise.

Using Functions to Set a Default Value

Now you will utilize some of the InfoPath functions to add more logic to the Home (default) view of the Blue Yonder procurement form. The specific functions you will use for this exercise are *concat* and *now*.

Your task is to create a unique value in the RequestID field. Among the many approaches to automatically generating unique values in data fields, one new option is to use the Document ID Service in SharePoint.

For this example, you are going to use the *now* and *concat* functions to set a default value on your Request ID text field. This will automatically generate a unique value in the RequestID field for each form instance the user creates. This unique value can be used for a variety of purposes: tracking/reporting, workflows, or to provide a unique name for the form when it is saved to SharePoint.

 SET UP In Design mode, open the Procurement form template that you saved from the previous exercise. Alternatively, you can open the **no rules Procurement** form template from the practice files.

1. In the form template, right-click the **Request ID** field, and then in the shortcut menu that opens, choose **Text Box Properties**. Click the **Display** tab, and then select **Read-only** in the **Options** area so that the user cannot change the ID that you are going to generate.

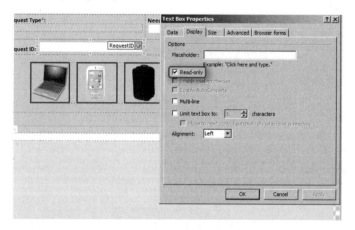

Tip The **Read-Only** property can also be set on the ribbon, as illustrated in the following. Select the control in the design surface, click the **Properties** tab, and then select the **Read-Only** check box.

2. In the **Text Box Properties** dialog box, click the **Data** tab. In the **Default Value** area, click the **fx** (for *function*) button.

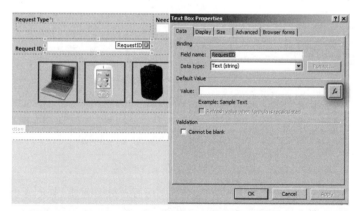

3. Select **Insert Function**, and then choose **Text** from the list. Double-click **concat** (which should be the first option).

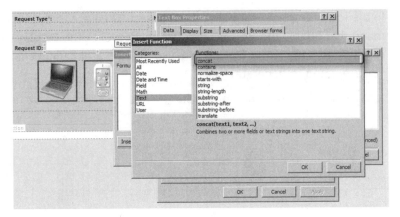

4. In the Insert **Formula** dialog box, place your cursor over each of the three links labeled **double click to insert field**, and then carefully delete each of them and the commas, leaving only **concat()**.

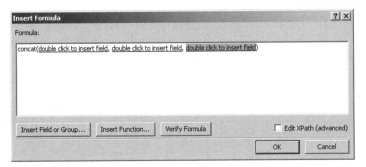

5. Place your cursor between the two parentheses, and then type **ID:** (including the colon).

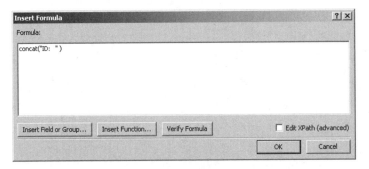

6. Type a comma directly after the last quote but just to the left of the closing parenthesis. Click the **Insert Function** button, choose **Date and Time**, click **now**, and then click **OK**. Your formula should look like the illustration that follows.

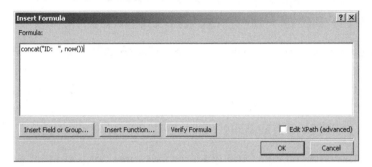

Tip Be sure to type formulas exactly as instructed. Many InfoPath formulas require precision to work correctly.

7. Click **OK**, and then click **OK** again. On the ribbon, click **Preview**; you should have an automatically generated ID number in the **Request ID** field.

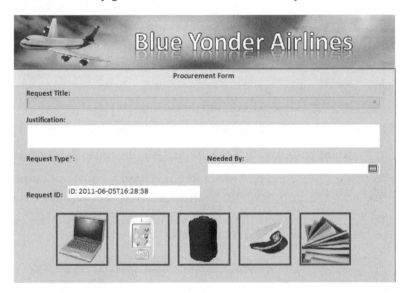

Using the **now()** function is a useful and simple way of generating field values that will almost certainly be unique because this function returns the system time including the seconds. Also notice that if you click inside the **Request ID field** and attempt to alter the text, you are unable to do so because you designated the field as read-only.

 CLEAN UP Close the preview, and then save your form template. Leave your template open in InfoPath Designer if you plan to continue on to the next exercise.

Adding Action and Formatting Rules

In the following exercise, you will add action rules to all the picture buttons in the procurement form. This will set the value of the RequestType field to match the appropriate product category that the user selects. Each picture button will also have a formatting rule that adds background color to the button currently selected. This will provide the user with a visual cue that indicates which button they've selected.

 SET UP In Design mode, open the Procurement form template that you saved from the previous exercise. Alternatively, you can open the **no rules Procurement** form template from the practice files.

1. In the **Procurement** form, ensure that you have selected the picture button of the computer.

2. On the ribbon, click **Manage Rules** to open the **Rules** pane.

3. In the **Rules** pane, create a new formatting rule called **Set Background Color**.

4. To create a new condition where **RequestType** is equal to **Computers**, choose **type text** from the drop-down list on the right, type in **Computers**, and then click **OK**.

   Tip Do not be concerned if you see InfoPath automatically putting quotations around text that you type in to formulas. That is expected behavior.

5. In the **Rules** pane, in the **Shading Color** tool, select **gold**.

6. In the **Rules** pane, create a new Action rule called **Set Request Type**.

7. Click **Add**, and then select **Set a field's value** from the drop-down list.

8. In the **Rule Details** dialog, click the **Field** button.

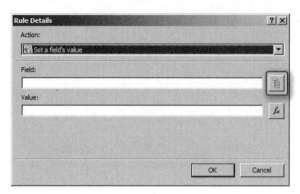

9. Select **RequestType**, and then click **OK**.

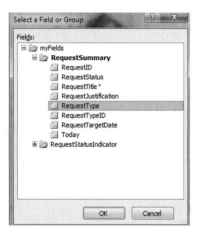

10. In the **Value** field, type **Computers**, and then click **OK**.

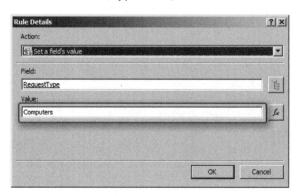

11. Select the **Preview** button for your form, and then click the **Computers** picture button.

You should see both of your rules take effect: the background color changes on the **Computer** picture button, and the **Request Type** field is set to **Computers**.

12. Repeat steps 3 through 10 for each of the other four picture buttons. Add the same two rules that you did for the **Computers** picture button, but set them equal to the following text for each picture button respectively:

- ○ **Cell phones**
- ○ **Luggage and gear**
- ○ **Apparel and uniforms**
- ○ **Training courses**

13. Preview the form by pressing **F5**, confirm your rules are working properly for each picture button, and then save your form template.

✖ CLEAN UP Leave your template open in InfoPath Designer if you plan to continue on to the next exercise.

Working with Sections and Conditional Formatting

Using conditional formatting on sections is very useful when you want to hide or applying formatting to all controls in that container via a rule. In the following exercise, you will work in the second view in the procurement form (View Request) and add conditional formatting rules to the form status sections. This will allow you to show *only* the current status of the form (Approved, Pending, and so on), while hiding all the other possible statuses. You will use the Request Status drop-down field to determine which status is currently in effect.

 SET UP In Design mode, open the Procurement form template that you saved from the previous exercise. Alternatively, you can open the **no rules Procurement** form template from the practice files.

1. On the ribbon, click **Page Design**, and then select **View Request** in the **View** selector.

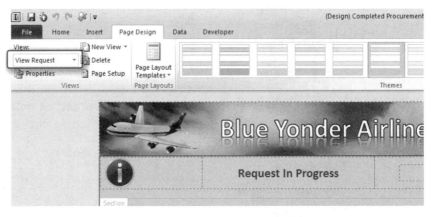

2. Click the **Home** tab, and then click the **Manage Rules** button to open the **Rules** pane.

3. In the **Request in Progress** section, click the **Section** button to make this section the active selection in the **Rules** pane.

4. In the **Rules** pane, add a new formatting rule called **Hide Section**.

5. Add a new condition, and then in the **Condition** dialog box, set the first drop-down field to **Select a field or group**.

6. In the **Select a Field or Group** dialog box, browse up to the **Request Summary** group, and then select the **RequestStatus** field.

7. In the **Condition** dialog box, finish the condition by setting your rule to **is not equal to**. Choose the **Type Text** option, type Processing, and then click **OK**.

8. In the **Rules** pane, in the formatting area, select the **Hide this control** check box.

   What the rule is logically telling the form is that if the user has not currently set the **Request Status** field to **Processing**, hide this entire section of the form.

9. On the ribbon, click the **Preview** button.

10. In preview mode, experiment with setting the **Request Status** drop-down field to **Processing** and then changing it to something else.

If you've properly completed the process, the **Request in Progress** section should disappear if you have selected anything other than **Processing** in the **Request Status** field.

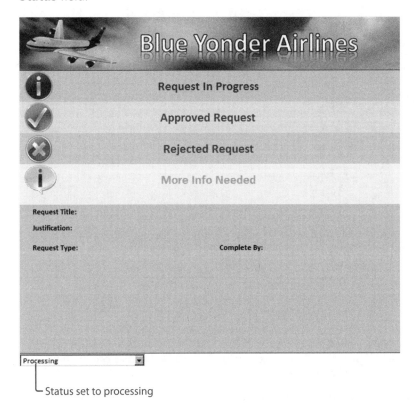

Status set to processing

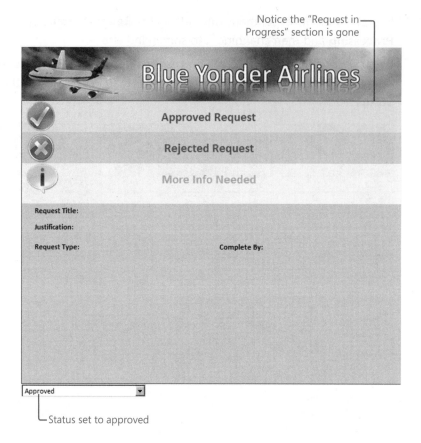

Notice the "Request in Progress" section is gone

Status set to approved

Note Following this logic, if you add the same **Hide Section** rule for every status section on your form, when a user picks a particular status from the Request Status field, that section will be the only one displayed on the form.

11. Add the same **Hide Section** formatting rule that you created (steps 3 through 8) to the **Approved Request**, **Rejected Request**, and **More Info Needed** sections.

   The text in the condition dialog box for each of these sections should be **Approved**, **Rejected**, and **More Info**, respectively, because that is the text we have set in the **Request Status Drop-Down List Box** control.

Tip InfoPath 2010 introduces the ability to copy rules. This can save you time when you need to apply the same rule to multiple sections or controls. Simply click the copy rule button (or copy all rules) in the **Rules** pane, as shown in the following screenshot. Then, navigate to the target control/section and paste the rule by using the paste button.

12. After you have added the rule for each of the remaining three sections, preview the form.

If you have performed the steps correctly, you should now see only the specific status section that matches the status that you select from your drop-down field. The following screenshot shows what your form should look like if you select **Approved** in the **Request Status** drop-down.

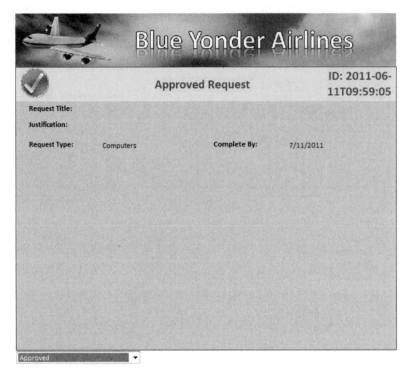

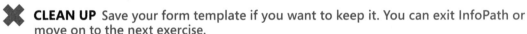

 CLEAN UP Save your form template if you want to keep it. You can exit InfoPath or move on to the next exercise.

Using Rules to Create a Wizard-Style Form with Multiple Views

In the following exercise, you will be working with a form whose purpose is to capture provisioning requests from Blue Yonder employees. These requests need SharePoint Records Management sites to support the document storage requirements. The form is mostly complete; you simply need to add a few remaining rules to finish it. By adding the final logic touches to the form, you will have a chance to explore the full potential of using InfoPath's rules to create a very rich, wizard-style form.

SET UP In Design mode, open the form called **Blue Yonder Records Management SharePoint Site Request** form.

On the default (Home) view of the form, you are collecting only a couple of basic pieces of information from the users: what types of records they need to save on their

SharePoint site, and a description of their purpose. Now, you will add a rule to the arrow image, which will allow the user to navigate to the second view of the form. The arrow is a picture button control, which means that we can add rules to it.

1. On the ribbon, open the **Rules** pane, and then click the arrow.

 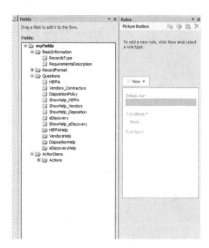

2. In the **Rules** pane, add a new action rule that switches the view to the **Formats** view. You can name the rule something like **Next Page**.

3. On the ribbon, click the **Page Design** tab, and then switch to the second view of the form, the **Formats** view.

> **Tip** Like many of the steps in this chapter, adding the rule to switch views could have been accomplished quickly by using the **Add Rule** button on the ribbon. As shown in the following illustration, it accomplishes the same switch views task as using the **Rules** pane, but with fewer clicks. Remember to always activate the control to which you want to add a rule by clicking it once, prior to clicking the **Add Rule** button on the ribbon.

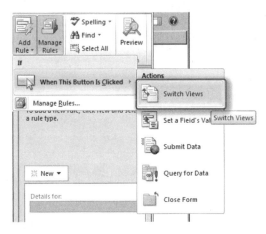

On the **Formats** view, the form again makes use of picture buttons to provide the user a richer experience. It displays arrows for providing navigation between the views of the form. If you click an arrow and look at its rules in the **Rules** pane as shown in the following screenshot, you can see the logic behind it.

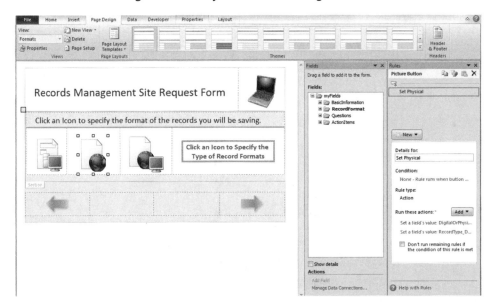

You will use the three picture buttons in the middle of the page to represent the current format of the records that the users will be saving in their SharePoint sites. The first button represents digital records only, the second, physical records only (documents that would be scanned), and the third button represents digital and physical records. The rules have already been added for the first two buttons. Your job is to add the rules for the third, the **Digital and Physical** button. Each of the first two buttons has one rule with two actions. The first action sets a hidden field called **DigitalOrPhysical** to the appropriate format, based on user selection. The second action sets the text inside the label to match whatever format the user has selected.

4. To get a feel for what the first two picture buttons do, first select each image and review their rules in the **Rules** pane. Now preview the form, and then click the buttons to see how they set the labels appropriately. Also notice, if you click the third button, nothing happens.

5. Close the preview, and then select the third picture button.

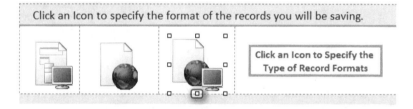

6. In the **Rules** pane, add a new action rule called **Set Digital and Physical**. Both of the actions you are going to create will be setting a fields value.

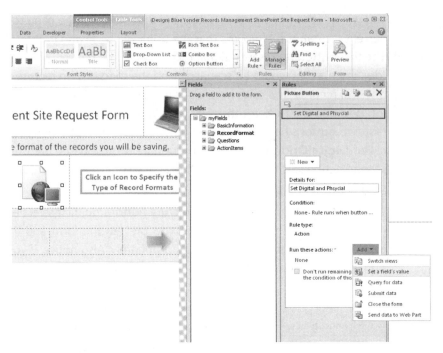

7. To set the **DigitalOrPhysical** field contained in the **Record Format** group, type **Digital and Physical** in the value field.

   Tip Notice that the **DigitalorPhysical** field is not actually shown on the design surface. This is a good example of a case where you need a field to store a variable data value, but you don't actually need it directly displayed on the form. You will find this to be a useful technique. A hidden field in your form can effectively serve the same function as a variable would in a programming language.

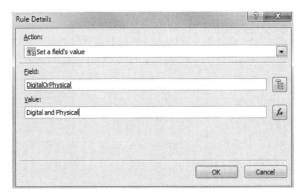

8. Type in the same value (**Digital and Physical**) for the **RecordType_DisplayLabel** field as well as in the **Record Format** group.

   You should now have two actions in your rule for the third picture button.

9. Preview the form by using either the **Preview** button on the ribbon or the **F5** key.

All three of the picture buttons should now set the label on the right appropriately, depending on which one you select.

10. On the ribbon, click the **Page Design** tab, and then switch to the third view of the form, the **Questions** view.

On this view, you will be presenting the form user with a series of questions related to records they are creating in their SharePoint site.

11. Preview the form, and then select **Yes** from the drop-downs on all the questions.

Notice that when you select **Yes** for the vendor/contractor question, an additional section of information becomes visible at the bottom of the form. Also, click the blue question mark icon next to the vendors/contractors question; you will see that help is available on demand. Both of these elements make use of rules to show and hide a section based on user input. Designing a form in this manner makes it more dynamic and rich, while also improving usability because you are not overwhelming the user with information they might not need.

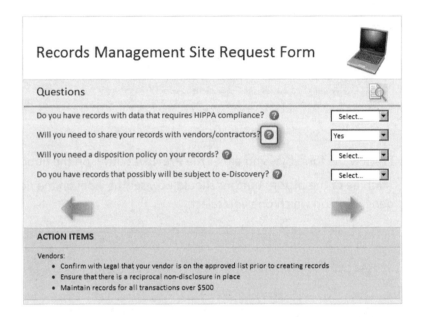

As with the previous two views, this one is already partially completed for you; your task will be to add the remaining rule. You might have noticed in Preview mode that the help content for the **e-Discovery** section appeared whether or not you clicked the help button. Therefore, you need to add a rule to hide the **e-Discovery** help section unless the **ShowHelp_eDiscovery** field is set to true. That is, unless the user has clicked the question mark for help on the **e-Discovery** section, keep it hidden.

12. Select the **eDiscoveryHelp** section.

13. Open the **Rules** pane, and then add a new formatting rule for this section. Add a condition where you select a field, and find the **ShowHelp_eDiscovery** field under the **Questions** group.

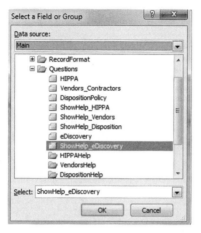

14. Set the condition **is not equal to** to **TRUE**.

15. In the **Rules** pane, select **Hide This Control**.

16. Preview the form.

    You will notice the **e-Discovery** help section is now hidden until you click the question mark button. This is an excellent example of using a formatting rule to provide a more interactive form experience.

17. On the ribbon, using the **Page Design** tab, switch to the final summary view shown in the following screenshot.

    As with the previous three views, this one is nearly complete. You will add the remaining rule. Before you do that, preview the form and become familiar with the functionality. The primary things to notice are the picture buttons on the page, which allow navigation to other parts of the form. The picture buttons just to the right of the summary questions allow the user to navigate back to the Questions view and edit their answers.

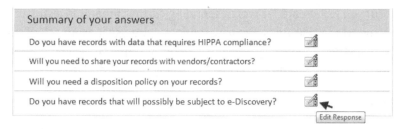

18. The fourth button on the question about e-Discovery does not have a rule applied to it yet. Therefore, using the **Rules** pane, add an action rule on the button that, when clicked, will transfer the user back to the Questions view.

Notice the use of ScreenTips to help the user understand the purpose of the button. The ScreenTips are in the properties of the picture button, which you can see by right-clicking and choosing **Picture Button Properties**. Look for the **Advanced** tab.

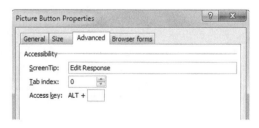

The form you just created is worth spending further time to investigate all the different action and formatting rules. Preview the form, and use it as an actual user would, filling it out completely and seeing how it works. As you do this, switch back into Design mode with the Rules and Fields panes open to clearly understand how everything fits together.

 CLEAN UP Save your form template if you wish to keep your changes, and close out of InfoPath Designer.

Key Points

- InfoPath provides multiple methods for easily adding logic and rules to your forms, without programming.
- InfoPath data validation is a powerful way to ensure users enter data correctly.
- InfoPath 2010 has improved the rules interface via the new Rules task pane.
- Creating navigation for forms with multiple views/pages is easily achieved using Action rules.
- Demonstrate the capabilities of building a user input form by simply using the Formatting Rules functionality.

Chapter at a Glance

Create a time off request form, **page 167**

Set up submit button actions, **page 177**

Concatenate field names to create a file name, **page 174**

Publish a form as a content type, **page 180**

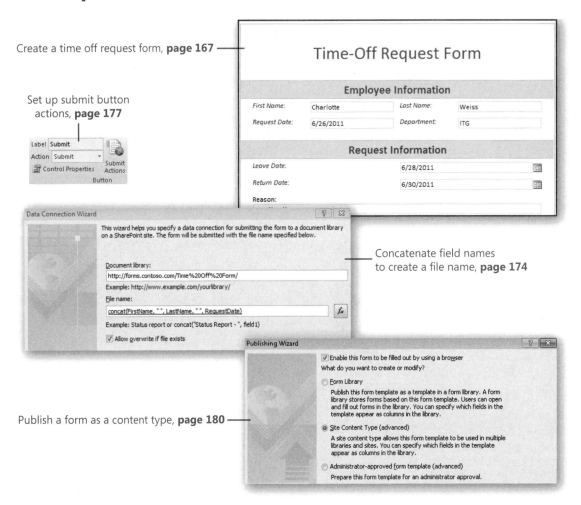

6 Publishing and Submitting Form Data

In this chapter, you will learn how to:

- ✔ Determine the right method to publish your form
- ✔ Publish a form library form to SharePoint
- ✔ Decide between publishing and saving a form
- ✔ Create a data connection to submit a file to SharePoint
- ✔ Understand the different methods of form publishing

When creating a Microsoft InfoPath form, publishing a form means to send the form template to a certain location as an XSN file. After a form has been published, it can be filled out and submitted to Microsoft SharePoint. You can use several different methods to publish a form, and the method that is selected depends on several different factors and requirements.

In this chapter, you will learn about the different ways to publish a form, along with the reasons to select each of these methods. The examples will walk you through publishing your own form, and you'll learn how important it is to create a data connection for the submittal of information to your SharePoint site. Furthermore, you'll understand how form fields can be promoted to SharePoint columns in document form libraries.

> **Practice Files** No practice files are required to complete the exercises in this chapter.

Publishing Methods

In previous chapters, you learned how to create an InfoPath form, how to add layouts and controls, and even how to create a simple SharePoint list form. Because this chapter mainly focuses on publishing methods, we will create simple forms, with the emphasis on the publishing and submission processes. The methods and best practices that you'll learn will apply in all forms that are created, except for SharePoint list forms. In Chapter 4, "Working with SharePoint List Forms," you might have noticed that the creation of data connections and the selection of a publishing method were not required because they were automatically built-in. The three different publishing choices are as follows:

- **Form library**   Publish to a SharePoint form library when the form needs to be filled out and submitted only to a single location. When a form is published to a form library, the form template's XSN file becomes the template for the library. Typically, when publishing to a library, the form will also be submitted to that same library.

- **Site content type**   Publish to a content type when the form will need to be used in multiple libraries. When a form has been published by using this method, the new form content type can be added to many different libraries in the site. When publishing as a content type to the top level of a site collection, the content type can be utilized in all of the sites and libraries in the site collection.

  Tip It is the data connection, not the content type, that determines where the forms are submitted after they are filled out. We'll cover more of that later.

- **Administrator-approved form template**   Publish a form as an administrator-approved template when it needs to be globally deployed across the farm or when customized code has been included in it. When this type of form is published, unlike when using the other two publishing methods, it is not automatically deployed in SharePoint. This method creates an XSN file as output, which then must be uploaded into InfoPath Forms Services by a server administrator.

Now that you have a basic understanding of the three different publishing methods, it's time to get to work on some exercises. At Contoso, all employees will navigate to the same form library in SharePoint, where every time-off request is collected in one SharePoint form library. When gathered, all of the company time requests can be sorted and filtered, and multiple views can be created. Because all of the forms must reside in one location for further reporting and dissemination, only a single form library is needed.

In the following exercise, you will create a company time-off request form. This form will be used in every exercise in this chapter.

SET UP In the web browser, open your SharePoint site so that a new list can be created. Create a new folder on your computer called C:\InfoPath Files.

1. To open the new file screen in InfoPath, from the **Start** menu in Windows, click **All Programs | Microsoft Office | Microsoft InfoPath Designer 2010**.

SharePoint Form Library

2. In the **Popular Form Templates** section, click to select **SharePoint Form Library**, and then on the right side of the screen, click **Design Form**.

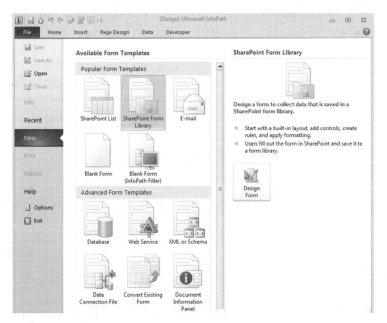

3. Before we add controls to the form, some fields can be created in the **Fields** pane on the right side of the screen. Right-click **myFields**, and then click **Add** to open the **Add Field or Group** dialog.

4. In the **Name** text box, enter **EmployeeInfo**. In the **Type** text box, enter **Group**, and then click **OK**.

The goal here is to organize all of our fields by group, into logical sections.

Tip Creating and keeping fields organized is beneficial to you, the form creator. This will make your job easier, especially with forms that have over 50 fields. Be sure that the organization of the fields is complete before the form goes live and is used in production. Rearranging fields later can cause loss of data.

5. In the **myFields section**, use the same method to create another group called **RequestInfo**, and then click **OK**.

6. Right-click **EmployeeInfo**, and then click **Add**. Name the field **FirstName**, with a type of **Field (element)** and a data type of **Text (string)**. Click **OK**.

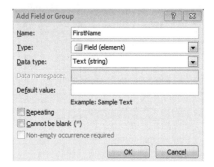

7. Use the following table to repeat step 6, creating the rest of the fields under each of the two groups that were created in steps 4 and 5.

Name	Type	Data Type	Under Group
LastName	Field (element)	Text (string)	EmployeeInfo
RequestDate	Field (element)	Date and Time (dateTime)	EmployeeInfo
Department	Field (element)	Text (string)	EmployeeInfo
LeaveDate	Field (element)	Date (date)	RequestInfo
ReturnDate	Field (element)	Date (date)	RequestInfo
Reason	Field (element)	Text (string)	RequestInfo

Tip If any fields are created in the wrong location in the structure, right-click the field to see additional options such as **Move**, **Move Down**, or **Move Up**.

8. Double-click the **RequestDate** field, and then click the function button next to the default value.

9. Click the **Insert Function** button. In the **Categories** section, choose **Date and Time**, in the **Functions** section, select **now**, and then click **OK**.

10. After the request date has been captured, you don't want the date in this field to change the next time the form is opened, so clear the **Refresh value when formula is recalculated** check box, and then click **OK**.

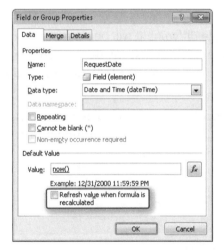

Tip The **now()** function can be used because this RequestDate field was created as a dateTime field. If the field had been created as just a Date field, the **today()** function could be used instead. In this case, we want the RequestDate always to be unique for each form. Therefore, capturing the date and time down to the second ensures that the field's value is unique.

11. Now we need to add some text to the layout. Click in the form's **Click to add title** field, and type **Time-Off Request Form**. Click in the first **Click to add heading** field, and then type **Employee Information**; in the second **Click to add heading** field, type **Request Information**.

Time-Off Request Form			
Employee Information			
Add label	Add control	Add label	Add control
Add label	Add control	Add label	Add control
Add label	Add control	Add label	Add control
Request Information			
Add label		Add control	
Add label		Add control	
Add label		Add control	

12. Drag the **FirstName** and **LastName** fields to the first row of the **Employee Information** section.

13. The **Request Date** field is a little different. It will be set as read-only. Because a date and time picker cannot be set as read-only, it will be inserted as a text field. In the far-left cell of the second row of the **Employee Information** section, type **Request Date:** (including the colon).

14. Press the **Tab** key on the keyboard so that the cursor is in the second cell of the second row. In the list of fields on the right, click the drop-down arrow on the **RequestDate** field, and then click **Text Box**.

15. Double-click the **Request Date** text box on the form, and then on the ribbon, on the **Properties** tab, select the **Read Only** check box.

16. Drag the **Department** field to the second row of the same section. Select the third row under this section, and then delete the entire row.

17. In the **Request Information** section, place the **LeaveDate** field in the first row, the **ReturnDate** field in the second row, and the **Reason** field in the third row. Merge the two cells in the third row.

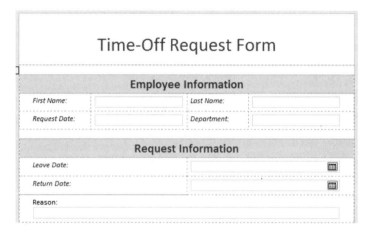

Now that the form has been created, it will be used as the basis of the rest of the exercises in this chapter.

 CLEAN UP Leave InfoPath Designer and the browser open if you are continuing to the next section of this chapter. Otherwise, click Save to save the XSN file to your computer, close InfoPath Designer, and close the browser.

In the following exercise, the time-off request form will be published to SharePoint as a form library.

 SET UP If the **Time Off Request** form is not currently open in InfoPath Designer 2010, navigate to the location on the computer where it was saved in the Clean Up of the previous exercise. Right-click the XSN file, and then select Design.

SharePoint Server

1. Click the **File** menu, click **Publish**, and then click **SharePoint Server**.

   The **Save As** screen appears, prompting you to save the XSN file. The XSN file is the template file of the new InfoPath form. The location that the file is being saved to is simply a backup copy of the file.

2. Select the folder called **C:\InfoPath Files**, and name the file **TimeOff.xsn**. This will start the Publishing Wizard.

   Note When it is time to work on the XSN file later, one method is to simply right-click the saved XSN file and select Design.

3. On the first page of the Publishing Wizard, type the URL of the SharePoint site where you would like the new form to be located, and then click **Next**.

   In this example, Contoso uses a site called forms.contoso.com, where all company forms are published.

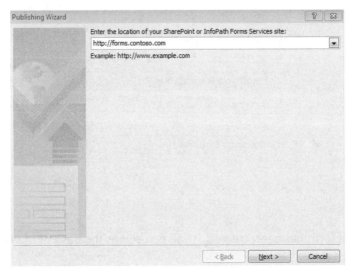

4. During the creation of this new form, the default compatibility level has been browser-based. Because the form will be used in only one form library and will need to be filled out in the browser, the default settings can be used on this screen. Click **Next**.

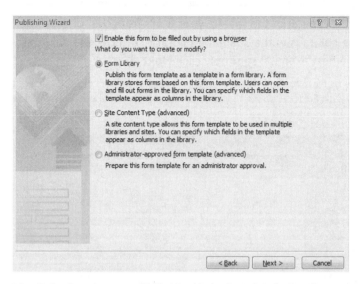

Tip If the form's compatibility level needs to be changed at any point other than during publishing, click File and then select Form Options. There is a compatibility section in the form options, where there are more settings.

5. Because this is the first time that this form is being published, select the **Create a new form library** option. Click **Next**.

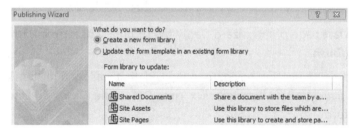

6. Type **Time Off Form** as the name of the form library. In the **Description** field, type **This is the time-off request form**. Click **Next**.

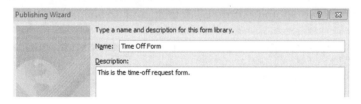

7. On the next page of the wizard, your fields from the form can be promoted to become columns in the SharePoint library. For now, the columns will be left out until the next exercise, so simply click **Next**.

Tip The bottom half of this screen is where parameters can be added. Chapter 8, "Using the InfoPath Form Web Part," which discusses the InfoPath Form Web Part, contains a section on parameters, with examples of how they can be used.

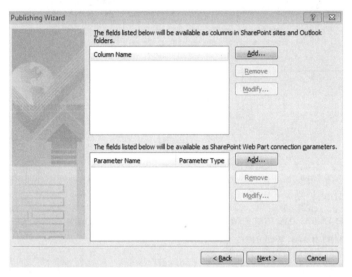

8. On the last page of the wizard, verify the summary of form information, and then click **Publish**.

 9. Open the browser and navigate to the URL that was used in step 3. In the left navigation panel under **Libraries**, click **Time Off Form**. Click **Add Document** to fill out a new form.

Notice that this very basic form leaves much to be desired. Several major improvements need to be made. One of the most glaring issues that we will cover in-depth in this chapter is that there is no Submit button by default, and no validation.

CLEAN UP Leave InfoPath Designer and the browser open if you are continuing to the next section of this chapter. Otherwise, click Save, close InfoPath Designer, and then close the browser.

Promoting Columns

Because there is a choice as to which fields are promoted, you'll want to identify the most important fields for promotion. Following are some essential considerations regarding fields and columns:

- **Reporting**   Think about the full life cycle of a form and what the most pertinent data is. Just as with any list or library in SharePoint, these columns can be used to quickly sort and filter information, and views can be created. Which fields will need to be readily available for these purposes?

- **Workflows**   If workflows will be used, what data does the workflow need?

- **Site columns**   For columns that are more common or will be used in other parts of the business solution as a whole, you have the option to create the columns as site columns (preferably before publishing the form), versus library columns.

Columns can be promoted in two different ways in InfoPath. One way is to click the File menu, choose Form Options, and then click the Property Promotion section. Another way is through the Publishing Wizard, as was demonstrated in the preceding exercise. The latter of the two provides additional options. The following illustration shows the settings available when adding each column.

Note The Publishing Wizard also has available options regarding the selection of fields to become parameters. Parameters are covered in depth in Chapter 8.

- **Field To Display As Column**   In this section, click to select the field that needs to be added as a column. It's always a best practice to organize the fields well and use good naming conventions.

- **Site Column Group**   This drop-down box allows for the selection of an existing site column group. This is the same set of groupings that are available if you click Site Settings | Site Columns. The groups are used to organize the columns, and this drop-down box is used to narrow the list of columns in the column name box. If the name of the currently selected column matches that of an already existing site column, the site column group will automatically be selected and the column name will default to the name of the existing column. If the name of the column does not already exist, this field will show the following entry: (None: Create New Column In This Library).

- **Column Name**   Type or select the desired column name in SharePoint. If a column of that name does not already exist, one will be suggested to you. This suggested field name can be changed. In the previous example screenshot, the column name suggestion is Leave Date, but it can be edited to be simply called Leave. If the name of the column matches an existing site column, that site column name will already be selected here as a drop-down box. In this case, the name can be modified. The option (None: Create New Column In This Library) is selected in the Site column group drop-down box.

- **Function**   This drop-down box is available only for fields that are in repeating controls. When multiple data values are being considered, there are options as to which of the values will exist in the SharePoint column when forms are submitted. The common functions are as follows:

  - **First**   The first value in the repeating control.

  - **Last**   The last (most recently added) value in the repeating control.

  - **Count**   A number count of all of the values in the repeating control field.

  - **Merge**   This is a space-delimited list of all of the values in the field of the repeating control.

  - **Sum, Average, Min, Max**   These functions are available only with number fields, and they perform the various functions. The result of the selected function will be the value shown in the column in SharePoint.

- **Allow Users To Edit Data In This Field By Using A Datasheet Or Properties Page**   This option allows the data in this field both to be displayed in a column and to be edited in SharePoint without opening the form in InfoPath. This setting is most often used when the data in the field needs to be changed via workflow.

When fields are modified from SharePoint, users can potentially view the form library in Datasheet view, or they can click to edit the properties of an item without actually opening the form in InfoPath.

Note By default, the Datasheet view is available. You can change this configuration to No in the configuration library's advanced settings so that items cannot be edited in the datasheet.

In the following exercise, you will promote fields from an InfoPath form to become columns in SharePoint.

SET UP In the web browser, open your SharePoint site and browse to the **Time Off Request** form that was created previously in this chapter. If the **Time Off Request** form is not currently open in InfoPath Designer 2010, navigate to the location on the computer where it was saved in the Clean Up of the first exercise. Right-click the XSN file, and select Design.

1. In the Time Off Request form in InfoPath Designer 2010, click the **File** menu, click **Publish**, and then click **SharePoint Server**.

2. Click **Next** three times, which will take you to the screen where columns and parameters are selected.

3. Click the **Add** button to add the first field.

4. Expand the **EmployeeInfo** group, and then click to select the **FirstName** field.

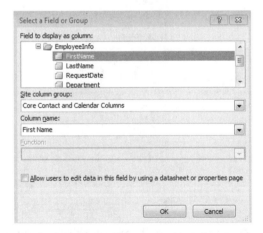

Because **First Name** is an already existing site column, InfoPath suggests this column by default. This is a field that is used when new contact lists are created in SharePoint, so it exists in the **Core Contact and Calendar Columns** group in the list of site columns. Click **OK**.

5. Click **Add**, but this time select **LastName**. Click **OK**.

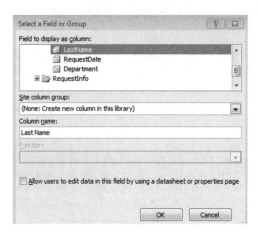

6. Click **Add**, click **Department**, and then click **OK**. Do the same for the **LeaveDate** and **ReturnDate** fields.

Notice that InfoPath has recognized where you used capitalization in the field names and has automatically added a space in the column names. Click **Next**.

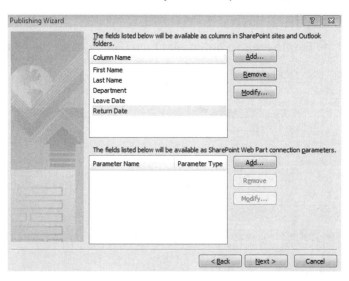

7. Click **Publish**, select the **Open this form library** check box, and then click **Close**.

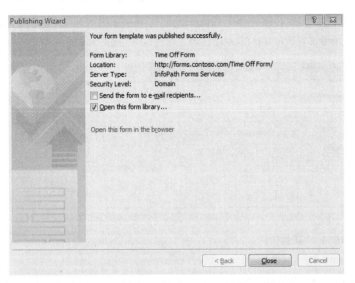

Add document 9. In the form library in the browser, notice that there are several new columns. Click **Add Document** to fill out a new form. Put your own name in the form, and then fill out the other fields.

Save

10. Click **Save** at the upper-left. Enter your name with the number 1 appended, as shown in the following illustration, and then click **Save**.

Save As

You can only save this file to the current site.

File name:*   Charlotte1

Save in: [http://forms.contoso.com/Time Off Form/]

Save   Cancel

Close

11. Click **Close** at the top.

✖ **CLEAN UP** Leave InfoPath Designer and the browser open if you are continuing to the next section of this chapter. Otherwise, click Save, close InfoPath Designer, and then close the browser.

Now that some columns have been promoted and a form has been filled out, it's obvious that some data is readily available to sort through. Some data, which might exist in large text boxes such as the Reason field, is better off left in the form and not as a column. Users can simply click to open a form to see more detailed information contained within it. Also notice the columns on the library settings page. The columns that were created new through the Publishing Wizard are shown here as gray text. The already-existing columns are editable. Therefore, during publishing, selecting columns that already exist has almost the same effect as choosing Allow Users To Edit Data In This Field By Using A Datasheet Or Properties.

Submitting to SharePoint

In the previous exercises in this chapter, the process of filling out a form probably seemed quite inefficient: saving a file, entering a name, and then clicking Close. Plus, the amount of clicks involved is cumbersome. It leaves a lot of room for error when end users have this much freedom. In this section, you will learn how to create a data connection to submit a form to a SharePoint form library. With a data connection, the file name and location can be controlled, as well as form validation. Understanding the proper method for creating a data connection for submission is important both for form accuracy and for the general end-user experience.

In form planning, the following factors should be considered before creating the data connection to submit to SharePoint:

- What field or combination of fields is unique to each form? For each form that is submitted, an XML file is created in a SharePoint form library. If you would like each form to be a unique file, which is usually the case, you need to ensure that each file name is unique in the library each time someone submits a form.

- After the form has been submitted the first time, does it ever need to be edited again? There is a setting that will enable you to ensure that the file is never over-written, but in most scenarios the form will be modified again. Think about form approval processes, or forms that contain additional "office use only" fields.

- Which fields are required when a form is initially submitted? If fields are going to be used as part of the file name, they should also be required fields. This way, all or part of the file name will not be missing.

- Will multiple views be used? In many cases, several different views are created, with each view having its own submit buttons. Each of these different submit buttons can have different rules behind it so that different actions are triggered depending on where you are in the form. If this is the case, the Default Submit Connection might not be something that you will want to utilize. This default button is auto-matically displayed on the ribbon on every view, negating any different rules that exist on different submit buttons on various views.

When creating a data connection to submit to the SharePoint form library, the page shown in the following illustration is an important part of the Data Connection Wizard.

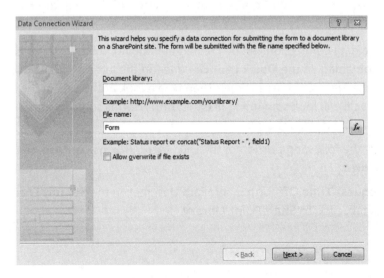

The available settings are as follows:

- **Document Library**   This is the URL to the document library (form library) where the forms will be submitted. It is recommended that the form be published to SharePoint before creating this data connection so that the location will exist before getting to this point. An example of the syntax is shown in the previous screenshot.

- **File Name**   This is one of the most misunderstood settings in InfoPath. By default, the file name is Form. This is not a setting that will ever need to be kept as default. If Form were used as the file name, only one form could be submitted to the form library. Typically, the syntax of this file name should be created so that it is unique to each form that is filled out. There's a function button to the right of the file name text box so that formulas can be utilized—for example, to concatenate multiple fields.

- **Allow Overwrite If File Exists**   Select this check box if the form will ever need to be edited after it has been initially submitted. If this box is left unchecked, an error will be encountered if resubmission of an existing file is attempted.

Now that you've read the high-level overview of settings, the next few exercises will teach you how to create a data connection to submit to SharePoint. You will learn some effects of creating a submit connection in different ways so that the best practices will become apparent.

SET UP   In the web browser, open your SharePoint site and browse to the **Time Off Request** form that was created previously in this chapter. If the **Time Off Request** form is not currently open in InfoPath Designer 2010, browse to the location on the computer where it was saved in the previous exercises. Right-click the XSN file, and then select Design.

1. Before the data connection can be created in InfoPath, the document library URL must be obtained. In the **Quick Launch** pane (on the left side of the page), click the name of the **Time Off Form** library. Then take a look at the URL in the browser's address bar. It will look something like this: http://forms.contoso.com/Time%20Off%20Form/Forms/AllItems.aspx.

   Copy *only* the following portion of the URL: **http://forms.contoso.com/Time%20 Off%20Form**.

2. In the **Request Time Off** form in InfoPath Designer, in the **Submit Form** section on the **Data** tab, click **To SharePoint Library**.

3. In the **Document library** text box, paste the URL that you copied in step 1.

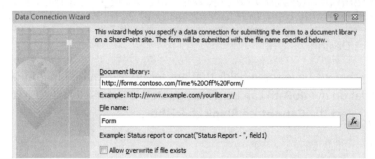

4. For demonstration purposes only, the rest of the default settings will be used. Click **Next**, and then click **Finish**.

5. Click the **Quick Publish** button. Leave InfoPath Designer open.

6. In the form library in the browser, click the **Add Document** button.

7. Fill out the first and last name fields with your own name, and then click **Submit**.

In the form library, notice that the name of the new XML file is **Form**. If you try to fill out another new form, an error occurs. This is because the data connection is saving every form as file name **Form**, and the **Allow overwrite if file exists** check box is not selected.

CLEAN UP Leave InfoPath Designer and the browser open if you are continuing to the next section of this chapter. Otherwise, click Save, close InfoPath Designer, and then close the browser.

The preceding exercise provides a very simple example of how to create a data connection that you can submit to a form. It is apparent that the file name syntax is something that needs to be thought through, because the default setting is not useful.

In the following exercise, you will modify a data connection so that file names are unique to each form, and another difference between saving and submitting will be demonstrated.

SET UP In the web browser, open your SharePoint site and browse to the **Time Off Request** form that was created previously in this chapter. If the **Time Off Request** form is not currently open in InfoPath Designer 2010, browse to the location on the computer where it was saved in the previous exercises. Right-click the XSN file, and then select Design.

1. Now that we have some fields that are set up as required in InfoPath Designer, validation in InfoPath can be demonstrated. Double-click the **First Name** text box, and select the **Cannot Be Blank** check box.

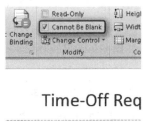

2. Repeat step 1 for the **LastName** field.

   The **Request Date** field will be mandatory, but because it's already been set with a default value and as read-only, it will always contain a value, so validation is unnecessary.

3. On the ribbon, on the **Data** tab, click **Data Connections**.

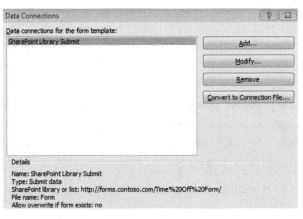

4. Select **SharePoint Library Submit**, and then click **Modify**.

   Modifying the data connection ensures that each file submitted will not be called **Form**.

5. Click the **fx** button next to the **File name** text box.

This is the area where functions and fields can be used to formulate a unique file name.

In this example, three fields will now be concatenated for the file name, with a space between each field name: **FirstName**, space, **LastName**, space, **RequestDate**.

6. Click the **Insert Function** button.

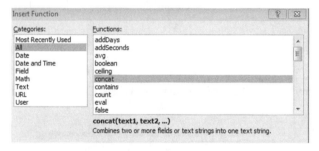

7. In the **Categories** section, select **All**, and then in the **Functions** section, select **concat**.

Notice that an example of the function's syntax is displayed in gray at the bottom. Click **OK**.

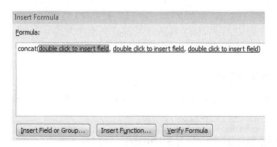

8. Double-click the first item that says **double click to insert field**. Expand the **EmployeeInfo** group, select the **FirstName** field, and then click **OK**.

9. With a concatenation, text and spaces can be placed between the fields. After **FirstName**, the second field will be a space, and the third field is **LastName**. After the **LastName** field, type a comma, click the **Insert Field or Group** button to insert the **RequestDate** field, and then click **OK**. Click **OK** when the formula is complete.

10. Select the **Allow overwrite if file exists** check box. Click **Next**, and then click **Finish**.

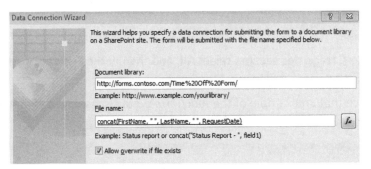

11. In the **Data Connections** dialog box, click **Close**.

12. Click the **Quick Publish** button.

13. Go to the form library in the browser, and then click **Add Document** to fill out a new form.

14. Fill out all of the fields, and then click **Submit**.

Take a look at the resultant file name. The fields have been concatenated to create a file name. As long as that combination of three fields is unique, none of the files will ever inadvertently overwrite existing files. By setting the request date default to the date and time that the form was created, you ensure that the form name is unique. Because the data connection has been set to allow overwrite, the submitted form can be opened later, modified, and submitted again. Fill out another new form and leave the last name blank. Take a look at the following error message:

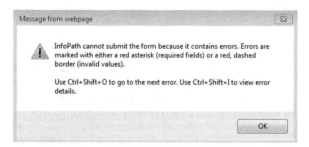

Tip If the Request Date had been set as a date field and not date/time, the form name might not be unique. For example, if a form was filled out with the employee name of John Smith and another form was filled out the same day with the name John Smith, the second form would be written over the first form. The full date and time might not be pretty to look at, but it is definitely unique.

When the submit data connection is used, forms cannot be submitted if required fields are empty. This is not the case with the **Save** and **Save As** buttons. Validation does not occur with these buttons.

15. Fill out yet another new form, and leave at least one required field empty. Click **Save**.

Notice that the same error message pops up regarding the required fields, but InfoPath still allows the file to be saved. The end user can name the file whatever she wants to.

16. Name your file **Test Stuff**, click **Save**, and then click **Close**.

17. Open the **Test Stuff** file again. Fill out the rest of the required fields, and then click **Submit**.

Back in the library, notice that there are now two different copies of the same form that was submitted.

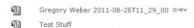
Gregory Weber 2011-06-26T11_29_00 ☑ NEW

Test Stuff

 CLEAN UP Leave InfoPath Designer and the browser open if you are continuing to the next section of this chapter. Otherwise, click Save, close InfoPath Designer, and then close the browser.

In the preceding exercise, you learned some differences between saving and submitting a form. Saving a form allows freedom in file naming, and form validation rules do not apply. Submitting a form allows tight control over the file name syntax and enforces validation rules and required fields. When end users can both save and submit forms, the resulting set of files in the library can become quite disorganized. There are potentially varying copies of any one file, in various stages of completion.

In the following exercise, you will learn how to disable the Save and Save As buttons. The Submit button will also be placed in a more obvious place, instead of only on the ribbon at the top left.

 SET UP In the web browser, open your SharePoint site and browse to the **Time Off Request** form that was created previously in this chapter. If the **Time Off Request** form is not currently open in InfoPath Designer 2010, browse to the location on the computer where it was saved in the previous exercises. Right-click the XSN file, and then select Design.

Form Options

1. In InfoPath, click the **File** menu to display the Backstage view, and then choose **Form Options**.

2. In the **Categories** section, click **Filler Features**, and then in the **Enable features** section, clear the **Save and Save As** check box.

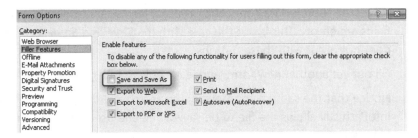

3. Again, in the **Categories** section, click **Web Browser**. Notice that the **Save** and **Save As** check boxes are now disabled. Click **OK**.

   Now it's time to add the submit button to the bottom of the form.

4. Put the cursor at the bottom of the **Time Off** form. On the **Home** tab in InfoPath, in the list of controls, click the **Button** control to add it to the form.

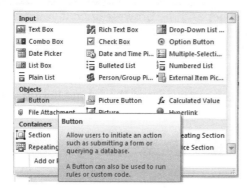

Now that a button control has been added to the form, double-click it. The ribbon will display the **Properties** tab, where properties of the button can be configured.

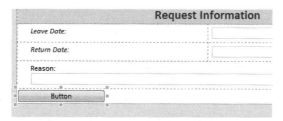

5. On the ribbon, on the **Properties** tab, click the **Action** drop-down box, and then click **Submit**.

As soon as the action drop-down is changed to submit, the **Label** box will automatically show **Submit**, and the button will now say **Submit**. For a visual enhancement, the button needs to be centered.

6. On the ribbon, on the **Home** tab, click the **Center** button in the **Format text** section.

7. Click the **Quick Publish** button. Leave InfoPath open.

CLEAN UP Leave InfoPath Designer and the browser open if you are continuing to the next section of this chapter. Otherwise, click Save, close InfoPath Designer, and then close the browser.

The next time a form is filled out, the user interface will be a lot more intuitive. The Save and Save As buttons have now been removed, and the Submit button is in a prominent place.

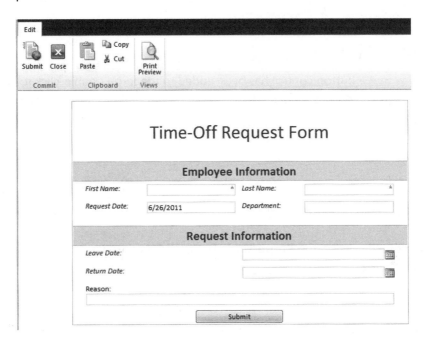

Publishing As a Content Type

Now that a form has been published to a form library and the submission methods have been covered, we can take a look at how to publish a form as a content type. This method will be used when the same form needs to be filled out in multiple libraries in a site collection. Furthermore, with this method, multiple form content types can potentially be used in a single form library.

Content types exist at the upper-level site collection and at each site. If a form will be needed throughout the site collection, it will need to be published at the root site of the site collection. As is inherent with all content types, the form content type will be available for use in all sites and libraries below the site to which the content type has been published.

When publishing a form as a content type, there will be a prompt to save the XSN file to a document library. By default, the root site in the site collection will contain a document library called Form Templates. This is the perfect place to save the file.

Note For more basic introductory information about content types, take a look at the following link on Office.com online help at *http://office.microsoft.com/en-us/windows-sharepoint-services-help/introduction-to-content-types-HA010121570.aspx.*

In the following exercise, you will learn how to publish a form to the site as a content type. Because a form has already been created, some small changes will be made so as to differentiate it from the form that was published directly to a form library. This will be a way of mimicking a completely different form, without spending the time to create a new form and new fields. The example is a Time Off Request form that will be filled out from each department's site so that each department can have its own separate library of these requests.

SET UP In the web browser, open your SharePoint site and browse to the **Time Off Request** form that was created previously in this chapter. If the **Time Off Request** form is not currently open in InfoPath Designer 2010, browse to the location on the computer where it was saved in the previous exercises. Right-click the XSN file, and then select Design.

For this exercise, the previously created form will be saved with a new name because you don't want to cause confusion with the form library to which the **Time Off Request** form has already been published.

1. With the **Time Off Request** form opened in Design mode, click **File**, and then click **Save As**.

2. Where the previous file was named **TimeOff**, this new copy can be named **Time Off CT**. Select a location on your computer, and then click **Save**.

3. In the header of the form, add the word Departmental so that the form is named **Departmental Time-Off Request Form**.

   Another quick visual way to differentiate it from the other form is to click the **Page Design** tab, and then select another color theme. In this example, **Professional - Mission** has been selected.

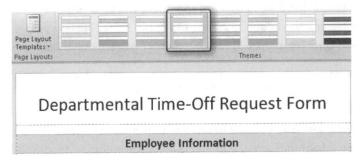

SharePoint
Server

4. Click the **File** menu, choose **Publish**, and then click **SharePoint Server**.

5. Enter the URL of the top level of your site collection, and then click **Next**.

Publishing Wizard

Enter the location of your SharePoint or InfoPath Forms Services site:

http://forms.contoso.com/

Example: http://www.example.com

Next >

6. Select **Site Content Type (advanced)**, and then click **Next**.

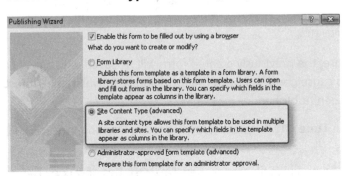

Publishing Wizard

☑ Enable this form to be filled out by using a browser

What do you want to create or modify?

○ Form Library

Publish this form template as a template in a form library. A form
library stores forms based on this form template. Users can open
and fill out forms in the library. You can specify which fields in the
template appear as columns in the library.

◉ Site Content Type (advanced)

A site content type allows this form template to be used in multiple
libraries and sites. You can specify which fields in the template
appear as columns in the library.

○ Administrator-approved form template (advanced)

Prepare this form template for an administrator approval.

7. Select **Create a new content type**, and then click **Next**.

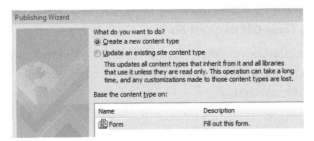

Publishing Wizard

What do you want to do?

◉ Create a new content type

○ Update an existing site content type

This updates all content types that inherit from it and all libraries
that use it unless they are read only. This operation can take a long
time, and any customizations made to those content types are lost.

Base the content type on:

Name	Description
Form	Fill out this form.

8. Name the content type **Dept Time Off**. For the description, type **This is the time off request form that can be filled out at each department site**. Click **Next**.

9. Specify a location and file name for the XSN file. This is where that default Form Templates library comes in handy. Click the **Browse** button, select **Form Templates**, and then click **Save**.

10. For the file name, type **Dept Time Off**, and then click **Save**.

11. In the Publishing Wizard, click **Next**.

12. On the page that lists the promoted columns, click **Next**, and then click **Publish**. On the last page of the wizard, click **Close**.

CLEAN UP Leave InfoPath Designer and the browser open if you are continuing to the next section of this chapter. Otherwise, click Save, close InfoPath Designer, and then close the browser.

In the following example, you will come to understand the power of publishing a form as a content type. The form can be opened and filled out by clicking a link directly to that XSN file in the Form Templates library. However, the submit data connection is still configured to submit the file to that original Time Off library. So even though the form is ready to be filled out, more work needs to be done so that the file can be submitted to the right locations. There is an accounting department site and a marketing site, and the employees in each of those departments will submit to their own library.

In the following exercise, you will create new Marketing and Accounting sites so that Time Off Request libraries can be created in each, and you will associate the new content type to the libraries.

SET UP In the web browser, open your SharePoint site that was used in the previous exercise.

1. From the same root-level site that the content type was published to in the previous exercise, click the **Site Actions** button, and then click **New Site**.

2. Select the **Team Site** template. Use **Accounting** as both the name and the URL of the new site, and then click **Create**.

3. Browse back up to the root site. Repeat steps 1 and 2, naming the second new site **Marketing**.

   Now you need to create form libraries in each subsite.

4. In the **Marketing** site, click **Site Actions**, and then click **More Options**.

5. Select **Form Library** as the template. Name the library **Time Off**, and then click **Create**.

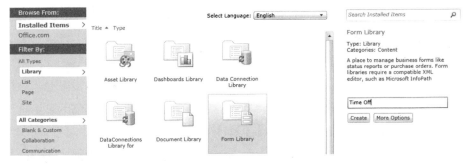

6. On the ribbon, on the **Library** tab, click **Library Settings**.

7. Click **Advanced settings**. Change **Allow management of content types?** to **Yes**, and then click **OK**.

8. In the **Content Types** section of the **Form Library Settings** dialog, click **Add from existing site content types**.

9. In the **Microsoft InfoPath** group, select **Dept Time Off**, click the **Add** button, and then click **OK**.

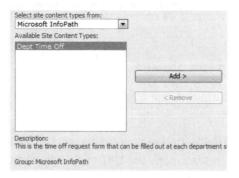

10. In the **Content Types** section in the **Form Library Settings** dialog box, click the name of the **Form** content type, and then click **Delete this content type**. Click **OK** to the confirmation message.

11. Browse to the new Accounting site, and then repeat steps 4 through 10.

Notice that in each of these new form libraries, as soon as the new content type was added, all of the promoted columns appeared in the library settings as columns in the library. Multiple libraries now exist so that Accounting and Marketing employees can go to their respective locations to fill out forms.

Editing the Template

After a form has been created and published as a content type, it will probably need to be modified later. How can you get to it, especially if you don't remember where the XSN file was saved on the hard disk, or if the person who created the form no longer works for the company? Good news! It's still possible. On the Accounting site, click Site Settings | Site Content Types, and then click the name of your content type. Click Advanced Settings, and then click the (Edit Template) hyperlink.

In the following exercise, you will create data connections to submit to the Accounting and Marketing form libraries.

SET UP In the web browser, open your SharePoint site that was used in the previous exercise. If the Time Off Request form Time Off CT is not currently open in InfoPath Designer 2010, browse to the location on the computer where it was saved in the previous exercises. Right-click the XSN file, and then select Design.

1. Navigate to the new **Time Off** library that was created on the **Accounting** site, and then from the browser's address bar, copy the URL to the clipboard.

2. In the **Departmental Time Off Request** form in InfoPath Designer, on the ribbon, click the **Data** tab, and then click **Data Connections**.

3. Select the **SharePoint Library Submit** data connection, and then click the **Modify** button.

4. In the **Document Library** text box, paste the URL of the Accounting document library, and then click **Next**.

   Tip Don't forget to remove the **Forms/AllItems.aspx** part of the URL.

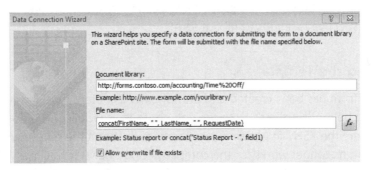

5. For the name of the data connection, rename it to **Accounting Submit**. Click **Finish**, and then click **Close** in the **Data Connections** dialog.

6. Another data connection needs to be created for submittal to the Marketing site. Navigate to the Marketing site that was created in the last exercise, and then click the **Time Off** form library. Copy the URL to the clipboard.

7. On the **Data** tab, click **To SharePoint Library**. Paste the URL to the Marketing site's time-off form. Use the same file name syntax as was used for the Accounting data connection, and then click **Next**.

   Note Follow steps 5–9 from the exercise on page 173 to create the formula for the data connection to submit.

8. Name this data connection **Marketing Submit**, and then click **Finish**.

9. Click **Close** in the **Data Connections** dialog.

The existing **Department** field will be used to determine the correct department to which to submit each form.

10. Right-click the **Department** text box, select **Change Control**, and then select **Drop-Down List Box**.

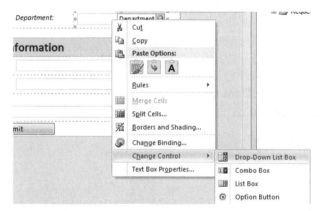

11. Click **Control Properties**, and then select the **Cannot be blank** check box.

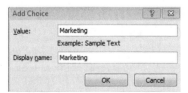

12. Click the **Add** button. Type **Accounting**, and then click **OK**. Add the Marketing department, as well.

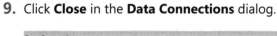

13. Click **Select**, and then click the **Set Default** button on the right.

The word **Yes** appears in the default column. Now, when people fill out this form, they are required to pick a department before submitting the form.

14. Click **OK**.

Submit
Options

15. On the ribbon, click the **Data** tab, and then click **Submit Options**. Select **Perform custom action using rules**, and then click **OK**.

16. In the **Form Submit Rules** pane, change the name of Rule 1 to **Accounting**. Under the word **Condition**, click the link text so that a condition can be added.

17. Create a condition stating that **Department is equal to "Accounting"**, as shown in the following screenshot. Click **OK**.

Tip This text is case sensitive, so if the beginning of the department name was capitalized in step 12, it also needs to be capitalized here.

This rule is done. It states that if the Accounting department is selected, the form will be submitted to the Accounting library.

18. While still in the **Rules** pane, click the **New** button, and then select **Action**. Name the rule **Marketing**, and then create a condition just like you did in step 17, except set the condition to **Department is equal to "Marketing"**.

19. Next to **Run these actions**, click the **Add** button, and then click **Submit Data**.

20. In the **Rule Details** dialog, in the **Data connection** field, select **Marketing Submit** from the drop-down box, and then click **OK**.

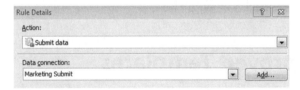

21. Click **Quick Publish**.

The resultant behavior is that when people fill out this form, it is submitted to the library for the department that is selected in the **Department** drop-down box.

Try this form out by browsing to the Accounting site's Time Off library. Fill out a new form. Notice that whichever department is chosen, the form is submitted to the appropriate library.

Tip Technically, a form can be submitted to any library, as long as it has been properly set up in the data connection. The key thing to remember with the content types is that all of the form's column data is populated when forms are submitted.

Administrator-Approved Templates

The administrator-approved template is the last of the three methods available for publishing forms. Under certain circumstances, the Publishing Wizard will allow only the option to publish the form as this type of template, with the other options disabled.

Important Microsoft Office 365 has no interface to upload an administrator-approved template, so this section does not apply to those of you who are using that product.

Reasons why an administrator-approved template would be necessary include the following:

- The form contains custom code (programming done by a developer) and needs to be a browser-based form.
- The form security has been set to Full Trust or Restricted.
- The form needs to be deployed globally, available to all site collections.
- The form utilizes data connections that connect to site collections other than the URL where the form is being filled out.

To deploy this type of template, an XSN file needs to be generated and given to the SharePoint server administrator to upload to forms services.

In the following exercise, you will create an administrator-approved template and upload it to central administration.

SET UP In the web browser, open your SharePoint site that was used in the previous exercise. If the **Time Off Request** form Time Off CT is not currently open in InfoPath Designer 2010, browse to the location on the computer where it was saved in the previous exercises. Right-click the XSN file, and then select Design.

1. With the **Time Off Request** form opened in Design mode, click **File**, and then click **Save As**.

   This file will be saved with a new name because you will be deploying it differently than the other forms in previous exercises.

2. Name this new copy **Time Off Admin**. Select a location on your computer, and then click **Save**.

3. In the header, rename the form **Global Time-Off Request Form**.

4. Click **File**, click **Publish**, and then click **SharePoint Server**.

5. Click **Next**. Select **Administrator-approved form template (advanced)**, and then click **Next**.

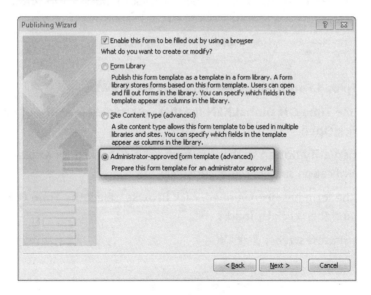

6. Specify a file name and location. This file can be saved to your hard disk and will be the file that is given to the SharePoint administrator. Click **Browse**, and then save the file to **C:\InfoPath Files**. Name it **Time Off Global**. Click **Next**.

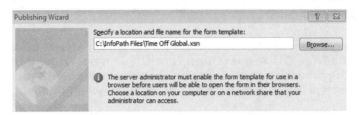

Tip This new file is not to be confused with the file that was saved in step 1. That file is the one that you can edit and do further design work, later on; the file generated in step 6 is the one that is to be uploaded to Central Administration. To give this file to the server administrator, you can either email it to him or put it in a shared network location to which you both have access.

7. Click **Next**. Click **Publish**, and then click **Close**.

8. Go to Central Administration. (This step must be performed by someone who has the necessary access to SharePoint's Central Administration site. In this exercise, it is assumed that you have this type of server access.)

9. Click **General Application Settings** on the left.

10. In the **InfoPath Forms Services** section, click **Manage form templates**.

11. Click **Upload Form Template**, and then click **Browse**.

12. Select the **Time Off Global.XSN** file that you created in step 6 of this exercise, and then click **Open**.

13. Click the **Verify** button so that the form will be checked for errors or issues. In the form verification success screenshot, click **OK**.

14. When the form has been verified, click **Browse**, select the **Time Off Global** file again, and then click **Upload**.

15. On the success screen, click **OK**.

Form Template Status

The form template has been successfully uploaded to the farm. To make the form template available in a site collection, activate the form template from the Manage Form Templates page or from the feature activation page in the site collection.

OK

16. Click the drop-down box on the newly uploaded form.

17. Click **Activate to a Site Collection**.

After it's been determined which site collections will need to have this form available, it can be activated to those site collections. When that is done, the form will exist as a content type at the top level of those site collections. The experience regarding association of the content type to form libraries will be the same as it was in the exercise in this chapter where we published a form as a content type.

Note Take a look at Chapter 12, "Managing and Monitoring InfoPath Forms Services," for more information about these global form templates and the concepts behind activating to a site collection.

Key Points

- There are three different methods for publishing a form library form to SharePoint: form library, site content type, and administrator-approved form template.

- Columns can be selectively chosen to promote to SharePoint as columns in a form library.

- When promoting columns, existing library or site columns can be selected, or new ones can be created.

- By default, the only way that new forms are added to a library is by using the Save functionality, with which end users can designate the file names.

- Form validation is not applicable when forms are saved instead of submitted.

- It is important to plan the syntax of the file names when creating a connection to submit to SharePoint.

- When the Save and Save As buttons are available, the form can be saved without validation, which means that required fields are not really required.

- In Form Options, there are settings with which you can disable specific ribbon buttons.

- When a form is published as a content type, it can be submitted to more than one library.

- When a form is published as an administrator-approved template, it can be deployed and used in multiple site collections.

Chapter at a Glance

Add a SharePoint list data connection to a drop down control, **page 196**

Work with Data Connection Libraries, **page 200**

Use the External Item Picker control, **page 204**

7 Receiving Data from SharePoint Lists and Business Connectivity Services

In this chapter, you will learn how to:

✔ Work with Microsoft SharePoint 2010 lists as data sources for your forms

✔ Benefit from maintaining data connections in a centralized Data Connection Library in SharePoint

✔ Configure and use the External Item Picker control and Business Connectivity Services to add information from external systems to your forms

---

Practice Files Before you can complete the exercises in this chapter, you need to copy the book's practice files to your computer. The practice files you'll use to complete the exercises in this chapter are in the Chapter 7 practice file folder. A complete list of practice files is provided in "Downloading the Practice Files and eBook," on page xxvi.

Receive Data Connections

In Chapter 6, "Publishing and Submitting Form Data," you learned about data connections for submitting Microsoft InfoPath forms to SharePoint. In this chapter, you will learn about using data connections for *retrieving* data from SharePoint lists. You will use standard SharePoint lists, and you will also work with the new External Item Picker control in your forms. The External Item Picker is used to select items from SharePoint's Business Connectivity Services (BCS). BCS is used to connect a SharePoint list to an external data source such as a customer or product database.

In this chapter, we will focus primarily on SharePoint list data connections. Chapter 9, "Working with the SharePoint User Profile Web Service," shows you how to use web service data connections to query data from SharePoint. InfoPath offers more data source options, such as XML files and databases, but those are beyond the scope of this book, because we want to focus primarily on the core SharePoint scenarios.

The deep integration between InfoPath and SharePoint gives InfoPath the ability to use SharePoint 2010 lists as secondary data connections to easily retrieve data into form controls. For many forms, an obvious benefit of using a SharePoint list data connection is that the data already exists and is maintained in a SharePoint list. Therefore, the form can always pull in the most up-to-date information from SharePoint rather than trying to duplicate the same information within your form. Also, if the data is maintained in SharePoint, it will be much easier to allow business users to provide updates to the information that your form consumes, without the need to actually modify the form.

Adding a SharePoint List Data Connection

In the following exercise, you will add a control on an existing form so that the form can receive information from a SharePoint list.

 SET UP In InfoPath Designer, in Design mode, open the form **Flight Delay Form Post Exercise 4** from the practice files location. This is the same form you created in the last exercise of Chapter 3, "Form Design Basics: Working with InfoPath Layout, Controls, and Views."

In the scenario behind this exercise, you have had a request to add another field of information to the Flight Delay form to capture the name of the flight's captain. One effective way to handle this requirement might be to add a SharePoint receive data connection because you already have a list of pilots' names in SharePoint.

1. Publish the **Flight Delay** form to a form library in SharePoint (if it is not already).

2. Create a new SharePoint custom list in the same site. Call the list **Pilot Names**.

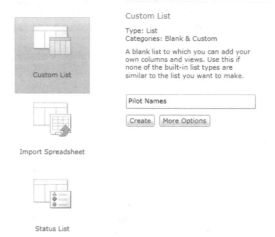

3. In the list, create one text column named **Pilot Name**.

4. On the ribbon, on the **List** tab, click the **List Settings** button. Set the **Require that this column contains information** option of the **Title** column to **No**.

5. Enter the following seven pilot names in your list:

Pilot Name

Jack Smith

Mary Johnson

Doug Black

Hannah Smith

Devin Jones

Sydney Johnson

Zoe Anderson

6. Switch back to the Flight Delay form in InfoPath Designer. In the table on the top part of the form, right-click in the area below the **Reason for Delay** field.

7. In the label area, add the text **Pilot Name**, and then insert a **Drop-Down List Box** control. In the control's properties, rename it **PilotName**.

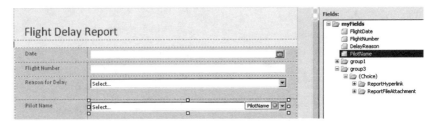

8. On the ribbon, on the **Data tab**, click the **From SharePoint List** button to create a receive data connection on your form.

The Data Connection Wizard opens.

9. Provide the required information in the wizard to add the **Pilot Names** list you added in step 2. On the third page of the wizard, select the check box to add the **Pilot Name** field.

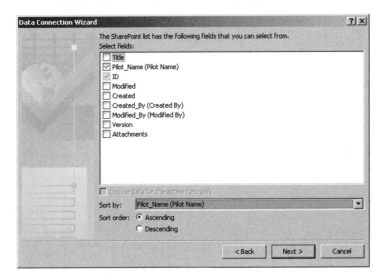

10. For the remainder of the wizard pages, accept the defaults, and then click **Finish**.

    Now you need to connect the SharePoint list receive to the **Drop-Down List Box** control.

11. In the properties for the **Pilot Name Drop-Down List Box** control, select **Get choices from an external data source** and ensure that **Pilot Names** is selected, as shown in the following screenshot.

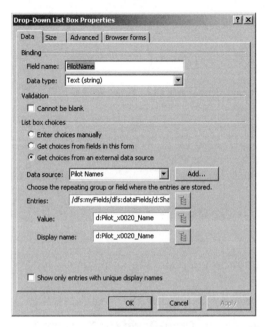

12. Click **OK**, and then press **F5** to preview the form.

    You should now have the information from the SharePoint list available in your **Pilot Name** field.

 13. Use the **Quick Publish** button to update the form library with your new and improved form.

Now, anytime a new pilot name is added in the SharePoint list, your form will automatically display the name in the **Drop-Down List Box** control.

 CLEAN UP You can leave InfoPath Designer open if you intend to continue on to the next exercise. Otherwise, save your form and close InfoPath.

Note For a more sophisticated example of consuming SharePoint lists in a form, read the blog article at *http://www.wonderlaura.com/Lists/Posts/Post.aspx?ID=129*, which describes how you can add multiple SharePoint list data connections in your form so that they connect and query one another.

Data Connection Libraries

Data connections from SharePoint lists generally work great in either InfoPath filler or browser forms. However, using data connections in browser-enabled InfoPath form templates introduces some potential management and authentication challenges that can be addressed by simply converting your data connections in InfoPath to Universal

Data Connection (UDC) files. UDC files abstract the data connection information from the form template and place the connection information in a special SharePoint library called a Data Connection Library (DCL), as shown in the following illustration.

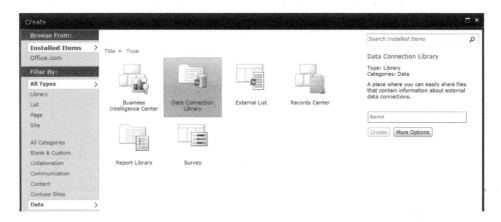

InfoPath 2010 uses data connections that adhere to the UDC file type. They have either a .udcx or a .xml file extension. You can connect to various types of data sources with UDC files, which are stored on the SharePoint server and then used as data connections in your form templates. Using a UDC file in a Data Connection Library offers several potential benefits, including the following:

- You can publish a form template that can access data sources in a different security domain (that is, another server). This is a very useful capability because browser form authentication can be very challenging when crossing security domains.

- It will be easy for you to configure data connections that work in both the InfoPath Filler client and in InfoPath Forms Services.

- You can easily modify the UDC file to redirect data connections to new or updated data sources without modifying all the forms that reference the UDC file. This is much easier than having to go back and update every form template.

- Last but definitely not least, you can have a single place to publish data connections that can be shared across multiple forms and even multiple servers. Think of a common data source you might use in your business that might be useful in many different forms—perhaps a list of department names, job titles, store locations, and so on. It would be much easier to maintain the data connection and security settings in one location for this type of information. All the forms in your business that need that information can reference one UDC. Combining a UDC file and a Data Connection Library is an excellent strategy for simplifying large or complex form environments.

The process for adding a UDC is actually quite simple. First, you need to have a Data Connection Library set up in SharePoint. Assuming one is in place, you add your data connection in InfoPath as usual. In the Manage Data Connection dialog, you simply use the Convert To Connection File button, which will walk you through a wizard to convert and save your connection as a UDC file.

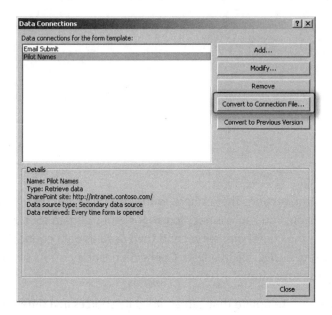

You will need to provide the location of the Data Connection Library in SharePoint. In the following screenshot, we are publishing the data connection as a UDC file named Pilots.udcx to a library named Pilot Information.

After you have done this, you can reuse the data connections in other new forms, by using the From SharePoint Server button on the ribbon's Data tab.

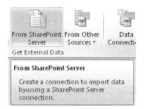

Next, browse for UDC files in Data Connection Libraries, and then pick the one you need for your new form.

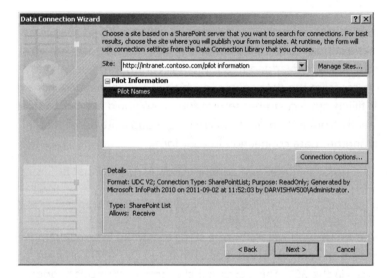

Now your new form can use the data from the Pilots Name SharePoint list data connection that you created in the previous exercise. However, it's now stored in a centrally managed Data Connection Library, and all your forms that require this information can reference a single UDC file for their data.

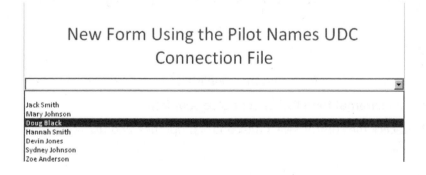

The External Item Picker and Business Connectivity Services

Many companies use BCS in SharePoint to connect to external systems such as customer or product databases and make that information available in SharePoint. BCS is different from the previous types of data connections we've discussed in one major way: the data resides in its own application rather than in a SharePoint list. BCS gives SharePoint (and thus InfoPath) a "view" into that data, but the data still resides natively in its own application (typically a database).

Fortunately, for situations in which your company is utilizing BCS in SharePoint 2010, InfoPath 2010 has a control called the External Item Picker that exists specifically for consuming data from BCS. When added to a form, this control provides an easy way for users to select items from the data source to which BCS is connecting. For example, perhaps the user is filling out a customer service form, and you'd like her to select the customer name directly from BCS rather than creating a duplicate list of that information in SharePoint and another data connection in your form.

BCS is typically set up by a SharePoint administrator. Assuming that BCS is in place for you to utilize, the External Item Picker has several unique advantages for the InfoPath forms designer, including a pre-built security and data access model.

In the following exercise, you will follow the steps to add an External Item Picker control on to a form and set the control properties so that you can select an item from an external data source via the BCS. This exercise makes some assumptions about configuration work that is already done on your system to set up an external content type (ECT) in BCS. The ECT uses XML to define data that is stored in an external system, such as a Microsoft SQL Server database. If you're not the SharePoint administrator, you will need to work with that person to gather some information that is required—and perhaps provide some instructions about how you need the ECT configured to make it work with InfoPath.

 SET UP Open InfoPath Designer.

1. Create a new blank form, and then publish it to a form library in SharePoint.

2. Add an **External Item Picker** control to your form.

3. Right-click the control, select the control properties, and then click the **General** tab.

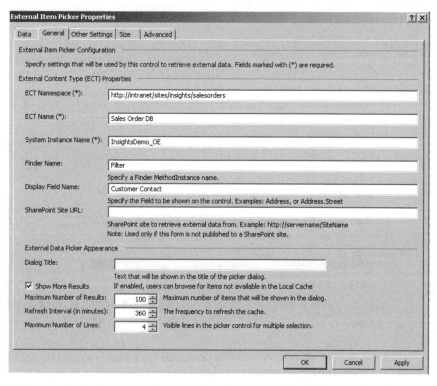

This page includes several properties that you will need to gather from your SharePoint System Administrator. The easiest way to collect these properties is by going to **Manage Service Applications** in **Sharepoint 2010 Central Administration** and choosing **Business Data Connectivity Services**.

4. Click the specific ECT to which you want to connect. The following screenshot, shows an ECT with the name **Sales Order DB**.

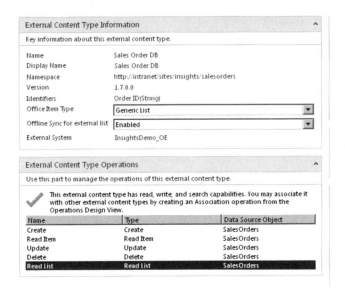

5. Gather the following information from the **External Content Type Information** page:

   ○ **Name**

   ○ **Namespace**

   ○ **External System**

6. Switch back to InfoPath, with the properties of the **External Item Picker** control still open. Then do the following:

   ○ Populate the **ECT Namespace** field with **Namespace**.

   ○ Populate the **ECT Name** field with **Name**.

   ○ Populate the **System Instance Name** with **External System**.

   ○ Skip the **Finder Name** for now; you will add that data in a later step.

   ○ Populate the **Display Field Name** with the actual database field that you'd like to use in the control. If your administrator used SharePoint Designer to create the ECT, you can easily go to the properties of the ECT in Designer and see all the available fields, as shown in the following screenshot. In this example, it is **Customer Contact**.

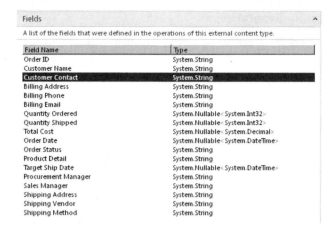

7. In the control properties dialog box, switch to the **Other Settings** tab. Ensure that the **Refresh on Open** check box is selected, and then switch the **Picker Mode** drop-down box at the bottom of the page to **Connect to External Data Source through SharePoint**. You need to set it that way because you are using BCS in SharePoint.

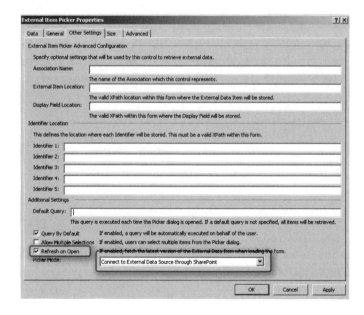

8. Switch back to the **General** tab.

   You are almost finished, but to have your control work properly, one very important field remains to be filled out: the **Finder Name** field. The **Finder Name** is equivalent to a filter on the ECT. This gives the user the ability to search for information in the control. If you do not configure a filter, the user will be presented with a list of all results from the database, and he will have to scroll through them all rather than simply searching.

9. If your administrator has already defined a filter on the **Read List** operation of the ECT, add the filter name to the **Finder Name** field in the **External Item Picker Controls Properties** dialog box. In this example, the filter name is simply **Filter**.

   Note If you do not have a filter on the ECT, see the instructions that follow this exercise for instructions on how to add a filter, and then return to step 9.

10. Click **Apply**, and then **OK**.

    You should be back on your form design surface. Use the **Quick Publish** button to update the form library with your new form. If you go to the form library and create a new form instance, you should be able to use the **External Item Picker** control to browse and search for data from the external system.

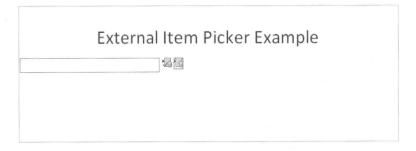

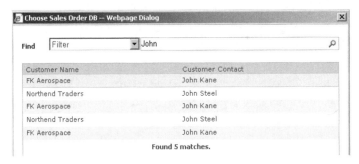

Tip Do not be discouraged if this control doesn't work properly on your first, second, third, or even tenth attempt. It is one of the most complex InfoPath controls. Several moving parts need to be set just right in SharePoint and InfoPath to make the External Item Picker work properly. Verify that you have entered everything accurately at every possible point along the way.

 CLEAN UP Save your form, and then close InfoPath Designer.

Adding a Filter to a Business Connectivity External Content Type

Part of the reason the External Item Picker control is so daunting for new forms designers is that it requires knowing exactly which information from the ECT in SharePoint must be added to the control properties so that everything works correctly. That information was covered in the previous exercise. In most cases, an ECT will be created either in Microsoft Visual Studio or SharePoint Designer 2010. In either case, the developer or administrator should be able to give you the necessary data. However, to make the External Item Picker work as intended, the one extra step that you might need to ask them to take is to add a wildcard filter so that your users can search for the information. The filter must be added in a very specific manner for it to work properly. The screenshots included in the following exercise are from an ECT that has been set up in SharePoint Designer. The instructions will provide the steps necessary for you or your SharePoint administrator to add the filter to new or existing ECTs.

 SET UP Open the SharePoint site you want to work with in SharePoint Designer.

1. Select the appropriate ECT; in this case, it is **Sales Order DB**.

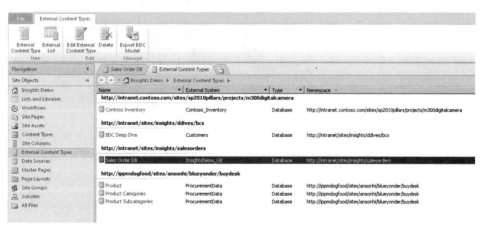

2. In the **External Content Type Operations** dialog box, double-click **Read List** to open the **Read List Operation Properties** Wizard.

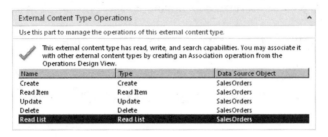

3. On the **Filter Parameters** page of the wizard, set your configuration as shown in the following illustration.

The name of the filter will be the same name that you use to populate the **Finder Name** field in the External Item Picker properties in InfoPath. The **Data Source Element** and **Filter** field should be set to the same field from the database as the one you want the picker control in InfoPath to display.

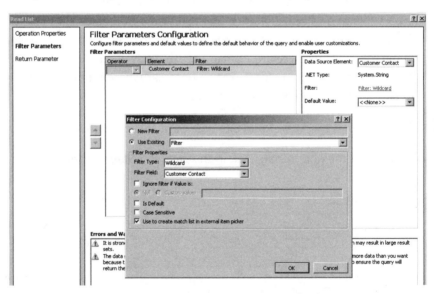

4. On the **Return Parameter** page, ensure that you have selected the appropriate **Data Source Element** option and that the **Show In Picker** check box is selected.

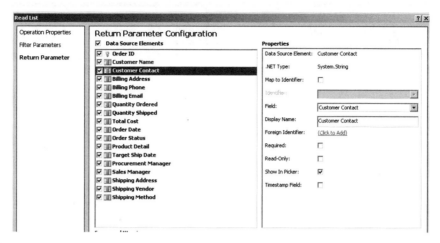

5. When you've completed the **Read List Operation Properties** Wizard, save your changes in SharePoint Designer. This will update the ECT properties in BCS and allow your form to filter on the data source.

✖ **CLEAN UP** Save your form, and then close SharePoint Designer.

Key Points

- InfoPath 2010 provides very tight integration with data in SharePoint lists.
- SharePoint lists are easily maintainable by business users and are thus a great way to ensure that the data in your forms is current.
- Data Connection Libraries make the administration of data sources much easier by centralizing security and management.
- By using the External Item Picker control, InfoPath can consume data from external systems through SharePoint 2010 BCS.

Chapter at a Glance

Create a simple feedback form, **page 223**

Configure the InfoPath Form Web Part, **page 221**

Learn about Web Part connections, **page 224**

Create an input parameter, **page 227**

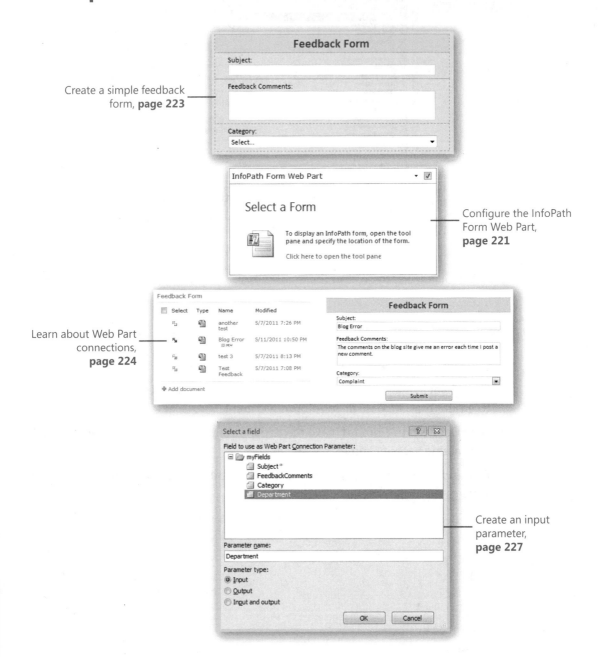

8 Using the InfoPath Form Web Part

In this chapter, you will learn how to:

✔ Configure Web Part settings

✔ Create Web Part connections

✔ Create form parameters

✔ Utilize other browser form parameters

Newly introduced in Microsoft SharePoint 2010, you can use the InfoPath Form Web Part to insert a browser-based form directly onto a page on any site in SharePoint Enterprise or Microsoft Office 365. These types of forms are not available in SharePoint Foundation. When you have the ability to display an interactive form directly on the site, it makes the form more readily accessible for users to fill it out. Any browser-based forms will be available for display in this Web Part. This includes administrator-approved templates that have been uploaded to forms services in Central Administration, forms that have been published as content types in the site, form library forms, and even SharePoint list forms that have been converted to use InfoPath.

> **Practice Files** No practice files are required to complete the exercises in this chapter.

When working with SharePoint lists whose forms have been customized by using InfoPath, the interface that is seen on the display, edit, and new forms is actually the InfoPath Form Web Part on a page. Not only can you fill out forms on these default pages, but custom Web Part pages and other ASPX pages can be created. These types of interfaces and mashups are very useful when creating custom business solutions.

Web Part Settings

After the InfoPath Form Web Part has been inserted onto a page in SharePoint, the Web Part settings are used to configure it further. Not only can the specific form from the site be selected, but a form view can also be chosen, along with even more customizations regarding the display and behavior of the form.

In this section, each Web Part setting will be described. The following illustration shows an example of the Web Part tool pane for the InfoPath Form Web Part properties that has been added to a page.

- **List Or Library**   This option allows for the selection of a form that has been previously published to the site. For a form name to exist in this list, one of the following conditions must be met:
  - A SharePoint list on the current site has been customized to use an InfoPath form instead of the default list form.
  - A form has been published directly to a form library on the current site.
  - A form that was published as a content type or an administrator-approved template has been added as a content type in at least one library in the current site.
- **Content Type**   If more than one form content type exists in the selected list or library, choose the name of the specific content type to be displayed in this Web Part.

- **Display A Read-Only Form (Lists Only)**   This option can be used only if the selected form is associated with a SharePoint list, as opposed to a library. Choose this if the form simply needs to be displayed on the page and not filled out.

- **Show InfoPath Ribbon Or Toolbar**   When this check box is selected, the contextual ribbon is enabled. This means that while the form is actively being filled out or selected, the ribbon at the top of the browser window displays context that is relevant to form submittal. The following illustration shows an example of the contextual toolbar when a list-based form is being filled out.

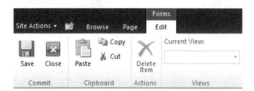

Tip   When this Web Part option is selected, the interface on the page is a bit awkward, especially if the InfoPath Form Web Part is not close to the top of the page. When the form is being filled out, the site visitor would need to look at the top of the page, on the Edit tab on the ribbon, to find the Save or Submit button when the form is ready to be submitted. To avoid confusion during form submittal, you can clear the Show InfoPath Ribbon Or Toolbar check box. In this case, a Submit button would need to be added to the form.

- **Send Data To Connected Web Parts When Page Loads**   This check box is relevant only when Web Part connections are used in relation to the InfoPath Form Web Part. When filter data is being sent from this Web Part to another, any default value that exists in the form when the page first loads is sent to the connected Web Part. This results in the consumer (receiving) Web Part being automatically filtered to show that default value in the form.

- **Select The Form View To Display By Default**   Select the desired form view to display in this Web Part. Read more about form views in Chapter 3, "Form Design Basics: Working with InfoPath Layout, Controls, and Views."

Tip   Because this Web Part will display the selected form view in its original size, a smaller view can be created specifically for use in this Web Part. In the form, create a new view and reduce the size by narrowing the tables and removing any unnecessary spacing. Learn more about views in Chapter 3.

- **Submit Behavior**   You can choose the action to be performed after the form has been filled out and submitted:

  ○ **Close The Form**   After the form is filled out, the form is replaced with the following gray text: The Form Has Been Closed.

  ○ **Open A New Form**   As soon as the form is submitted, a new blank form appears.

○ **Leave The Form Open** The form is submitted to the list or library, but it remains open with no indication that the data was submitted. Site visitors might end up submitting the same form multiple times if it's not obvious that the form submission occurred.

Tip If the Submit options in the Form Library form are not enabled, the Submit Behavior drop-down box will be disabled. In that case, the defined actions behind the form's Submit button rules will apply.

In the following exercise, you will create a new SharePoint 2010 sample site and a simple form library form that will be used to capture website feedback from site visitors. This form will be used in the rest of the exercises in this chapter.

SET UP In the web browser, open your sample SharePoint site so that a new subsite can be created.

1. Click **Site Actions**, choose **New Site**, and then create a site using the **Document Workspace** template. Name the site **Test Feedback**.

2. From your computer's **Start** menu, open InfoPath Designer 2010. On the **New** menu (on the left), select **SharePoint Library** in the **Popular Form Templates** section.

3. Click **Design Form** on the right.

4. In the **Fields** pane on the right side of the screen, right-click **myFields**, and then choose **Add**.

5. Create the fields listed in the following table by repeating step 4 for each, with **Subject** being the only required field.

Name	Data Type
Subject	Text
FeedbackComments	Text
Category	Text

6. In the main area of the form, press **Ctrl+A** to select everything on the form, and then press **Delete** to delete the form content so that the form is completely blank.

7. On the ribbon, on the **Insert** tab, click to expand to see more tables, and then select the table called **Single-Column Stacked 2**.

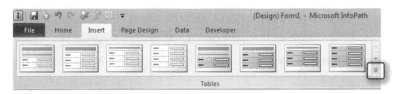

8. In the heading of the table you just inserted, type **Feedback Form**.

9. On the **Layout** tab, narrow the entire table to a width of **410** px, using the **Width** button, and then click **OK**.

10. From the **Fields** pane on the right side of the screen, drag the **Subject** field to the next row of the table, under the heading.

11. Drag the **Feedback Comments** field to the next row down, and then double-click to select this **Feedback Comments** text box. On the ribbon, check the **Properties** tab, and then change the height of the text box to **50** px.

12. Click the **Control Properties** button, and then on the **Display** tab of the text box properties, select the **Multi-line** check box and click **OK**.

This ensures that if more than two rows of text are typed, the box will expand to accommodate more text.

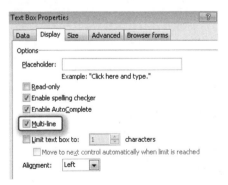

13. Drag the **Category** field to the last row of the table.

14. The **Category** field needs to be a drop-down box instead of a text box, so right-click the text box, choose **Change Control**, and then choose **Drop-Down List Box**.

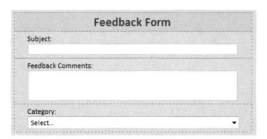

15. To add the category choices, click to select the **Category Drop-Down List Box** control. Press **Alt+Enter** to quickly open the control properties.

16. In the **Drop-Down List Box Properties** window, use the **Add** button to add two choices: **Suggestion** and **Complaint**. Click **OK**.

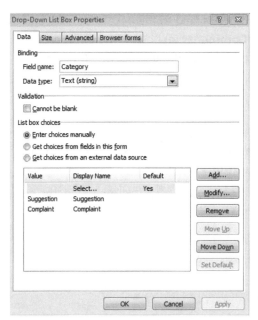

Now the form is ready to publish to SharePoint.

SharePoint
Server

17. On the ribbon, click the **File** tab, choose **Publish**, and then choose **SharePoint Server**.

18. Publish the form to a new SharePoint form library called **Feedback Form** on the site that was created in step 1.

For more information about details of the publishing process, please refer to Chapter 6, "Publishing and Submitting Form Data." When you are prompted to save a copy of the XSN file to the file system, be sure to remember that location. On the Property Promotion page of the wizard, add all three fields in the form to be promoted.

 CLEAN UP Leave InfoPath Designer and the browser open if you are continuing to the next section of this chapter. Otherwise, close InfoPath Designer and the browser.

Now that the basic feedback form has been created, it can be used to gather feedback information. However, the form does not have any submit functionality yet. The next step in this process is the creation of a data connection so that the form can be filled out and submitted to SharePoint.

In the following exercise, you will create a data connection, and then you will add the InfoPath Form Web Part to the home page of your site so that it is intuitive and easy for users to fill out the form.

 SET UP In the web browser, browse to the Test Feedback SharePoint site that was created in the previous exercise. Open the previously created form in Design mode by using InfoPath Designer 2010. In step 18 in the previous exercise, the XSN file was saved to the file system. To open the form in Design mode, right-click this XSN file and then choose **Design**.

To SharePoint
Library

1. In InfoPath, on the **Data** tab, click **To SharePoint Library**.

2. Create a submit connection to the **Feedback Form** library that was created in step 18 of the preceding exercise. (More detailed information about data connections can be found in Chapter 7, "Receiving Data from SharePoint Lists and Business Connectivity Services.") In the **Data Connection Wizard**, be sure to select the default setting of **Set as the default submit connection**.

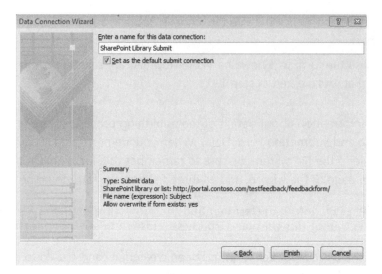

3. On the **Data** tab, click the **Submit Options** button.

4. Click the **Advanced** button, and then select the **Show this message if the form is submitted successfully** check box. For the **After Submit** drop-down box, change the selection to **Open a new form**, and then click **OK**.

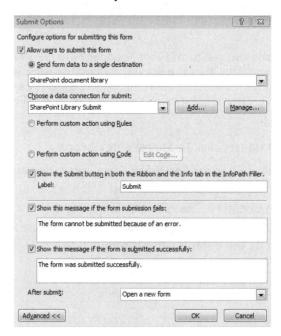

5. Use the blue **Quick Publish** button to publish the latest changes to the form.

6. On the home page of the **Test Feedback** site, click **Site Actions**, and then choose **Edit Page**.

7. In the right zone of the page, click **Add a Web Part**.

8. In the **Categories of Web Parts**, on the left, select **Forms**. In the **Web Parts** section on the right, click the name of the InfoPath Form Web Part to select it, and then click the **Add** button.

9. Now that the Web Part has been added to the page, it needs to be configured to show the Feedback Form that has been published to the site. Click the **Click here to open the tool pane** link.

10. In the Web Part tool pane on the right side of the screen, in the **List or Library** drop-down box, choose **Feedback Form**. The **Content Type** field will have a default value of **Form** because it is the only content type in the library.

11. Verify that the **Show InfoPath Ribbon or toolbar** check box is selected. The **Views** drop-down box will default to **View 1** because that is the only view in the form. In the **Submit Behavior** drop-down box, choose **Open a new form**.

12. Expand the **Appearance** section in the Web Part tool pane. In the **Title** box, type **Feedback Form**. At the bottom of the InfoPath Form Web Part tool pane, click **OK**.

 CLEAN UP Leave InfoPath Designer and the browser open if you are continuing to the next section of this chapter. Otherwise, close InfoPath Designer and the browser.

Now that a form has been created and inserted on the home page as a Web Part, it can be tested. Fill out the form with some test information. On the ribbon in the browser (at the top left of the screen), click Submit.

When a form must be submitted by using the default submit button on the Toolbar, it can be a bit confusing to end users, depending on the location of the form Web Part on the page. In the following exercise, the form will be modified so that the submit button is on the form itself, and not the ribbon.

 SET UP In InfoPath, open up the **Feedback Form** created in the previous exercise, and make sure that the form is in Design mode. The following exercise is a continuation of the steps that were already completed.

1. In the InfoPath form, position the cursor in the last cell of the table that contains the **Category** drop-down box. Press the **Tab** key on the keyboard to create a new cell at the bottom of the table.

2. On the ribbon, on the **Home** tab, click the **Button** object to insert a button on the form.

3. Also on the **Home** tab, with the new button selected, in the **Format Text** section, click the **Center** text button to center the text, which will align the button in the center of the bottom row of the feedback form.

4. Double-click the new **Button** button, which will open the **Properties** tab in the ribbon. In the **Action** drop-down box, choose **Submit**.

This automatically changes the **Label** value to **Submit**.

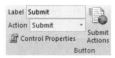

Quick
Publish

5. Click the **Quick Publish** button to publish the changes to SharePoint.

6. Now that the form has been modified and published, in the browser, refresh the Test Feedback site home page. Click the drop-down box at the upper-right corner of the Feedback Form Web Part, and then choose **Edit Web Part**, which will open the Web Part tool pane on the right side of the screen.

7. In the Web Part tool pane, clear the **Show InfoPath ribbon or toolbar** check box, and then click **OK**.

 CLEAN UP Leave InfoPath Designer and the browser open if you are continuing to the next section of this chapter. Otherwise, close InfoPath Designer and the browser.

Notice that now when the form is filled out, you have an obvious submit button to click, which will make more sense to people visiting the site. When the form is filled out and submitted, the data will be stored in the Feedback Form form library.

Feedback Form

Feedback Form
Subject:
Feedback Comments:
Category:
Select...
Submit

Web Part Connections

In the first part of this chapter, you learned how to add one Web Part to a page. When multiple Web Parts are placed on a page, Web Part connections can be created between Web Parts. These connections allow the passing of filter data or parameters from one Web Part to another.

In this section, you will learn how to connect an InfoPath form Web Part to another Web Part, and you will see that you have several methods for accomplishing this. The following options are available when a new connection is created:

- **Send Data To**   This flyout menu will display choices of all of the Web Parts on the page that this Web Part can send data to. This option is to be used with form library forms that contain output parameters.

  Note Parameters are described later in this chapter, in the "Parameters" section.

- **Get Form From**   When this option is selected, the Web Part will be filtered to show one form that already exists in the list or library. The Web Part selected must be a list view Web Part of the form library in which this form is located. The end result is that the desired form is selected in the list view, which will display the associated filled-out form in the InfoPath Form Web Part. The black double-arrow icon in the Select column on the left, as shown in the following illustration, is the selected item indicator.

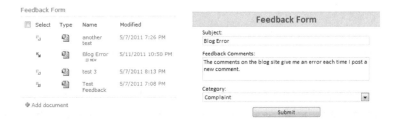

  Note If a non-form library Web Part is selected in this connection, the following error will be displayed: The Web Part Cannot Find An InfoPath Form In The Specified Location.

- **Get Data From**   This option can be used only if parameters have been defined in the InfoPath form, and this applies only to form library forms. InfoPath forms based on SharePoint lists cannot receive form data. You cannot receive data from more than one Web Part on a page.

Parameters

What are parameters in InfoPath? A *parameter* is data that is passed from outside of the form, to be consumed by the form. This piece of information is received in the form, either affecting the behavior of the form as a whole or being passed into one of the fields that has been deemed one of the form parameters.

Parameters are defined during the publishing process and can be set as input, output, or both. The top section of the following screenshot is the familiar property promotion area, and the section on the bottom, new in SharePoint 2010, is used for the creation of parameters.

Tip Parameters are not an option in SharePoint list forms.

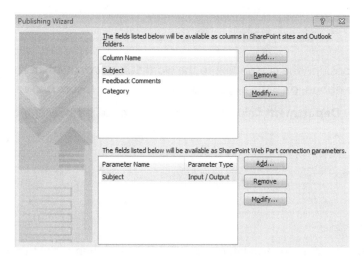

To send data from the form, one Web Part to another Web Part, an output parameter must be used. To retrieve data from other Web Parts, an input parameter must be used.

In the following exercise, you will create a new field in the previously created form, making this field a Web Part connection parameter. Then you will pass a parameter from the Current User Filter Web Part to the InfoPath Form Web Part on the home page. The current user filter Web Part will be used to capture the department name of the currently logged-on user, passing it into the form.

Tip In the following example, you will be displaying the value of the passed parameter as a text box on the form. This part is not required, because the form can still receive the parameter information without the need to display that information in the form.

SET UP Open the previously created **Feedback Form** in Design mode. This exercise builds on the previous exercises in this chapter.

1. In the list of fields in the pane on the right side of the screen, right-click the **myFields** group, and then click **Add** to open the **Add Field or Group** dialog.

2. Name this new field **Department**, and then click **OK**.

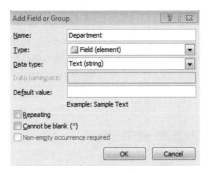

Insert
Above

3. In the form, position the cursor next to the word **Subject** in the third row of the table. On the ribbon, click the **Layout** tab, and then click **Insert Above**.

4. Drag the new **Department** field from the **Fields** pane to the new empty row of the table.

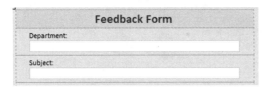

SharePoint
Server

5. Click the **File** menu at the top left, choose **Publish**, and then click **SharePoint Server**.

   Note In this exercise, you will be using the Publishing Wizard instead of the Quick Publish button, because the option to select parameters is one of the steps in the Publishing Wizard.

6. Click **Next** through three screens of the Publishing Wizard, until you see the page in which you can select fields to publish as columns.

7. Click the **Add** button to add the new **Department** field to the top list of columns. Do the same for the **Subject**, **FeedbackComments**, and **Category** fields.

8. Also click **Add** to add the **Department** field as a parameter in the bottom section. **Department** will be an input parameter. Click **OK**.

Four columns appear in the top section and one parameter in the bottom section.

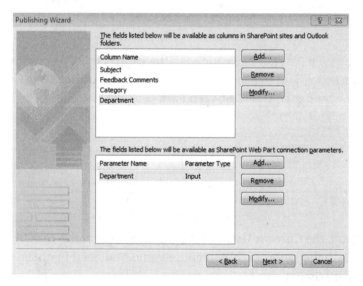

9. Click **Next**.

10. Click the **Publish** button, and then click the **Close** button.

11. Go back to your **Test Feedback** site in the browser. When you refresh the web page, you'll see that the **Feedback Form** Web Part has now been updated to display the new **Department** field. Click **Site Actions**, and then choose **Edit Page**.

12. In the right zone on the page, click **Add a Web Part**.

You will be adding the **Current User Filter Web Part** to the page, and it does not matter which zone it is placed in because it will not actually be seen on the page.

13. In the **Categories** list on the left, select **Filters**. In the **Web Parts** list, select **Current User Filter**, and then click **Add**.

14. After the Web Part has been added to the page, it must be configured before it has any functionality. In the upper-right corner of the **Current User Filter** pane, click the arrow, and then click **Edit Web Part**.

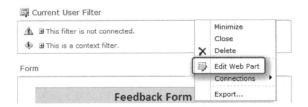

By default, the **Current User Filter** stores the value of the current user's logon name, with the syntax of DOMAIN\username. You need to obtain the logged-on user's department name.

15. Change the **SharePoint profile value for current user** drop-down box to **Department**.

16. Click **OK** at the bottom of the **Web Part** tool pane.

Now you need to create a Web Part connection between the filter Web Part and the form Web Part.

17. With the page in Edit mode, in the upper-right corner of the **Feedback Form** (the form itself, not the list of forms), click the black drop-down arrow. On the flyout menu, select **Connections | Get Data From | Current User Filter**.

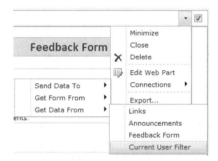

18. On the **Configure Connection** page, the consumer field name of **Department** will already be selected because Department is the only input parameter that has been created for this form. Click **Finish**.

With the page still in Edit mode, in the connection that has been created, the filter Web Part will now indicate the name of the Web Part to which it is sending information. Also, the **Department** field in the form will now display the department name of the currently logged on user. In this example, the current user is in the IT department.

19. Click **Stop Editing** at the upper-left of the web page.

Stop Editing

CLEAN UP Save the form and close InfoPath Designer. Close the browser.

Now that the steps are complete, notice that even though you cannot see the current user filter Web Part on the page, it is capturing information and passing it to the form Web Part. Try submitting a new feedback form. When you click the name of the Feedback Form library in the quick launch on the left side of the page, you'll see all of the submitted forms, and the Department column will show the name of the department of whoever submitted each form.

Note Another method for pulling user information into an InfoPath form entails creating a data connection to the UserProfileService web service. This method is covered in detail in Chapter 9.

The Query String (URL) Filter Web Part

The Current User filter is one of the simplest ways to pass information to the form. Another extremely useful filter Web Part is the Query String (URL) Filter. A query string puts together a URL so that it includes information that is passed into Web Parts on a page, to filter them. The query string part of the URL is placed at the end of the name of the ASPX SharePoint page, after a question mark. The syntax is **Field=Value**.

The following example shows a URL to a site page on a Team site called Accounting. This site page has been created as a project dashboard for Accounting projects. The purpose of this example is to convey the URL syntax:

http://www.contoso.com/accounting/sitepages/ProjectDetails.aspx?Project=23

To break down the preceding URL example:

- ProjectDetails.aspx is the name of the Web Part page.
- Project is the name of the field.
- 23 is the value.

When this query string filter Web Part is used on a page, it will look at the current URL and the desired query parameter. In the Web Part properties, the Query String Parameter Name must match the field in the URL, so in this URL example, the value would be Project. Just as with the Current User Filter, this Web Part needs to have Web Part connections to other Web Parts in order to pass that filter information to them.

Other Parameters

The ability to pass parameters to an InfoPath form is very powerful when it comes to creating custom business solutions. Often, when an InfoPath form is being created, it is part of an overall business solution, such as a site for new employee onboarding, travel requests, or project management. The ability to create useful page interfaces for visitors to the site and for people filling out forms is very important for ensuring that the site makes sense to them. The concept of the user interface will be covered in further depth in Chapter 13, "SharePoint Views and Dashboards."

Following are additional parameter concepts to know when working with InfoPath browser-based forms:

- **Source**   The source parameter tells the form what URL to navigate to after someone has submitted or closed a form. By default, this parameter contains the URL of the default view of the form library. In situations where it is not necessary to send users to the form library, this parameter can be modified to more tightly control where in the site you end up after filling out a form. Following are two examples of situations in which a customized source URL is desirable:

    - A link is created on the home page so that site visitors can click once to fill out a form. When this custom link is clicked, someone fills out the InfoPath form and submits it and then she is immediately directed back to the home page of the site where they began.

    - An email is sent as part of a workflow, with a URL link to a specific form. When the email recipient clicks the link to open the form, the form is viewed and closed or it is submitted. The person is then immediately directed to the home page of the form site.

- **DefaultView** The default view parameter is used for navigating directly to a specific view in the form, other than the view that is set as the default in the form. Add the DefaultView parameter to the end of the URL with the following syntax: **&DefaultView=View Name**. Another method for controlling switching between views is to use Form Load action rules in the form, with conditions set up to determine when the view should be switched, using the Switch Views action.

  Note See Chapter 14, "Advanced Options," for more information about form load rules.

- **URL Dissection** To understand how some typical URLs are constructed when working with browser-based forms, two different types of URLs will now be taken apart, with each parameter explained in a table.

  ○ **New Form example full URL:** http://portal.contoso.com/testfeedback/ _layouts/FormServer.aspx?XsnLocation=http://portal.contoso.com/testfeedback/ FeedbackForm/Forms/template.xsn&SaveLocation=http%3A%2F%2Fportal% 2Econtoso%2Ecom%2Ftestfeedback%2FFeedbackForm&Source=http%3A%2F %2Fportal%2Econtoso%2Ecom%2Ftestfeedback%2FFeedbackForm%2FForms %2FAllItems%2Easpx&DefaultItemOpen=1

  ○ **Link to an existing form URL:** http://portal.contoso.com/testfeedback/ _layouts/FormServer.aspx?XmlLocation=/testfeedback/FeedbackForm/Blog %20Error.xml&Source=http%3A%2F%2Fportal%2Econtoso%2Ecom%2Ftestfee dback%2FFeedbackForm%2FForms%2FAllItems%2Easpx&DefaultItemOpen=1

Part of URL	Description
FormServer.aspx	This is the URL to your SharePoint site with /_layouts/Form-Server.aspx, which is part of forms services and renders the form to browser-based.
XsnLocation	This is the URL to the XSN template file that the form uses. In this example, the form has simply been published directly to a form library.
SaveLocation	This is needed only if the Save or Save As buttons need to be utilized. This path is the default location that the form will save to if the user filling out the form clicks Save or Save As.
Source	Again, this is the URL of where the user will be redirected to after submitting the form.
DefaultItemOpen=1	This indicates that the request is from a library that has the Open In The Browser setting under Advanced Settings.
XmlLocation	This is the URL to the XML file name. In this example, the file name is constructed in the data connection to simply use the Subject field of the feedback form.

Note For more information about InfoPath 2010 query string parameters, see the MSDN article at *http://msdn.microsoft.com/en-us/library/ms772417.aspx*.

Key Points

- Using the InfoPath Form Web Part, you can insert a browser-based form directly onto a page on any site in SharePoint Enterprise or Office 365.

- In the Web Part settings, the form's content type and view can be selected, as well as ribbon settings and form submission behavior.

- When the form's submit options are not enabled, the form submit behavior in the Web Part is disabled.

- The form's default submit button location can be awkward because it exists only in the ribbon unless a submit button is explicitly inserted on the form.

- With a Web Part connection, other Web Parts on a page can send data to input parameters in the InfoPath Form Web Part.

- With a Web Part connection, a Web Part that displays a list view of the form library can send connection information to open each specific form on the same page.

- With a Web Part connection, other Web Parts can get filter data from the current InfoPath Form Web Part.

- Parameters cannot be created in SharePoint list forms.

- Filter Web Parts can send data to the InfoPath Form Web Part on the same Web Part page.

- Only one parameter at a time can be passed to the InfoPath form Web Part.

- The Query String (URL) Filter Web Part can pass URL information through to the InfoPath form Web Part.

- Other InfoPath browser-based parameters can be utilized, such as the Source and DefaultView parameters.

Chapter at a Glance

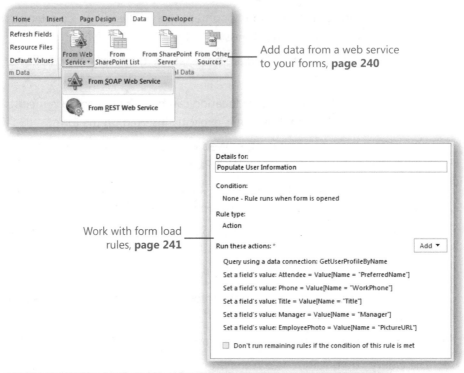

Add data from a web service to your forms, **page 240**

Work with form load rules, **page 241**

Create an event registration form, **page 238**

9 Working with the SharePoint User Profile Web Service

In this chapter, you will learn how to:

✔ Work with the SharePoint User Profile web service

✔ Use form load rules to prepopulate a form with data from a SharePoint user profile

✔ Connect controls to data returned from a web service

✔ Integrate the people picker control with the SharePoint User Profile web service

If you've never worked with XML web services before, this chapter will give you a solid introduction to understanding and learning the techniques involved in consuming data from a web service into an InfoPath form. Even if you have worked with web services in the past, you should still find this chapter useful in your work with InfoPath.

The content in this chapter focuses on specific tactics for integrating data from the SharePoint User Profile web service. The basic idea of web services is to take advantage of two very common standards (XML and HTTP) and build on top of them a technology that allows communication and interoperability between software applications. The primary technical components of a web services platform are as follows:

- Simple Object Access Protocol (SOAP) or REST (Representational State Transfer)
- Universal Description, Discovery and Integration (UDDI)
- Web Services Description Language (WSDL)

Web services are typically created by software developers or built in to packaged software applications so that people like you, who are doing data integration work, can easily consume data from those applications. SharePoint 2010 publishes many of its various data sources via web services in an easy-to-consume format, including the data in lists and libraries. Because so much integration is already built-in between SharePoint and

InfoPath, for most forms you might not need to resort to directly implementing web services in your solution. However, for InfoPath + SharePoint scenarios, one common scenario for which you need to use web services comes up frequently: when you need to query SharePoint for specific properties about a user that are above and beyond what the people picker control provides.

The people picker control in InfoPath 2010 provides a built-in method with which your forms can easily interact with user account names from SharePoint. But what if your form requires more information? What if you need a way to populate fields with the name of a user's manager, a user's phone number, or their work email address? These types of data properties about a user can easily be added to your form by creating a web services data connection to SharePoint. You can use this to supply your InfoPath form with a variety of information about any user who exists in your SharePoint user database (typically, all the users in Active Directory).

The particular web service that "advertises" the user profile properties via web services is called the User Profile web service. The specific operation of this web service, which returns all of the user profile information, is the *GetUserProfileByName* method. You will have ample opportunity to work with the *GetUserProfileByName* method in this chapter's exercises.

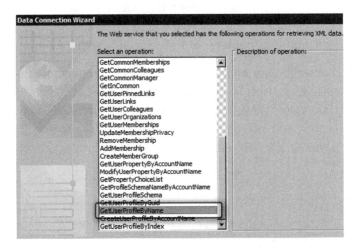

The User Profile database in SharePoint is the same data source that is used to populate the My Sites, so some of the user properties available to you are things that you might already be familiar with—for example, Work Phone and Job Title. The following screen-shot of a SharePoint My Site page shows some of the typical SharePoint user profile properties that you might want to reuse in your forms.

Tip You don't need to use a SharePoint My Site to take advantage of the SharePoint User Profile web service. It is used here purely for the purpose of illustrating the user properties.

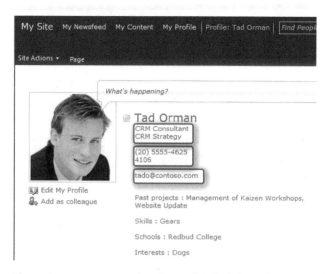

If you have access to the Central Administration console in SharePoint, you can go to the Manage User Properties page to see most of the properties that are available via the User Profile web service. The following screenshot shows some of the most common user properties from the User Profile database.

Central Administration › Manage User Properties

Use this page to add, edit, organize, delete or map user profile properties. Profile properties can be mapped to Active Directory or LDAP compliant directory services. Profile prope

📇 New Property 📇 New Section 📄 Manage Sub-types Select a sub-type to filter the list of properties: [Default User Profile Subtype ▾]

Property Name	Change Order	Property Type
> Basic Information	∨	Section
Id	∧ ∨	unique identifier
SID	∧ ∨	binary
Active Directory Id	∧ ∨	binary
Account name	∧ ∨	Person
First name	∧ ∨	string (Single Value)
Phonetic First Name	∧ ∨	string (Single Value)
Last name	∧ ∨	string (Single Value)
Phonetic Last Name	∧ ∨	string (Single Value)
Name	∧ ∨	string (Single Value)
Phonetic Display Name	∧ ∨	string (Single Value)
Work phone	∧ ∨	string (Single Value)
Department	∧ ∨	string (Single Value)
Title	∧ ∨	string (Single Value)
Job Title	∧ ∨	string (Single Value)
Manager	∧ ∨	Person

Practice Files No practice files are required to complete the exercises in this chapter.

Building the Foundation of the Event Registration Form

In the following exercise, you will begin to create an event registration form that can be used in almost any business scenario for which users need to register for an event, such as training, travel, conferences, and so forth. The form will have five fields of employee data pulled from the SharePoint User Profile SOAP web service: user name, picture, phone, title, and manager. Later in the chapter, you will configure the form so that all the information is pre-populated by using Form Load rules. In the final exercise in this chapter, you will add a button and a people picker control with which the form user can populate the form with data about any user from your SharePoint environment.

 SET UP This exercise assumes that you have access to a SharePoint server with user profiles.

1. Open InfoPath Designer, and create a new blank form. Change the title to **Event Registration** form. With your cursor active in the bottom row of the table, on the ribbon, click the **Insert** tab. Insert the **Four Column with Emphasis 3 – Subheading** table. Change the subheading to **Attendee Information**.

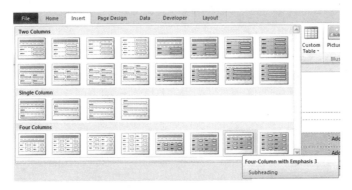

2. Add labels for the six fields as follows: **Event Name, Attendee, Phone, Title, Manager**, and **Employee Photo**.

3. For event name, add a **Drop-Down List Box** control. For **Attendee**, **Phone**, **Title**, and **Manager**, add text fields. For **Employee Photo**, add a **Picture** control. When you insert the **Picture** control, make sure that you choose the **As a link** option.

4. Rename the fields as follows, by using either the **Control Tools** tab or the **Fields** pane:

   ○ **EventName**

   ○ **Attendee**

   ○ **Phone**

   ○ **Title**

   ○ **Manager**

   ○ **EmployeePhoto**

5. On the properties of the **Event Name Drop-Down List Box** control, add a few event types, such as Annual Sales Conference, Company Meeting, and Holiday Dinner Party. Your form and fields should now appear as shown in the following illustration.

6. Add a data connection to the User Profile web service. On the ribbon, on the **Data** tab, choose **From SOAP Web Service**.

7. In the Data Connection Wizard, enter the URL for the SharePoint User Profile web service.

The format of the URL is as follows: http://*sharepoint*/_vti_bin/UserProfileService. asmx?WSDL (replace *sharepoint* with the URL to your SharePoint website). Click **Next**.

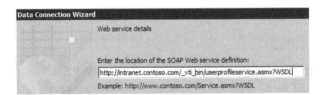

8. On the next page, you are presented with all the operations that the User Profile web service provides. Scroll down and select **GetUserProfileByName**.

This is the operation that you will use to pull the user properties from SharePoint.

9. Click **Next** three times. Do not change anything from the defaults until you get to the final page of the **Data Connection Wizard**.

   On the final wizard page, clear the **Automatically retrieve data when form is opened** check box. This is done primarily for performance reasons so that the form isn't trying to load too much data unnecessarily. Click **Finish**, and then close out of the **Data Connections Wizard**.

The form now has a connection to the SharePoint User Profile web service, although you haven't yet actually invoked any specific data from the web service in the form. In the following exercise, you will add rules that will connect specific fields in the form to the appropriate XML data being returned by the web service. This will require some fairly extensive navigation of the data source.

 CLEAN UP Be sure to save your form template. You will continue building on it in the following exercises of this chapter.

Now that you have created a data connection to the User Profile web service in the previous exercise, you can connect the fields in the form to their respective counterparts in the SharePoint User Profile. You can accomplish this in a variety of ways. Because the web service is simply a secondary data connection in your form, you can populate the fields in the same manner that you can with any other receive data connection—via rules, default values, or controls that provide lookup capabilities. For the event registration form, the goal is for the form to pre-load information about the user who is currently logged on. This minimizes the amount of information that the user must input manually. The best way to achieve this is through the use of **form load rules**, which you will add in the next exercise.

Creating Form Load Rules on the Event Registration Form

In the following exercise, you will add form load rules that connect the four text box fields and the picture control to the User Profile web service. When using the User Profile web service, you are required to bind the controls on your design surface to the appropriate fields from the web service. This process requires navigation and filtering of the user profile schema to retrieve to the proper data. You will perform those steps in the next exercise.

When you query the User Profile web service, it returns user profile information in repeating *PropertyData* nodes in the form's secondary data source. The Name field stores the name of the property. The corresponding value is contained in the Value field, located within the *ValueData* node. This terminology might seem confusing and abstract right now, but after you have added the connections a few times in the exercise, the picture will become more clear. Essentially, you will pass a filtered parameter to tell the web service which specific user profile property you want—for example, "Work Phone". Each control that you want to populate with user profile data will need to make this connection to the web service; typically, rules are the most effective way to accomplish this.

SET UP In InfoPath Designer, open the Event Registration form that you saved from the first exercise in this chapter. Alternatively, you can open the file Event Registration Post Exercise 1.xsn from the practice files. This exercise assumes that you have access to a SharePoint server with user profiles.

1. On the ribbon, on the **Data** tab, click the **Form Load** button.

2. In the **Rules** pane, create a new Action rule called **Populate User Information**.

   The condition should be that the Attendee field is blank. You don't want the original attendee's information overridden next time someone else opens the form. These fields only need to be populated when the form is being filled out for the first time.

3. If you recall from the last exercise, you cleared the check box in the **Data Connection Wizard** that asked whether to automatically retrieve data every time the form was opened. Because you cleared that check box (for performance reasons), you now need to add a **Query for Data** action as the first action in the form load rule. This will query the **GetUserProfileByName** secondary data connection so that the data is readily available to be used in the form.

4. Select the **GetUserProfileByName** data connection.

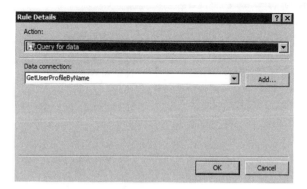

5. Add five **Set a Field's Value** action steps for the form load rule, one for each of the five user data fields that you will pull from the User Profile web service.

Each one of the action steps will require you to connect the respective control to the appropriate XML node from the web service. Add a **Set a Field's Value** step, and then select the **Attendee** field from the **Main** data source as the one you want to work with.

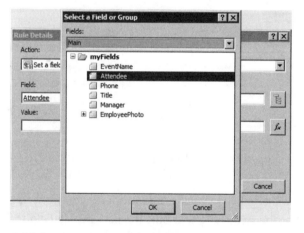

6. Add the correct entry from the web service to the **Value** field of the **Rule Details**. Click the formula button, and then select **Insert Field or Group**.

7. In the **Select a Field or Group** dialog box, change the drop-down box to the **GetUserProfileByName(Secondary)** data source.

8. In the **dataFields** folder, expand everything in the tree until you can access the **Value** field; select it, but *do not* click **OK** yet.

To get at the specific field of data that matches **Attendee**, the **Value** field requires you to pass a filtered parameter.

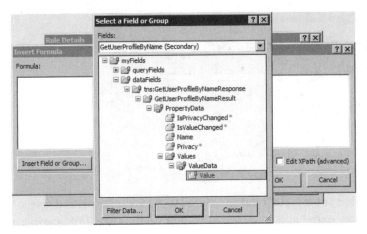

9. Click the **Filter Data** button, and then click **Add**. In the first drop-down, click **Select Field or Group**. The **Name** field is the one that we will filter on for all the user profile properties. Select the **Name** field within the **PropertyData** folder, and then click **OK**.

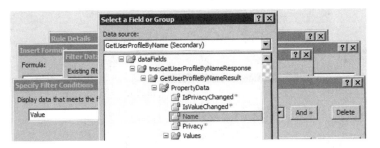

10. Leave the second drop-down set at **is equal to**. In the third drop-down, select **Type Text**.

In this field, you will enter the specific data property you want to pull from the user profile service. For the **Attendee** text box, the user profile field that makes the most sense is **PreferredName** because it is basically in the general "first name last name" format. Therefore, enter the text **PreferredName**, and then press the **Tab** key.

Tip InfoPath automatically inserts quotes around the text you enter, so do *not* type the quotes yourself.

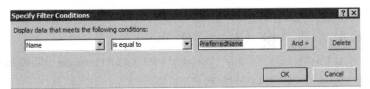

11. Click **OK** several times until you get back to the Design surface.

If you preview your form now, you should see that the **Attendee** field is filled in with whatever user account you are currently logged on with. Remember, you need to be on a system that has access to a SharePoint site with user profiles for this to work.

Tip The preceding steps must be performed exactly as instructed; the web service is very specific in the manner that you navigate and connect to it. Do not be frustrated if you need to retry the steps a few times to make sure you've done everything properly.

12. Now you need to add four more action steps to the rule, repeating steps 5–11 for each one for the remaining fields of user data. When you get to step 10 in the exercise, replace the **PreferredName** text in the condition filter with the following values:

- For the **Phone** field, use the text **WorkPhone**.
- For **Title**, use **Title**.
- For **Manager**, use **Manager**.
- For **Picture**, use **PictureURL**.

If you've done the rest of your steps properly, the rule in your **Rules** pane should now look as shown in the following illustration:

13. Preview your form. It should now appear as shown in the following screenshot, except all the values will be replaced by the relevant values for the logged-on SharePoint server user.

> **Tip** Notice that the **Manager** data comes back in the SharePoint user account name format (domain\username). This option is available for the currently logged-on user also, if you'd rather have the current user name in account name format rather than the standard name, use **AccountName** in the filter conditions rather than **PreferredName**.

Congratulations! You now have an event registration form that pre-populates five fields with user data from the SharePoint User Profile Service.

 CLEAN UP Be sure to save your form template. You will continue building on it in the next exercise of this chapter.

Adding a People Picker and Submit Button to the Event Registration Form

At this point, the registration form is great for a scenario in which whoever is currently logged on is filling out the registration form for themselves. But what if you would like to give the option for the person who is logged on and performing the data input to register someone else? The form, in its present configuration, has been designed to populate on form load with the information of the *currently* logged-on user. So how do you make that transition to populating a different user's profile data in the form? The tactic in this exercise is to utilize a people picker control along with data from the User Profile web service, and we'll also add a button that will drive another set of rules.

 SET UP In InfoPath Designer, open the Event Registration form from the previous exercise in this chapter. Alternatively, you can open the file **Event Registration Post Exercise 2.xsn** from the practice files. This exercise assumes that you have access to a SharePoint server with user profiles and that you have published the Event Registration form to a SharePoint form library.

1. Add a **Person/Group Picker** button on the form below the table. Also add a line of instruction to inform your users why the people picker control is there.

2. Add a button control below the people picker. In the button properties, change the text to **Click to load user data**, or something similar.

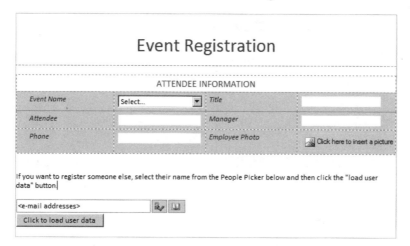

3. Make the button the active selection, and then open the **Rules** pane.

   You will use this button to invoke a new set of rules on the form to reload the five profile fields with the user data for whomever is selected in the people picker.

Note You can accomplish this in several ways—a generic button is perhaps not the most aesthetically pleasing. However, for the sake of instruction, it is useful to use a button so that you can easily see what is happening.

4. Add an Action rule for the button named **Load Alternate User Data**.

5. Add an action to set a field's value in the rule.

6. In the **Field** dialog box, navigate to the **GetUserProfilebyName(Secondary)** data source and drill into the **queryFields** group until you get to the **AccountName** node. Select it, and then click **OK**.

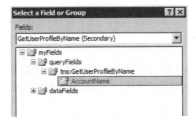

7. Click the formula button, and then choose **Insert Field or Group**. Browse to the **group_1 group** (or whatever your **Person/Group Picker** group is named), and then select the **AccountID** node.

Important The preceding rule enables the subsequent rules to populate the form fields with data about a user selected in the people picker control, rather than the user who is currently logged on.

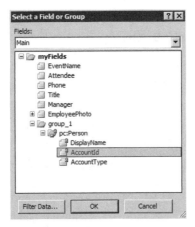

The second rule is also critical. You need to instruct the button to refresh the connection to the User Profile web service so that your subsequent rules can find the necessary data.

8. Add a **Query for data** step for your **GetUserProfile ByName** data connection. That should be all that's needed to ensure that the form will have a fresh connection to the web service when the button is clicked.

9. Now that you've used a rule to tell the form to look to the people picker to determine which user's data to use, you must add the same rules that you added for the form load in the previous exercise in this chapter. Specifically, you need to perform steps 5–11 of that exercise.

These rules will reload the appropriate data for each field when the button is clicked. You can either refer to the previous exercise or see the steps summarized below:

   ○ Add a **Set a Field's Value** step, and then select the **Attendee** field from the **Main** data source as the one you want to work with.

   ○ Click the formula button, and then choose **Insert Field or Group**.

   ○ In the **Select a Field or Group** dialog box, change the drop-down box to the **GetUserProfileByName(Secondary)** data source.

   ○ In the **dataFields** folder, expand everything in the tree until you can access the **Value** field; select it, but do *not click* **OK** yet. The **Value** field requires you to pass a filtered parameter to get at the specific field of data that matches **Attendee**.

   ○ Click the **Filter Data** button, and then click **Add**. In the first drop-down box, choose **Select Field or Group**. The **Name** field is the one that we will filter on for all the user profile properties. Select the **Name** field underneath the **PropertyData** group, and then click **OK**.

   ○ Leave the second drop-down set at **is equal to**. In the third drop-down box, choose **Type Text**. In this field, you will enter the specific data property that you want to pull from the User Profile Service. For the **Attendee** text box, the profile field that makes the most sense is **PreferredName**. So enter the text **PreferredName**, and then press the **Tab** key.

   ○ Click **OK** several times until you get back to the Design surface. Preview your form now. Select a user other than yourself in the people picker control. You should see that the **Attendee** field is filled in with whatever user account you have selected in the people picker.

10. Add four more action steps to the rule, repeating the steps for each of the remaining fields of user data.

    Just as in this chapter's previous exercise with the form load rules, when you get to the formula step in each rule, replace the **PreferredName** text in the condition filter with the values as follows:

    ○ For the **Phone** field, use the text **WorkPhone**.

    ○ For **Title**, use **Title**.

    ○ For **Manager**, use **Manager**.

    ○ For **Picture** use **PictureURL**.

    If you have entered your action steps properly, your rule should now appear as shown in the following illustration.

> Details for:
> Load Alternate User Data
>
> Condition:
>   None - Rule runs when button is clicked
>
> Rule type:
>   Action
>
> Run these actions: *   Add ▼
>
>   Set a field's value: AccountName = AccountId
>   Query using a data connection: GetUserProfileByName
>   Set a field's value: Attendee = Value[Name = "PreferredName"]
>   Set a field's value: Phone = Value[Name = "WorkPhone"]
>   Set a field's value: Title = Value[Name = "Title"]
>   Set a field's value: Manager = Value[Name = "Manager"]
>   Set a field's value: EmployeePhoto = Value[Name = "PictureURL"]
>
>   ☐ Don't run remaining rules if the condition of this rule is met

11. Save the form, and then on the ribbon, click **Quick Publish** to update the form library with your changes.

12. Preview the form. Select a different user in the people picker, and then click the button. Your form should load up with the other user's information, as shown in the following illustration:

Event Registration

ATTENDEE INFORMATION

Event Name	Select... ▼	Title	Sr. Business Developmen
Attendee	Julian Isla	Manager	CONTOSO\mollyc
Phone	(425) 555-0184	Employee Photo	

If you want to register someone else, select their name from the People Picker below and then click the "load user data" button.

Julian Isla

Click to load user data

Now if you want to finish off the form for real-world usage, you would definitely want to add a **Submit** button to the form with a connection to the form library in which it is hosted.

Congratulations! You have a functional event registration form that utilizes the SharePoint User Profile web service!

 CLEAN UP Save your form template if you want to keep your changes, and then close out of InfoPath Designer.

Key Points

- SharePoint User Profiles are a rich source of information that can be used to populate data in your forms.

- InfoPath can connect to various types of web services, including SOAP web services such as the SharePoint User Profile web service.

- Form load rules are a great technique to pre-populate a form with data.

- Connecting form fields to web services is not difficult but requires careful navigation of the secondary data source.

- The InfoPath people picker control, along with rules, can be used to populate a form with user data from a SharePoint user profile.

Chapter at a Glance

Integrate InfoPath forms in workflows, **page 254**

Customize an initiation form to look more polished, **page 262**

Update forms when fields change, **page 268**

Use task actions in workflows to generate a task form in the workflow, **page 275**

10 InfoPath Integration with SharePoint Designer Workflows

In this chapter, you will learn how to:

✔ Create a workflow initiation form

✔ Allow a workflow to be manually triggered

✔ Create a custom action button

✔ Use the task process designer

✔ Modify a workflow task form

Microsoft SharePoint Designer 2010 is a free download from Microsoft, and it is used for further customization of SharePoint. SharePoint comes with many built-in capabilities. Much of SharePoint can be customized without SharePoint Designer or custom code. However, in some situations, customizations need to be made beyond the built-in browser-based functionalities, which is when using SharePoint Designer is imperative.

> **Practice Files** No practice files are required to complete the exercises in this chapter.

Introduction to Workflows

In this chapter, you will learn about the integration points between Microsoft InfoPath 2010 and SharePoint Designer 2010. Most of the integration points that will be covered in this chapter are in workflows. Workflows are used to automate processes in lists and libraries. Some of the common functionalities of workflows are assigning approval tasks, sending emails, and setting field values. In SharePoint Designer, each workflow consists of a series of conditions and actions that execute in a certain order. Workflows can be created just for use in one specific list or library, or they can be created as reusable, which means that they can be associated with one or all content types.

After a workflow has been published for the first time, the associated InfoPath forms are listed in the Forms section of the main workflow settings screen.

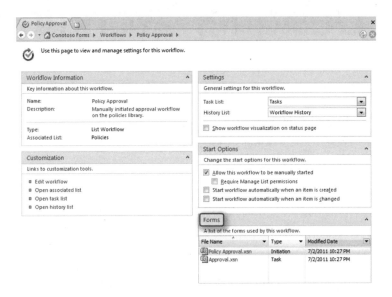

The two different types of forms that can be displayed in the Forms section are the *initiation* and *task* forms. Both will be covered in this chapter.

Tip Not every SharePoint Designer workflow will contain both types of forms. The criteria for each form will be covered in the examples in this chapter.

Workflow Initiation

When creating a workflow, one of your first considerations is deciding what will trigger the workflow.

- **Start Options**   The settings in the workflow that determine how it will be triggered are called Start Options, which consist of the following:
  - **Allow this workflow to be manually started**   When selected, this check box enables a user to click a button to explicitly start the workflow when desired. Associated to this is the **Require Manage List** permissions check box. When selected, only certain people can manually start the workflow. **Manage List** is a specific permission, and by default it is part of the Design and Full Control permission levels.

○ **Start workflow automatically when an item is created**   When this check box is selected, the workflow automatically runs as soon as an item is created in the list or library.

○ **Start workflow automatically when an item is changed**   When this check box is selected, the workflow runs every time each item in the list or library is modified.

You can select multiple start options.

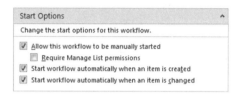

Manage List Permissions

What exactly is a Manage List permission, and where can I find it? It is part of the Design and Full Control permission levels, but here is a quick way that you can create a custom permission level just for managing lists:

1. From the root level of the site collection, click **Site Actions**, and then click **Site Permissions**.

2. On the ribbon, click **Permission Levels**, and then click **Add a Permission Level**.

3. Name this level **Manage Lists**, and then place a check box next to it.

4. Click **Create**.

Now you have a custom permission level. Whoever has this permission on the list or library where you create the workflow can manually run workflows for which the **Require Manage List** permissions check box is selected.

The following workflow initiation concepts are important to understand:

● If the workflow is to be manually started, an InfoPath form is automatically created as part of the publishing process. This form is called the initiation form because it is used upon workflow initiation. By default, the initiation form simply contains two buttons: Start and Cancel. If you want to require some information from the person starting the workflow, initiation parameters can be added.

- *Initiation form parameters* are fields that are added to the initiation form. The types of fields available are similar to the types of columns that can be created in a SharePoint list, such as text, dates, and choices. When these parameters have been created, they automatically appear in the InfoPath initiation form.

Typically, workflows are not triggered manually; instead, they are completely automated and operate behind the scenes. SharePoint site users do not need to know that they are running nor what they are doing. Also, the users don't need to worry about forgetting to run the workflow. Initiation forms are used only for the forms where a user is expected to start the workflow manually.

At our example company, Contoso, all of the company policies are documents stored in a single document library. A few people are in charge of editing policies, while most employees of the company can see only read-only files. When the editor of a policy has determined that edits are complete, the policy needs to go through an approval process before document changes are made available for public consumption. Policy editors have the freedom to select the approver of any given policy. For the Contoso company policies, they make use of SharePoint's built-in content approval settings. Therefore, when a document is approved, the content approval is automatically set to Approved.

In the following exercise, you will create a simple approval workflow. Using documents as the example, it can be demonstrated that workflows are applicable to any kind of SharePoint item, whether it be a list item, document or spreadsheet in a library, or an InfoPath form that has been submitted.

SET UP In the web browser, open your SharePoint site so that a new library can be created. Also, open your SharePoint site in SharePoint Designer 2010.

1. Create a new document library on your site, name the library **Policies**, and then type the description **This library contains all of the company policies**. Leave the rest of the settings as default, and then click **Create**.

Name and Description	
Type a new name as you want it to appear in headings and links throughout the site. Type descriptive text that will help site visitors use this document library.	Name: Policies Description: This library contains all of the company policies.

Library
Settings

2. Go to **Library Settings**. In the **General Settings** section, click **Versioning settings**. Next to **Content Approval**, under **Require content approval for submitted items?**, select **Yes**, and then click **OK**.

Content Approval

Specify whether new items or changes to existing items should remain in a draft state until they have been approved.   Learn about requiring approval.

Require content approval for submitted items?
● Yes   ○ No

New
Document ▾

3. Before the workflow is created, take a look at the built-in content approval functionality. Create a new document in the library, and name it **Dress Code Policy.docx**. The file will be saved to the **Policies** library.

Notice that the **Approval Status** column in the library says that the document's status is **Pending**.

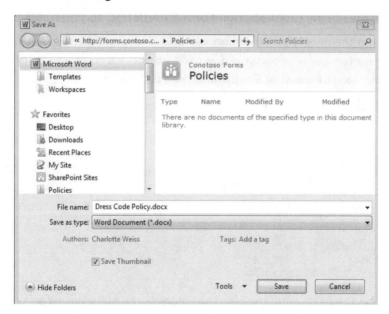

Now it's time to create the workflow.

Workflows

4. In SharePoint Designer, in the Navigation pane on the left side of the screen, click **Workflows**.

List
Workflow ▾

5. The new workflow will be created specifically for the **Policies** library, so on the ribbon, click **List Workflow**, and then choose **Policies** from the drop-down menu.

6. Name the workflow **Policy Approval**. Type the description **Manually initiated approval workflow on the policies library**, and then click **OK**.

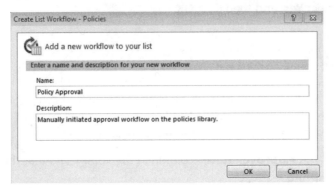

7. On the ribbon, click **Initiation Form Parameters**, and then click the **Add** button.

8. Using the people picker option, call it **Approvers**. Type the description **Select one or more people who should approve this document**. In the **Information type** field, select **Person or Group**, and then click **Next**.

9. Fill in the field's settings using the values in the following table. When complete, then click **Finish**, and click **OK**.

Setting	Value	Description
Show Field	**Account**	This is the user profile property.
Allow selection of	**People and Groups**	Should the approvers be restricted to individuals only, or do you want to allow the selection of both people and groups?
Choose from	**All Users**	The control will be a people picker, but if a specific SharePoint group is selected here, only members of that group can be chosen. For example, all people who can approve documents could exist in a SharePoint policy approvers group, and when initiating the workflow, you would be able to pick only one of those people.
Allow blank values	Not selected	Is the field required or not?
Allow multiple values	Selected	Can multiple entities be selected in the people picker? These entities can include a mixture of people and groups if **People and groups** is chosen under **Allow selection of**.

10. Now that the initiation parameter has been created, you need to kick off an approval process. On the ribbon, click the **Action** button, and then under the **Task Actions** section, select **Start Approval Process**.

This type of action is called the **Task Process Designer** and is an entire workflow inside of a workflow.

11. Click **these users** to select the approvers.

12. In this case, participants will be the approvers, so the initiation form parameter called **Approvers** will be selected as the participant. Click the **Address** icon next to **Participants**, and double-click **Workflow lookup for a user**.

13. In the **Data source** field, select **Workflow Variables and Parameters**. In the **Field from source** field, select **Parameter: Approvers**, and then in the **Return Field as** field, select **Login Names, Semicolon Delimited**. Click **OK** to close the **Lookup for Person or Group** dialog box, and then click **OK** in the **Select Users** dialog.

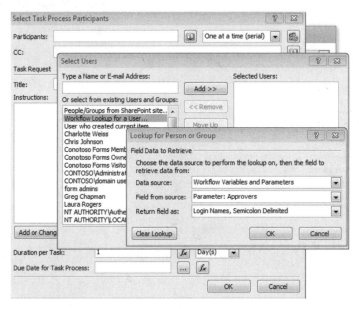

14. In the **Title** field, type **Policy for approval**, and then under **Instructions**, type **Please take a look at this policy, and approve or reject it**. In the **Duration per Task** field, type the number **1** (the default is days). Click **OK**.

Tip When the duration per task is one day, if the assigned task is not completed within one day, the assignee will receive automatic "overdue" emails.

15. On the ribbon, click the **Publish** button.

16. Go back to the **Policies** library in the browser, click the drop-down box for the **Dress Code Policy** document, and then click **Workflows**.

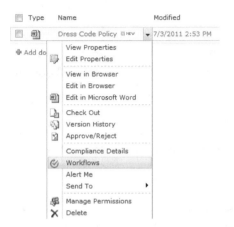

17. In the **Start a new workflow** section, click **Policy Approval**.

The initiation form presents a text box, in which you can fill in the names of the designated approvers.

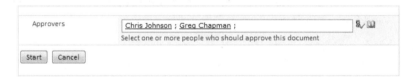

18. Fill in the names of one or more people, and then click **Start**.

Important If the SharePoint server's outgoing email settings have been set up correctly by the administrator, workflow emails will automatically be sent to the approvers and to the initiator.

 CLEAN UP Leave SharePoint Designer and the browser open if you are continuing to the next section of this chapter. Otherwise, close SharePoint Designer, and then close the browser.

The first time a workflow is started, a new column that has the same name as the workflow is automatically added to the library. In the Policies library, notice that there is a new column called Policy Approval. The workflow has been started, so it shows as In Progress, next to the Dress Code Policy document. When you click the In Progress link, you are taken to the Workflow Status page. This shows who the current task is assigned to, as well as a workflow history that lists each activity that has happened in the workflow so far. Now that the initiation form has been created (the form that was filled out in step 17 of the preceding exercise), it can be easily customized because it is an InfoPath form.

In the following exercise, you will customize the initiation form for the policy approval workflow so that it looks a bit more polished.

SET UP In the web browser, open your SharePoint site. Also, open the same SharePoint site in SharePoint Designer 2010. Open the Policy Approval workflow that was created in the previous exercise.

1. Go to the main workflow settings screen for the **Policy Approval** workflow. In the breadcrumb trail at the top of the workflow, click **Policy Approval**.

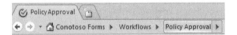

2. In the **Forms** section at the lower-right, click the **Policy Approval.xsn** form.

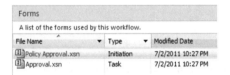

   Note Anytime a workflow has the manual start option selected, when it is published, the initiation form will be generated, and it will have the same name as the workflow.

3. Put the cursor in the empty row above **Approvers**, and then type Policy Approval Workflow.

4. On the ribbon, click the **Home** tab, and then using the **Font Styles** section, change the font to **Title**. Center the title across the page.

5. Again, on the ribbon, go to the **Page Design** tab. In the **Themes** section, click to select the theme called **Playground - Cay**.

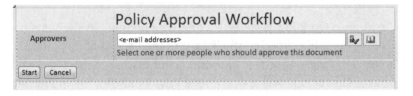

6. Now the form can be published. Click the **Quick Publish** button at the upper-left. InfoPath prompts you to save a backup copy of the form to your hard disk before publishing. Select a file location on the **Save As** screen, and then click **Save**.

7. When the template has been published successfully, click **OK**. Exit InfoPath.

8. Upload another document to the **Policies** library, and manually initiate the workflow by following steps 15–17 from the previous exercise. You'll see the new, modified initiation form in place.

> **Tip** Notice that it was not necessary to republish the workflow to implement the newly published InfoPath form.

 CLEAN UP Leave SharePoint Designer and the browser open if you are continuing to the next section of this chapter. Otherwise, close SharePoint Designer and close the browser.

To build the content approval into the workflow, the goal is to automatically set content approval to Approved if a document is approved; and otherwise, set it to Rejected. This entails adding a new condition to the workflow.

In the following exercise, you add the functionality to communicate with the library's content approval. When content approval is used on its own without a workflow, the only way to receive notification of items needing approval is to set up SharePoint alerts on that list or library. With this solution, only the specific approvers will get the email.

 SET UP In the web browser, open your SharePoint site. Also, open the same SharePoint site in SharePoint Designer 2010. Open the Policy Approval workflow that was created in the previous exercise.

1. Position your cursor on the line under the **Start Approval Process** action, type the word **If**, and then press the **Enter** key. This will show a list of all of the optional conditions. Select **If any value equals value**.

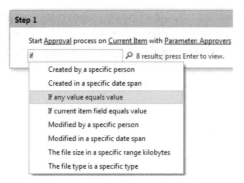

The first condition that you will set is to verify that the item has been approved. The approval process that took place in the first action has a variable that you will use.

2. Click the name of the first blue value, and then click the function (**fx**) button. Select **Workflow Variables and Parameters** as the data source; select **IsItemApproved** as the field name, and then click **OK**.

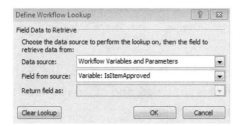

3. For the second value, after **is equal to**, select **Yes**.

 4. Select this first condition, and then on the ribbon, click the **Else-if Branch** button.

Now you have a structure, but actions need to be added after each condition in the statement.

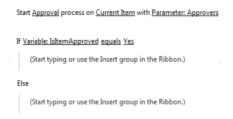

5. Position your cursor in the first section that says **(Start typing or use the Insert group in the Ribbon)**. On the ribbon, click the **Action** button, and then choose **Set Content Approval Status**.

6. Set the content approval status to **Approved**, with the comment **This policy has been approved**.

7. Under the **Else** statement, add another action to **Set Content Approval Status**. Set the content approval status to **Rejected**, with the comment **This policy has been rejected**.

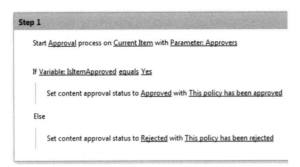

8. Publish the workflow.

9. Add a new document to the library, and then manually trigger the workflow again. Click the drop-down box on the document in the library, and then select **Workflows**. Click the name of the **Policy Approval** workflow. Enter one approver's name on the initiation form. In the **Policies** library, click **In Progress** in the **Policy Approval** column.

10. To open the workflow task, click the title of the assigned task—in this case, **Policy for approval**.

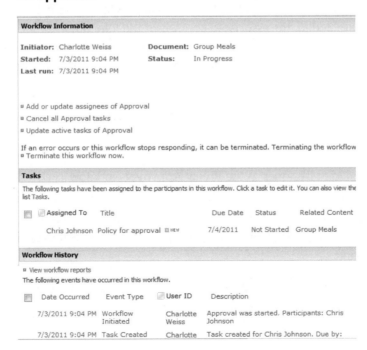

11. Click the **Approve** button on the task. Go back to the **Policies** library by clicking its name in the **Quick Launch** pane.

	Type	Name	Modified	Modified By	Approval Status	Policy Approval
☐	📄	Dress Code Policy ☐ NEW	7/3/2011 2:53 PM	Charlotte Weiss	Pending	
☐	📄	Group Meals ☐ NEW	7/3/2011 9:11 PM	Charlotte Weiss	Approved	Approved

➕ Add document

 CLEAN UP Leave SharePoint Designer and the browser open if you are continuing to the next section of this chapter. Otherwise, close SharePoint Designer, and then close the browser.

The Approval Status column has been set to approved, and the Policy Approval (workflow) column also shows as Approved. The benefit of using content approval is that each company policy can be worked on by policy editors, but the changes are not available for public consumption until the item has been approved.

This has been a fairly simple set of exercises so far, demonstrating what an initiation form is and how one is customized. However, in the real world, workflows are created, changed, published again, and then changed some more, and they go through multiple iterations. It is important to demonstrate the form publishing behavior when aspects of a workflow are modified.

In the following exercise, you will add a new initiation form parameter. When new parameters are added, the associated controls of the InfoPath initiation form are not automatically modified. You will learn how to work in the real-world scenario of having multiple changes to a workflow. A High Priority check box will be added so that the due date varies depending on the priority.

 SET UP In the web browser, open your SharePoint site. Also, open the same SharePoint site in SharePoint Designer 2010. Open the Policy Approval workflow that was created in the previous exercise.

1. In SharePoint Designer, in the **Policy Approval** workflow, click the **Initiation Form Parameters** button. Click **Add** to add a new parameter.

2. Name the field **High Priority**. In the **Description** field, type **Is this a high priority approval?**. In the **Information type** field, select **Yes/No (check box)**, and then click **Next**.

3. Select a default value of **No**, click **Finish**, and then click **OK**.

   If a policy is high priority, the approval task will be due in one day; otherwise, five days is the deadline.

Local
Variables

4. On the ribbon, click the **Local Variables** button, and then click the **Add** button.

5. Name the new variable **Due in Days**. Define the **Type** as **Number**, and then click **OK**.

6. Above the action that starts the approval process in the workflow, add a new condition: **If any value equals value**. For the data source, choose **Workflow Variables and Parameters**; for the source field, choose **Parameter: High Priority**. Click **OK**.

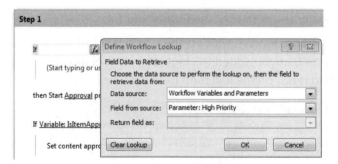

7. For the value after **equals**, choose **Yes**.

8. On the ribbon, click the **Else-If Branch** button.

9. If the approval is high priority, the approver will have one day to complete the task; otherwise, the approvers get five days. Under the first part of the else-if branch, insert an action to **Set Workflow Variable**. For the variable, select **Variable: Due in Days**, and then set it to **1**.

10. Under **Else** (not high priority), set the same variable to **5**. In the **Start Approval Process** action, click the link **Parameter: Approvers**.

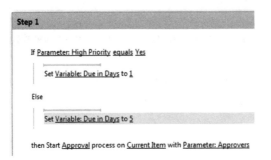

Note A variable is a way to temporarily store a value during the time a workflow is running. Now that we have obtained the desired number of days and are holding onto it in a variable, it can be used where we need it.

11. Next to the **Duration per Task** text box, click the function button. For the data source, select **Workflow Variables and Parameters**; for the field, select the variable **Due in Days**. Click **OK**.

12. Click **OK** again, and then click the **Publish** button.

An error message displays, which is the whole point of this exercise. The error message indicates that you added the high-priority initiation form parameter, but that the new field is not on the initiation form yet. Click **OK** to close the message box.

You have two different ways to address the error, both of which need to be done from the workflow settings dialog box for the workflow.

**Workflow
Settings**

13. On the ribbon, click the **Workflow Settings** button.

Notice in the **Forms** section, under **File Name**, that the **Policy Approval.xsn** (the initiation form) "needs update."

One way to get past this would be to simply delete the form. The next time the workflow is published, it would be regenerated automatically. Another way is to open the form and manually add the new high-priority field to the form. When you get to this error, you simply need to weigh your options. How much customization has been done to the form, versus how many field changes have there been since it was last published? Is it faster to redo the customization (in this case it's the title and colors), or is it more efficient to keep the existing form and manually add (or remove) any changed fields? Let's go for option number two: modify the form.

14. Open **Policy Approval.xsn** by clicking its name.

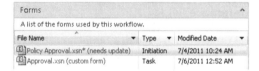

15. The message shown in the following illustration pops up to alert you that a field has changed. Click **OK**.

16. In the form's layout, insert a new row below the **Approvers** row, and then drag the high-priority field to the new row. Next to the text box, type **Is this a high priority approval?**.

17. Save the form by clicking **Quick Publish**, and then close InfoPath.

18. In SharePoint Designer, on the **Workflow Settings** tab, publish the workflow again. No error will occur this time.

CLEAN UP Leave SharePoint Designer and the browser open if you are continuing to the next section of this chapter, but close the policy approval workflow. Otherwise, close SharePoint Designer, and then close the browser.

Now that the workflow has been improved, try it out in a couple of different ways. Add another document, and follow steps 16–18 in this chapter's first exercise to manually start the policy approval workflow. Try starting one as high priority, and notice that the due date of the associated tasks are automatically set as one day from the date that the task is assigned. Alternately, when you start a workflow and it's not high priority, each approver has five days from the date of assignment.

In the preceding exercise, you learned that when an InfoPath form that is associated with a workflow has been customized, it is not automatically updated when the form's fields change. Weigh your options, and determine whether it's more efficient to delete the InfoPath form and let SharePoint Designer automatically recreate it or to open the form and modify the layout to add or remove fields.

Important The people who are set up to approve the documents must have permissions to approve list items in order for the workflow to run correctly. Recommendations on security on the Policies library are as follows:

- Give all employees of the company Read permissions.
- Give the policy editors Contribute permissions.
- Give the policy approvers Design permission, or a custom level that contains the Approve items permission.

Tip If approvers are not given permissions to approve items, this workflow can still be accomplished by using an impersonation step in the workflow; however, this is beyond the scope of this chapter.

Custom Actions

When manually starting the workflow each time, several clicks are involved. When fine-tuning the user experience in SharePoint, you need to put yourself in the shoes of the people who will be using the site daily; thus you need to think about making things easy and obvious for them. Having to go through three clicks to start a workflow is not very easy or intuitive. Custom actions are buttons that you can create as a way to help the site users. When creating custom actions, determine where the button needs to appear in the interface and what the button will do.

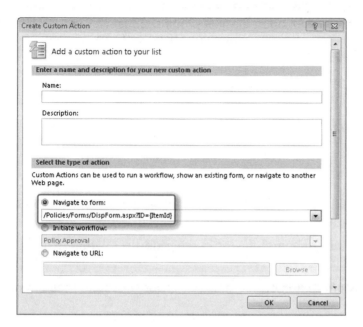

The custom action button can be added in the following places:

- List Item menu
- Display Form ribbon
- Edit Form ribbon
- New Form ribbon
- View ribbon

The following are the actions that can be taken when the button is clicked:

- **Navigate to form**   Open a specific form that is associated with that list or library
- **Initiate workflow**   Start a workflow that has been configured to be initiated manually
- **Navigate to URL**   Go to any specific website

At Contoso, when it is time for a policy to be approved, the user interface needs to be easy and obvious. A custom action button is the perfect solution to this requirement.

In the following exercise, you will add a custom action to the policies library that you will configure to start the policy approval workflow. A button will be added to the list item menu on each document.

SET UP In the web browser, open the SharePoint site that was used in the previous exercises in this chapter. Also, open the same SharePoint site in SharePoint Designer 2010.

 1. In SharePoint Designer, in the **Navigation** pane on the left, click **Lists and Libraries**.

2. In the **Document Libraries** section, click **Policies**.

3. On the settings page for this library, in the **Custom Actions** section at the bottom right, position the cursor in the white part inside of this section.

Notice that on the ribbon, at the top of the page, the **Custom Actions** tab is selected.

4. Click the **Custom Action** button, and then choose **List Item Menu** from the drop-down menu.

5. Type **Policy Approval Workflow** as the name; for the description, type **Start this workflow to select approvers for a policy**. In the **Select the type of action** section, select **Initiate Workflow**. Select **Policy approval** as the workflow.

6. Scroll down to **Button Image URL**, enter **/_layouts/images/itgbcirc.png**, and then click **OK**.

7. Go to the **Policies** library in the browser. Click the drop-down box on any policy to see the new task button called **Policy Approval Workflow**. The icon next to it is the PNG file that you defined in step 6. Click the **Policy Approval Workflow** button.

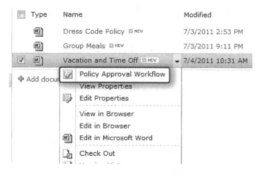

8. Adding this button takes you straight to the custom initiation form. Select some approvers, and then click **Start**.

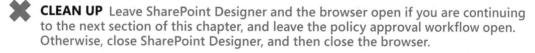 **CLEAN UP** Leave SharePoint Designer and the browser open if you are continuing to the next section of this chapter, and leave the policy approval workflow open. Otherwise, close SharePoint Designer, and then close the browser.

After performing all of the preceding exercises in this chapter, you now have an understanding of what an initiation form is, how a workflow can be triggered manually, and how one of these forms can be modified.

Workflow Task Forms

Another type of InfoPath form that is built into SharePoint Designer workflows is the task form. Six different task actions can be used in the Enterprise version of SharePoint, and each of these tasks comes with its own custom InfoPath form.

- **Assign a form to a group**   Assign a task to one or multiple groups and users. In this form, you can define the task title and other fields.

- **Assign a to-do item**   Assign a very simple task to one or multiple groups and users. Define the task title but no other fields.

- **Collect data from a user**   This task action returns the task ID as a variable but can be assigned only to a single person or a single group. In this form, you can define the task title and other fields.

- **Start approval process**   This type of task has built-in approve and reject buttons and is used to pass an item through an approval process.

- **Start feedback process**   This task has a button to submit feedback as well as a text box to enter comments.

- **Start custom task process**   Unlike the preceding two task process actions, this type is empty and must be fully customized.

The "task process designer" is a workflow inside of a workflow, which was introduced with SharePoint Server 2010 (Enterprise version). The latter three of the preceding six tasks have the task process designer built in. All of the workflow's emails are built in, and these types of actions are great to use for tasks with deadlines. When a task is overdue, an email will be generated and sent to notify the appropriate people. When the whole process has ended, more notifications are sent. All of these emails can be customized in SharePoint Designer.

How does each task action have its own InfoPath form? Each time a new task action is added to a workflow, a new content type is automatically created at the site level. If multiple tasks of the same action type are added on a site, parentheses with a number are automatically added to the name of the action. Although the same task list can be used for multiple types of tasks, each of these different task actions uses a different form interface to that same list. Each form is associated with a different content type.

A plethora of functionality is automatically built in, especially with the task process designer. The following illustration shows an example of an approval form, with descriptions of the associated fields:

- **Status**   This is the status of the individual task. It has an initial value of Not Started. When the task is done, it will be Completed. This is read-only.

- **Requested By**   This is the name of the person who initiated the workflow. This is read-only.

- **Consolidated Comments**   This is a description that includes the initiator's name, date, and the description of the task itself. With multiple approvers, all of their comments will also be concatenated here. This is read-only.

- **Due Date**   Use this to define a date, not the time, that the task is due. This is read-only.

- **Comments**   The task assignee can optionally type in comments before clicking one of the buttons at the bottom. These comments are stored in the workflow's history.

- **Approve and Reject Buttons**   These are called *outcomes*. Within the task process, any outcomes can be created; these are just the most common. In the task process designer, these are listed under the Task Outcomes section.

- **Request Change**   This button allows the task assignee to make a change request to the initiator or to any other person of their choosing. When this is done, the current task is automatically set to Completed, and a new task is created for the person from whom the change is being requested. This setting is optional, which means that you can disallow change requests from the workflow settings.

● **Reassign Task**   Use this button to reassign the task to someone else. The existing task will be automatically completed, and a new task will be assigned to the new person. This setting is also optional.

Tip   The custom task form also has several built-in views, which the change request and task reassignment utilize.

In the following exercise, you will explore the task process designer and associated InfoPath form that was created in the last exercise.

SET UP   In the web browser, open the SharePoint site that has been used in the previous exercises in this chapter. Also, open the same SharePoint site in SharePoint Designer 2010, and open the policy approval workflow.

Before we delve into the task form, let's explore the task process designer further.

Edit
Workflow

1. In the **Policy Approval** workflow, click **Edit Workflow**.

2. In the approval process action, click **Approval**.

then Start Approval process on Current Item with Parameter: Approvers

Welcome to the task process designer. The task form fields are extra fields that you would like the approvers to fill out. Task outcomes will be the buttons available to approvers. The settings section contains a security setting as well as check boxes to enable assignees to reassign or request change requests. In this exercise, you want the approvers to be able to reassign their tasks to someone else or to make change requests back to the initiator.

3. Select both the **Reassignment** and **Change Requests** check boxes.

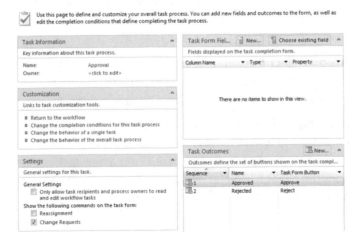

The three links—**Change the completion conditions for this task process**, **Change the behavior of a single task**, and **Change the behavior of the overall task process**—are all more workflows. This is where all of the workflow's emails are set up, and a lot more.

4. Click **Return to the workflow**.

5. Click **Workflow Settings** to return to the main screen for the **Policy Approval** workflow.

   Notice that the **Approval.xsn** file has an asterisk next to it. This indicates that the form has a pending change. The change was made to the check boxes in step 3, so the form needs to be updated to include both buttons.

6. Publish the form. This process automatically regenerates a new task form.

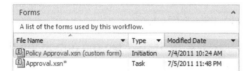

File Name	Type	Modified Date
Policy Approval.xsn (custom form)	Initiation	7/4/2011 10:24 AM
Approval.xsn*	Task	7/5/2011 11:48 PM

 CLEAN UP Leave SharePoint Designer and the browser open if you are continuing to the next section of this chapter, and leave the policy approval workflow open. Otherwise, close SharePoint Designer, and then close the browser.

In the following exercise, you will modify the task form. A few common fields are read-only but do not appear as such. Basically, when you're filling out a task form, it can be confusing because fields that might seem editable are not editable.

 SET UP In the web browser, open the SharePoint site that was used in the previous exercises in this chapter. Also, open the same SharePoint site in SharePoint Designer 2010, and open the policy approval workflow.

1. On the main workflow settings dialog box of the **Policy Approval** workflow, click **Approval.xsn** in the **Forms** section at the lower-right.

   This is an example of how the task form looks when a user opens it; it is readily apparent what each field looks like.

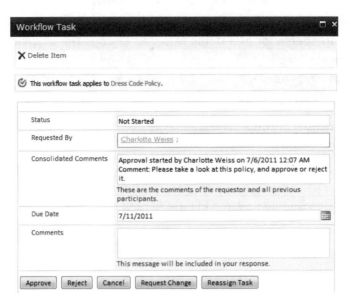

2. In InfoPath, select the text box next to **Status**. On the ribbon, on the **Layout** tab, click **Shading**, and then choose **No Fill**.

3. Delete the **Requested By** people picker control.

   This doesn't need to be a people picker, because people aren't being picked here—they're only being displayed.

4. From the list of controls on the **Home** tab, click **Calculated Value**.

5. Click the function button, and then click **Insert Field or Group**.

6. Click **Show Advanced View**.

7. Select the **DisplayName** field under **Requested By**, and then click **OK**.

8. Click **OK**, and then click **OK** again on the **Calculated Value Properties** screen.

9. Right-click the text box next to **Consolidated Comments**. Select **Change Control**, and then click **Calculated Value**.

10. Right-click the date picker control next to **Due Date**. Change it to a calculated value. On the ribbon, on the **Properties** tab, change the width of this box to **165** px.

11. You will put two different controls on the form, one for date and one for time. Copy the **Due Date** field, and then paste the copy next to it.

12. Select the second calculated value, and then on the ribbon, on the **Properties** tab, click **Data Format**. Change it to a time format, and then click **OK**.

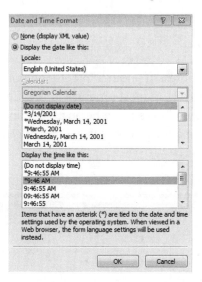

13. Click **Quick Publish**, and then close InfoPath.

14. Manually start the **Policy Approval** workflow on a document in the policies library.

Notice that the task form looks nicer, and it is more obvious that the **Comments** box is the only area that is editable.

 CLEAN UP Close SharePoint Designer, InfoPath, and the browser.

Just as with initiation forms, any time the task process is modified, the form needs to be updated. When the publish button is clicked, a prompt indicates that the form must be updated.

External List Forms

Besides workflows, external list forms represent another integration point between SharePoint Designer and InfoPath. Typically, in most organizations, different systems and databases are used for different purposes. There could be an accounting database on one server and a personnel database on another one. Many times, these islands of data are not connected or integrated with one another. In SharePoint 2010, the concept of external content types was introduced. With external content types, connections can be created to many different data sources, and the data can be presented to the end user as if it were in one location.

External lists are created from external content types. When users edit the data in one of these lists, the appearance is that the data is in SharePoint, but it is not. Each time an External list is created, a prompt opens to automatically generate an associated InfoPath form for the list.

Important The button to modify the form with InfoPath is not available via the browser, as it is with regular list forms.

In SharePoint Designer, in the Lists And Libraries section, External lists are in their own grouped section called External Lists. When you click the name of an External list, take a look at the ribbon. Click the Design Forms In InfoPath button. The form can now be customized just like any other InfoPath form.

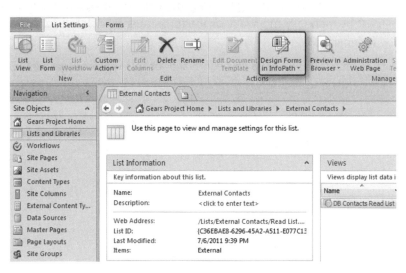

Key Points

- There are several InfoPath integration points in the SharePoint Designer 2010 software.

- SharePoint Designer 2010 is free to download and install.

- There is a forms panel on the workflow settings page, where associated forms are listed.

- There are three different start options for workflows; one or more can be selected.

- Initiation form parameters are fields that are on the initiation form when a workflow is manually triggered.

- A workflow can work in conjunction with a list or library's content approval settings.

- It can be a cumbersome process to manually trigger a workflow. Custom action buttons can be created to simply this action.

- When the form fields are changed after the workflow is published, the InfoPath form must be manually modified, or the form must be deleted so that a new one will be regenerated.

- Certain permissions will need to be in place for this type of approval workflow to be used efficiently and securely.

Chapter at a Glance

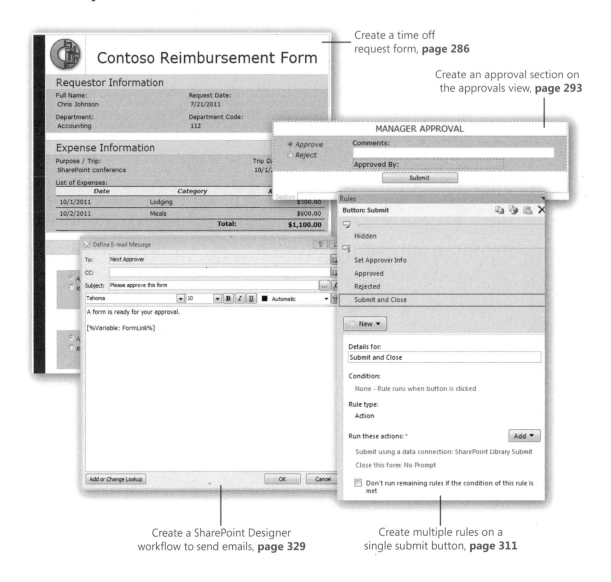

Create a time off
request form, **page 286**

Create an approval section on
the approvals view, **page 293**

Create a SharePoint Designer
workflow to send emails, **page 329**

Create multiple rules on a
single submit button, **page 311**

11 Building an Approval Process

In this chapter, you will learn how to:

- ✔ Create a simple interface for form approvers
- ✔ Set up form load rules to switch views
- ✔ Build out multiple approval sections
- ✔ Create a read-only view for completed forms
- ✔ Create a workflow to send emails at each stage of approval

---

Typically, when a form is filled out and submitted, an approval process is associated with the form. A common process involves obtaining management approval of a completed form. The number of approvals and the level of complexity can vary greatly from form to form. In planning out approvals, the process requirements will dictate the way that the form is created in InfoPath. The more information that is gathered at the beginning, the more efficient the form creation process will be. When you hear the term *workflow*, you might initially think about SharePoint Designer workflows, but much of the workflow can be built right in to InfoPath, using logic. Not to say that other workflows are unnecessary, but a form's workflow can be used in conjunction with SharePoint Designer workflows. Workflows such as those created with SharePoint Designer will add benefits that are not found within the InfoPath form logic alone.

In this chapter, you will learn how to create an approval process within an InfoPath form. Conditions and rules are powerful tools that can be used to create a workflow inside a form. Some basic approval process requirements will be discussed, and you will build on an existing form. New fields will be added, and views for approvers will be configured. This is a more advanced chapter, building on the principles that you have learned so far in this book.

The following screenshot shows a form that has gone through the approval process.

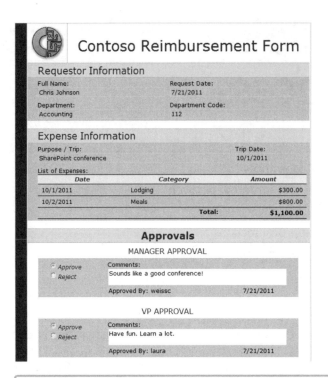

> **Practice Files** Before you can complete the exercises in this chapter, you need to copy the book's practice files to your computer. The practice files you'll use to complete the exercises in this chapter are in the Chapter 11 practice file folder. A complete list of practice files is provided in "Downloading the Practice Files and eBook," on page xxvi.

Gathering Requirements

When you create a new form in InfoPath that will need to go through an approval process, you need to gather some basic information. Having this information will not only help you build the form according to requirements but it will save time in the long run. Following is a list of basic requirements:

- **Workflow diagram**   Draw out a diagram of what the workflow process should be. Use Microsoft Visio, Microsoft Word, Microsoft PowerPoint, or just draw it on a whiteboard. All parties involved should come to a consensus as to the order and flow of the approvals.

- **Security considerations**   With InfoPath, you can create views to hide and show certain information. Views in SharePoint can also be used as filters to show people what you want them to see. This can be considered "security by obfuscation."

There's no true security involved with this method. Alternatively, item-level permissions can be used in SharePoint and assigned through a workflow. Determine which method is appropriate for the form. For example, a form that contains Social Security numbers or salaries needs tighter security.

- **List of approvers**   Who will approve each form, and how will their names be obtained? Will the form be routed to a name that is dynamic, like the logged-on user's manager? Can each person pick the next approver by using a people picker control? Maybe a special SharePoint group exists, and the approval email should be sent to the entire group. All three of these are common scenarios, and sometimes there is a combination of several methods within a single form.

- **Form lifecycle**   What will happen to the form after it has been approved? Commonly, the form is set to read-only after it has been approved. How long does each form need to be kept? Library views can be filtered so that completed forms are not displayed.

- **User interface**   When users visit the SharePoint site, what will their experience be? Plan the Web Parts and views that will be created. Some common filtered views are My Forms and Active Forms. Chapter 13, "SharePoint Views and Dashboards," will cover these considerations more thoroughly.

Contoso Reimbursement Form

At Contoso, after meeting with the reimbursement department, the following requirements have been gathered:

- There will be two levels of approval: Manager and VP.
- After final approval, the form will be read-only.
- Approvers cannot modify any of the original data that was submitted.
- If a form is rejected by anyone, the approval process is over and the form is set to read-only. To resubmit a form, the initiator must start from a new form.

Form Views

When working with multiple views of an InfoPath form, remember to keep it simple. Views are extremely useful, but the more of them you have, the more work you could be creating for yourself. The best practice is to create one view, with the form's' layout and fields finalized before copying them to other views. For a situation in which a field is displayed across multiple views and the name of the field's label needs to be modified, this text will need to be edited in each separate view.

The following three views will be used in the Contoso Reimbursement form for the exercises in this chapter:

- **New**   When a new form is filled out for the first time, this is the default view.
- **Approvals**   Approvers use this view to reject or approve a form as well as to include comments. The approvers cannot modify any of the original information in the request.
- **Read Only**   When the form has gone through the approval process or has been rejected, this view is used to display all the information, but nothing can be modified.

During form approval, you do not want the approvers to be able to modify the information that was submitted. These fields can be set to read-only. However, you do not want the entire view to be read-only, so this setting must be applied to each individual field, as needed.

The three views have already been created in the Contoso Reimbursement request form. The controls on the approvals view have each been set to read-only, and each control's background has been set to no fill. Because the fields are read-only, the background has been changed so that they do not appear editable.

Approval Fields

When a form reaches the approval stage, the approver will open the form, select to approve or reject the form, and type his comments. For accountability, when the submit button is clicked, the user's name and the date will be saved. For each level of approval that is required, there will be four fields:

- **Approval**   This is a radio button that has the value of Approved or Rejected.
- **Comments**   This is a text box in which the approver can type comments. Comments will be required if the form is rejected.
- **Approver**   The name of the approver will be stored in this field and will be displayed as read-only the next time the form is opened.
- **ApprovalDate**   The date of the approval will be stored in this field and will be displayed as read-only.

The Contoso reimbursement form will have two levels of approvals; therefore, it will have eight approval fields.

In the following exercise, you will create the Approvals table and add the approval information to the bottom of the form.

 SET UP Open the **ContosoReimbursementform.xsn** in Design mode, and then switch to the Approvals view. (On the Page Design tab, click the View drop-down box, and then select the Approvals view.)

1. In the **Approvals** table, put the cursor in the first white row of the table under the word "**Approvals**". In the list of fields on the right, in the **Approvals** section, click the drop-down box on the **Manager_Approval section**, and then click **Section** to insert a new, empty section on the form.

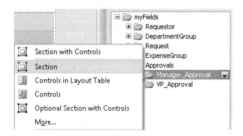

2. With the cursor inside the newly inserted section, press **Delete** two times to remove as much extra space as possible.

3. On the **Insert** tab on the ribbon, in the list of tables, select the table called **2 Column Offset With Emphasis 3**.

4. With the cursor in the area that says **Click to add subheading**, type Manager Approval.

   The approval fields have been pre-created in the template, and the beginning of the approval section has been started.

5. Position the cursor in the first green row under the **MANAGER APPROVAL** header, where it says **Add Label**. In the list of fields on the right, click the drop-down box on the **ManagerApproval** field under the **Approvals / Manager_Approval node**. Select **Option Button**.

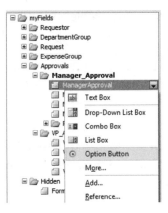

6. For the number of option buttons to insert, select **2**, and then click **OK**.

7. Next to each option button on the form, type the words **Approve** and **Reject**.

8. Select the **Approve** option, and then press **Alt+Enter** to open the control properties. In the **Value when selected** field, type **Approved**. Select the **This button is selected by default** check box, and then click **OK**.

9. Select the **Reject** option, and then press **Alt+Enter** to open the control properties. In the **Value when selected field**, type Rejected, and then click OK.

10. From the list of **Manager_Approval** fields on the right, drag the **ManagerComments** field to the table in the cell next to the **Approve** and **Reject** buttons. Change the label text to Comments.

Approvals	
MANAGER APPROVAL	
◉ Approve ○ Reject	Comments:

11. Click to select the **Comments** text box. Press **Alt+Enter**, and then in the control's properties, go to the **Display** tab. Select the **Multi-line** check box, and then click **OK**.

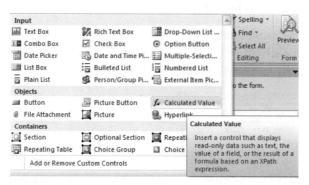

12. With the cursor to the right of the **Comments** text box, on the ribbon, click the **Home** tab. In the list of controls, click **Calculated Value**.

13. Click the function button to edit the formula. Type **concat(**, and then click the **Insert Field or Group** button. In the **Manager_Approval** section, select the **ManagerApproval** field, and then click **OK**.

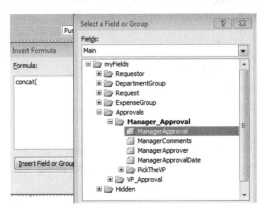

14. The formula will concatenate **ManagerApproval By:** and **ManagerApprover**, so complete the full formula, click **OK**, and then click **OK** again.

15. With the cursor to the right of the calculated field that was just inserted, click the drop-down box on the **ManagerApprovalDate** field, and then from the list of **Manager_Approval** fields, select **Text box**.

16. Select the **ManagerApprovalDate** text box, and then on the ribbon, click the **Properties** tab. Select the **Read-only** check box, and then use the **Shading** button to set the background to **No Fill**.

17. The widths of the calculated field and date field will now be modified so that they fit neatly next to each other. With the **ManagerApprovalDate** text box selected, on the **Properties** tab, and then change the **Width** value to **96** px.

18. Change the width of the calculated field (the one labeled **Approved By**) to **293** px.

19. Delete the last two green empty rows of the table.

Borders

20. With the **ManagerApprovalDate** text box selected, on the ribbon, click **Borders**. Click **None**, and then click **OK**.

Notice that the date field is no longer visible. This is because you just removed the background and borders.

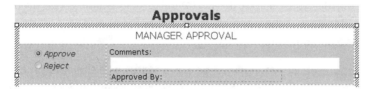

With the first approval section created, you can copy it and use it as a basis for the other approval sections. But before you do that, several rules will be created on each control.

 CLEAN UP Leave InfoPath Designer open if you are continuing to the next section of this chapter. Otherwise, click the Save button to save the XSN file to your computer, and then close InfoPath Designer.

The Status Field

Before you create rules on each approval section, you first need to understand the basis for how the logic will work for the form as a whole. To reiterate, the form will have its own workflow, which will be created by using form load rules and many different formatting and action rules. There will be a field called Form Status, which will be the foundation for much of the form's logic.

The Form Status values will be changed as the form goes through the approval process. The status levels are as follows:

- **New** This is the first status. It will be the initial default value.
- **Manager Approval** As soon as a form is submitted for the first time, because the manager is the first approver, the status will immediately be set to this.
- **VP Approval** This is the status after the manager approves a form.
- **Completed** When the VP has approved a form, the process is over and the form is complete.
- **Rejected** If any of the approvers reject the form, this is the status.

This Form Status field will also be promoted to be a column in the SharePoint form library on which it can be filtered and sorted. Any SharePoint workflows that send emails will use the status as a workflow condition.

When thinking about the big picture and creating many different forms and approval processes, you will discover that the Form Status field will be a common element in your architecture. Because of the need to use it across forms and in workflows, this field can be created as a site column.

In the following exercise, you will create Form Status as a site column and as a field in the reimbursement form. Then, the two will be tied together by publishing the form and promoting the field to SharePoint as a column.

For InfoPath fields that are also used for workflows and other activities transparent to the end users, it is a good practice to keep them in a pre-defined place within the list of fields so that you can find them quickly, later on. A group of fields called Hidden will be created in the form, which is where the form status will be.

 SET UP Open ContosoReimbursementform.xsn in Design mode. Decide to which of your test SharePoint sites you will publish this form. In the following example, the site will be http://forms.contoso.com. Open your SharePoint site in the browser.

 1. In SharePoint in the browser, click **Site Actions**, and then select **Site Settings**.

2. In the **Galleries** section, click **Site Columns**.

 3. Click the **Create** button.

4. Name the column **Form Status**, and then select **Single line of text**. Scroll down, to **Put this site column into**. In the **New group** field, type **Contoso Forms**. Leave the rest of the information as default, and then click **OK**.

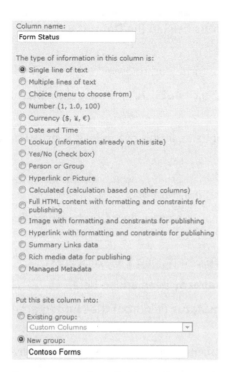

5. Repeat steps 3 and 4, creating another text column called **Next Approver**. In the **Existing Group** drop-down box, choose **Contoso Forms**. Both of the new fields are in the Contoso Forms group in the list of site columns.

6. In InfoPath Designer, create the group for hidden fields and the form status field inside it by clicking the drop-down box on **myFields**, and then clicking **Add**.

7. The name should be **Hidden**, and the type is **Group**. Click **OK**.

8. Click the drop-down box on the new **Hidden** group, and then click **Add**.

9. Name the field **FormStatus**, as a text data type, and then click **OK**.

10. Repeat steps 8 and 9, creating a field called **NextApprover**.

11. Double-click the new **FormStatus** field. In the **Default value** box, type **New**, and then click **OK**.

This value is important because form load rules will depend on it later.

12. On the **File** tab at the top, and click **Publish**, and then click **SharePoint Server**. This is the Publishing Wizard.

13. Type the URL of your SharePoint site. In this example, it is **http://forms.contoso.com**. Click **Next**.

Note For more information about publishing and submitting forms to SharePoint, see Chapter 6, "Publishing and Submitting Form Data."

14. Select **Form Library**, and then click **Next**. Select **Create a new form library**, and then click **Next**.

15. Name the new library **Reimbursement**, and then click **Next**.

Notice that several fields have already been added here.

16. Click **Add**, select the new **FormStatus** field from the **Hidden** group, and then click **OK**.

Notice that the **Site column group** drop-down box automatically shows the value of the **Contoso Forms** group, and the **Column name** drop-down list shows **Form Status**—this is the site column.

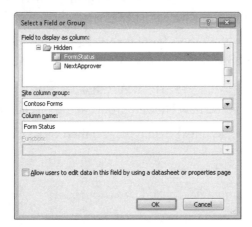

Tip InfoPath recognizes that the name of the field you selected has the same name as the existing site column. If the field in InfoPath had been named FormStatus (with a lowercase s), the field would not have been automatically matched up with the site column because InfoPath sees a capital letter or an underscore character as a word delineator.

17. Repeat step 16, adding the **NextApprover** field as another column.

18. Click **Next**. Select the **Adjust data connections to new location** check box, and then click **Publish**.

Important It is important that this check box is selected, because the template provided to you contains data connections to locations that do not exist in your own environment. When you allow InfoPath to adjust the data connections automatically, both the existing submit connection and the user profile service connection will be changed to point to your own site.

> You are moving this form from http://forms.contoso.com/Reimbursement/ to the location above. If the data sources this form uses are also moving, click the checkbox below so they continue to work.
>
> ☐ Adjust data connections to the new location. This will only affect connections to data sources within the same server (for example a SharePoint list).

19. After the Publishing Wizard has completed publishing the form, click **Close**.

The form now has a status field, and the site column called Form Status is being used in the reimbursement form library. This status will be changed each time a submit button is clicked, and its value will be used in form load rules.

Adjusting Data Connections

When the form has been published for the first time, it might be necessary to manually modify the data connections if they do not automatically adjust themselves. On the Data tab, click **Data Connections**. Select the **SharePoint Library Submit** connection, and then click the **Modify** button. Replace the document library URL with that of your own library, and then click **Next** through the rest of the wizard. (See Chapter 6 for detailed information about submitting to SharePoint.) The **GetUserProfileByName** data connection can be modified also, by changing the URL to point to your own site. (See Chapter 9, "Working with the SharePoint User Profile Web Service," for detailed information about this web service.)

 CLEAN UP Leave InfoPath Designer and the browser open if you are continuing to the next section of this chapter. Otherwise, click the Save button to save the XSN file to your computer, and then close InfoPath Designer. Close the browser.

Form Load Rules

In Chapter 5, "Adding Logic and Rules to Forms," you learned about form rules and logic. Each button and control can have rules applied to it. Not only can rules be created on individual controls but action rules can be created, which run each time a form is opened. These are called *form load* rules. For forms that go through an approval process and in this chapter's example, these types of rules can be used as sort of a workflow within InfoPath. Each rule can have its own conditions and actions. For example, one rule can take certain actions on new forms, another rule can be used for the approval process, and another rule can be created for forms that have been approved and completed.

On the ribbon, on the **Data** tab, click the Form Load button to open the Manage Rules pane on the right. You will notice that one form load rule has already been created; this rule will be addressed later in the chapter.

In your form, you do not want the end users to have the ability to switch between the form's views. The reimbursement form's process can be outlined as follows:

- When a new form is filled out, the default value of FormStatus is New.
- The first time the Submit button is clicked on the New view, the value of the FormStatus field will be set to Manager Approval.
- Use the following form load rule: If FormStatus contains Approval, switch to the Approvals view.
- As each person approves and submits the form and the FormStatus value goes from Manager Approval to VP Approval, each submit button will set the value of the FormStatus.

- Because the CEO is the last approver, when she approves and clicks Submit, the FormStatus value is set to Completed.

- If anyone along the way rejects the form, the FormStatus field is set to Rejected.

- Use the following form load rule: if FormStatus equals Completed or FormStatus equals Rejected, switch to the Read-only view.

In the following exercise, you will create the two new form load rules so that views will be switched automatically.

SET UP Open ContosoReimbursementform.xsn in Design mode.

1. On the ribbon, click the **Data** tab, and then click the **Form Load** button.

2. Click the **New** button, and then select **Action**.

3. In the **Details for** box, type **Approvals**.

   This is the name that you are giving the rule for your own reference later.

4. In the **Condition** section, click the **None - Rule runs when form is opened** link.

5. In the **myFields** drop-down box, click **Select a field or group**.

6. Expand the **Hidden** group, select **FormStatus**, and then click **OK**.

7. In the second drop-down box, select **Contains**.

8. In the third drop-down box, select **Type text**. Type **Approval**, and then click **OK**.

9. Click the **Add** button next to **Run these actions**, and then select **Switch views**.

10. Select the **Approvals** view, and then click **OK**.

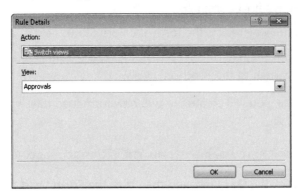

Now that the approvals rule has been created, the rule for completed or rejected forms can be created.

11. Again, in the **Form Load** pane, click the **New** button, and then select **Action**.

12. In the **Details for** dialog box, type **Read Only**. In the **Condition** section, click the **None-Rule runs when form is opened** link.

There are two conditions: **FormStatus is equal to** "**Completed**" and **FormStatus is equal to "Rejected"**. Notice the **or** condition in the drop-down box at the end of the first line.

13. Click **OK**. In the **Run these actions** section, click **Add**, and then select **Switch views**.

14. Select the **Read Only** view, and then click **OK**.

Even with two levels of approvals available, having one view for approvals will be efficient because our form load rules can be kept simple. Keep in mind that conditions are case sensitive, so be sure to follow the instructions carefully.

 CLEAN UP Leave InfoPath open if you are continuing to the next section of this chapter. Otherwise, click the Save button to save the XSN file to your computer, and then close InfoPath Designer.

So far, we have created some approval fields, one approval section, and a couple of form load rules. The next task is to tie together all of this functionality with some customized submit buttons and more rules.

Approval Sections

The layout of a single approval section was created in an earlier exercise, but it doesn't do anything yet. It's time to utilize the power of InfoPath rules to control the functionality of each approver's interface. The Approve and Reject radio buttons as well as the Comments box will be disabled after the form moves to the next approver status. The approver's name and date will be saved when he clicks the Submit button, and then the next approvers will see that read-only information. After each approver submits the form, the Submit button is hidden in that approver's section.

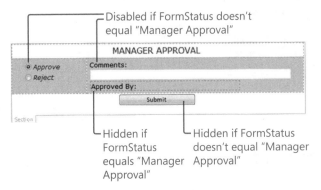

Disabled if FormStatus doesn't equal "Manager Approval"

Hidden if FormStatus equals "Manager Approval"

Hidden if FormStatus doesn't equal "Manager Approval"

In the following exercise, you will create several rules on the Submit button in the New view. Formatting rules will be created on controls in the manager approval section.

SET UP Open ContosoReimbursementform.xsn in Design mode, and then switch to the New view.

1. Double-click to select the **Submit** button, and then on the ribbon, click **Manage Rules**.

2. Click the **New** button, and then select **Action**.

3. In the **Details for** dialog box, type **Set Fields**. Click the **Add** button, and then select **Set a field's value**. In the **Field** text box, select **FormStatus**. In the **Value** text box, type **Manager Approval**, and then click **OK**.

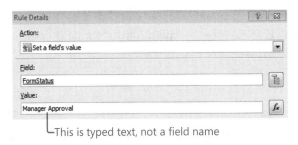

This is typed text, not a field name

4. Click the drop-down box for the **Set Fields** rule, and then select **Move up**; you want this rule to apply before the **Submit** rule.

5. Switch to the **Approvals** view. In the **Manager Approval** section, select the **Approve** option. In the **Rules** pane, click the **New** button, and then select **Formatting**.

6. Call this rule **Disabled**. Create the following condition: **FormStatus is not equal to Manager Approval**. Select the **Disable this control** check box.

7. Now you can copy and paste this rule to other controls. With the **Disabled** rule selected, at the top of the **Rules** pane, click the **Copy Rule** button.

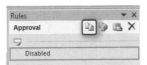

8. Select the **Rejected** option. In the **Rules** pane, click the **Paste Rule** button.

9. Click to select the **Comments** text box, and then click the **Paste Rule** button.

   Now, all three controls have the same rule. They will all be disabled if the **FormStatus** is not **"Manager Approval"**.

   At this point, formatting rules can be created on the controls that are under the **Comments** box.

10. Click to select the calculated field (with the **Approved By** text in it), click the **New** button in the **Rules** pane, and then choose **Formatting**. Create one condition, which is **FormStatus is equal to "Manager Approval"**. Select the **Hide this control** check box.

11. At the top of the **Rules** pane, click the **Copy Rule** button.

12. Select the **ManagerApprovalDate** text box, and then in the **Rules** pane, click the **Paste Rule** button.

    Note An identical copy of the rule has been copied from one control to another. You do *not* want the manager to see these two empty fields, which is why they are now hidden. When the form is routed to the next approver after the manager, these filled in fields will be visible. The manager's name will be captured when the manager clicks the **Submit** button, which is why the controls are read-only.

13. Add the **Submit** button by placing the cursor at the bottom of the **Manager Approval** section, and then on the **Home** tab, from the list of controls, click to add a button to the form.

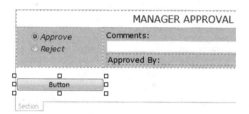

14. Also on the **Home** tab, click the **Center** button. Double-click the new button. In the label box, type **Submit**. Leave the **Action** drop-down default of **Rules and Custom Code**.

    Note The **Rules** pane should still be showing on the right. If it is not, click the **Rules** button. The last rule in this exercise will be the formatting rule for the **Submit** button. It will be similar to the rules on other controls in the manager approval section.

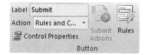

15. Select the **Submit** button, and then create a formatting rule with the condition that the button is hidden if the **FormStatus** is not equal to **"Manager Approval"**.

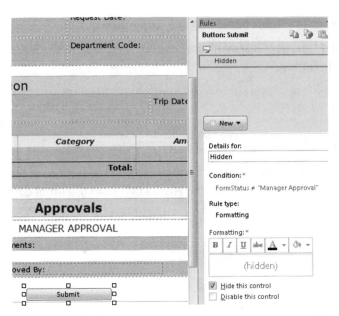

Only one approval section has been created so far, but the formatting rules have been created on each control in the section. When all rules have been created, this section can be copied to create the other level of approval.

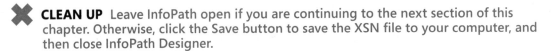

CLEAN UP Leave InfoPath open if you are continuing to the next section of this chapter. Otherwise, click the Save button to save the XSN file to your computer, and then close InfoPath Designer.

Submit Button Actions

With each different approval, different actions will take place in a specific order. Also, different actions will take place depending on whether the form is approved or rejected. However, whether the form is approved or rejected, the logged-on user's name and the current date will be saved. Here is how the form will behave according to the rules that you will define:

- **No conditions** When the submit button is clicked, the following actions will occur:
  - The Approver field will be set with the value of the currently logged-on user name.
  - The Approval Date field will be set with the value of the current date.

- **Approved**   When a form is approved, the FormStatus value will be set to "VP Approval". The VP will be the next person to approve this form, and the VP approval section will be below the manager approval.

- **Rejected**   When a form is rejected, the FormStatus value will be set to "Rejected".

In the following exercise, you will create action rules that will be carried out when the Submit button is clicked.

SET UP Open **ContosoReimbursementform.xsn** in Design mode, and then switch to the "Approvals" view.

1. Double-click to select the **Submit** button. If the **Rules** pane is not already showing on the right side of the screen, then on the ribbon, click the **Manage Rules** button.

Manage Rules

2. In the **Rules** pane, click the **New** button, and then select **Action**. In the **Details for** box, type **Set Approver Info**.

3. Next to **Run these actions**, click the **Add** button, and then select **Set a field's value**.

4. Click the field picker button adjacent to the **Field** box.

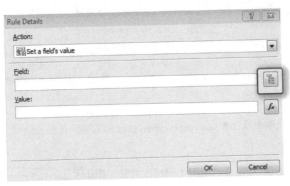

The **Select a Field or Group** dialog box opens.

5. In the **Manager_Approval** section, select the **ManagerApprover** field, and then click **OK**.

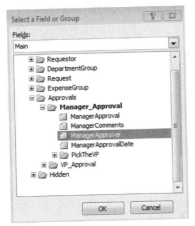

6. Click the function button next to the **Value** box, and then click the **Insert Function** button.

7. Select the **userName** function, and then click **OK**. Also, click **OK** on the **Insert Formula** window.

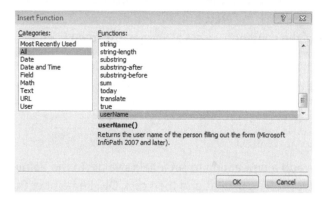

8. In the **Rule Details** dialog box, click **OK**.

9. In the **Rules** pane, click the **Add** button again, and then select **Set a field's value**.
Repeat steps 4–7, except that the field should be **ManagerApprovalDate** and
the value should be the **Today()** function.

10. In the **Rules** pane, click the **New** button, and then select **Action**. Name this rule **Approved**. For the condition, select **ManagerApproval is equal to Approved**. Click **OK**.

11. For the action, add a new action to set a field's value. In the **Value** text box for **FormStatus**, type **VP Approval**, and then click **OK**. Remember that the typed text here is case-sensitive.

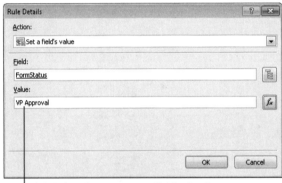

└This is free-form text, not field selection

12. Click the **New** button to create another action rule. Name this rule **Rejected**, and then set the condition as **Manager Approval is equal to Rejected**.

This action sets the **FormStatus** field to **"Rejected"**.

Note Just as in step 11, you are typing free-form text in the Value box. Simply type the word Rejected; you do not need to click the function button next to the Value box.

13. After all of these values are set, the form needs to be submitted and closed. Click **New** again, and then select **Action**. Name this rule **Submit and Close**. There are no conditions. Create two actions: the first one submits the form to SharePoint (**Submit Data**), and the second closes the form.

You now have five rules on the **Submit** button.

As you've seen so far, there is a lot going on behind the scenes to automate this form. All this complexity will be transparent to the people filling out the form. The approval process will be easy to understand and very simple.

✗ CLEAN UP Leave InfoPath open if you are continuing to the next section of this chapter. Otherwise, click the Save button to save the XSN file to your computer, and then lose InfoPath Designer.

In the following exercise, you will copy the Manager Approval section to create the other approvals.

➡ SET UP Open the **ContosoReimbursementform.xsn** in design mode, and switch to the "Approvals" view.

1. Using the cursor, select the entire **Manager Approval** section. At the lower-left corner, click **Section**. Press **Ctrl+C** to copy this selection to the clipboard.

2. Press the right-arrow key on the keyboard until the cursor is positioned to the immediate right of the section. Press **Ctrl+V** to paste the copy.

3. In the heading of the new section, change the word **Manager** to **VP**. Now that the section has been copied, all of the VP fields need to be used instead of the manager fields. Right-click **Section** at the lower-left of the **VP** section, and then select **Change Binding**.

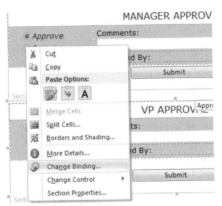

4. The control needs to be bound to the **VP Approval** section instead of **Manager Approval**, so select the **VP_Approval** section, and then click **OK**.

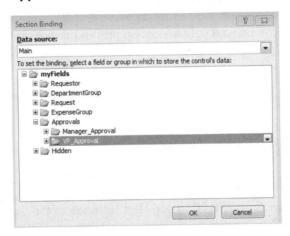

Now each individual control needs to have its binding changed.

5. In the **VP Approval** section, right-click the **Approve** option, and then select **Change Binding**. In the **VP_Approval** section, select the **VPApproval** field, and then click **OK**.

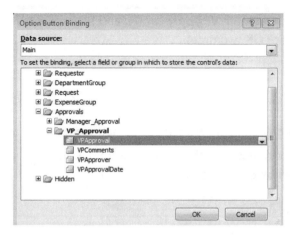

6. Using the same method as in step 5, change the binding for the following controls to that listed in the following table.

Control	New Binding
Reject (radio button)	**VPApproval**
Comments (text box)	**VPComments**
ApprovalDate (hidden text box)	**VPApprovalDate**

7. The calculated **Approved by** field is a bit different. Click to select this control, and then press **Alt+Enter** to open the properties. The **XPath** field will show as empty, so the calculation needs to be recreated. If the XPath is not empty, clear out the existing value. Click the function button next to the **XPath** box.

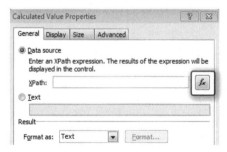

8. The formula will concatenate **VPApproval By:** and **VPApprover**, so create this formula (again). Click **OK** two times.

The **Approve** option needs to be set as the default radio button again.

9. Select the **Approve** option, and then in the control's properties, select the **This button is selected by default** check box. Click **OK**.

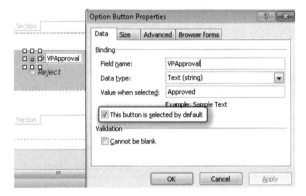

Now the rules need to be modified slightly.

10. Double-click to select the **Approve** option again. If the **Rules** pane is not already displayed, click the **Manage Rules** button. There is one rule, called **Disabled**. Click the link to go to the rule's condition.

11. Modify the condition by changing the text from **"Manager Approval"** to "VP Approval".

12. Modify each of the six controls in the approval section to have a formatting rule exactly the same as the manager approval rules, with the exception that the condition needs to be "VP Approval".

13. The **Submit** button's action rules also need to be modified. In the **VP Approval** section, select the **Submit** button. In the **Rules** pane, click the **Set Approver Info** rule. Under **Run these actions**, click **Set a field's value: ManagerApprover = username()**.

14. The field needs to be changed so that instead of **ManagerApprover**, it shows **VPApprover**. Click **OK**, and then click **OK** again to save the action.

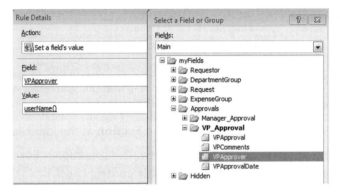

15. Do the same thing with the **Approval Date** action by selecting the **VPApprovalDate** field.

16. The conditions behind the **Approved** and **Rejected** rules also need to be modified. In the **VP_Approval** section, change the field in each rule so that it is the **VPApproval** field.

17. In the **VP Approval** section, click to select the **Submit** button. In the **Rules** pane, select the **Approved** rule. Set the **FormStatus** field value to **Completed**.

When the Manager is filling out approval information, you don't want to see the **VP Approval** section yet.

18. Select the **VP Approval** section by clicking **Section** at the lower-left of the control.

19. Create a new formatting rule called **Hidden**. The condition is **FormStatus is equal to Manager Approval**. Select the **Hide this control** check box.

The form's approval process is almost complete. After the form is submitted for the first time, it automatically switches to the Approvals view the next time it is opened. Lastly, the read-only view will need to be configured. Take a look at the progress that has been made on this view.

Approvals

MANAGER APPROVAL | ApprovalSection

- Approve
- Reject

Comments:

Approved By:

Submit

VP APPROVAL

- Approve
- Reject

Comments:

Approved By:

Submit

 CLEAN UP Leave InfoPath open if you are continuing to the next section of this chapter. Otherwise, click the Save button to save the XSN file to your computer, and then close InfoPath Designer.

As part of the form's lifecycle, you do not want any of the form's data to be edited after the form has been completed and approved. Therefore, you use a read-only view and the form load rule so that when the form's status is completed, it automatically switches over to that view. This maintains the integrity of the data.

In the following exercise, you will copy the approvals view over to the read-only view.

 SET UP Open **ContosoReimbursementform.xsn** in Design mode, and then switch to the "Approvals" view.

1. Press **Ctrl+A** to select everything on the **Approvals** view, and then press **Ctrl+C** to copy this information to the clipboard.

2. On the ribbon, on the **Page Design** tab, select the **Read Only** view from the **View** drop-down box. Press **Ctrl+V** to paste the information from the clipboard onto this view.

3. Again, on the **Page Design** tab, in the **Views** section, click **Properties**.

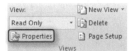

4. On the **General** tab of the view settings, select the **Read-only** check box, and then click **OK**.

5. Click the **File** menu, and then click **Quick Publish**.

Now the read-only view is truly read-only. Keep in mind that when the last approver approves the form, the Submit button sets the FormStatus value to Completed. Then a form load rule automatically switches over to the read-only view if the FormStatus value is equal to Completed or Rejected.

Tip If you are using the attachment control, the attachments cannot be opened or viewed at all when they are put in a read-only view. The workaround is to *not* select the read-only check box if attachment controls are involved. Instead, set each individual control on the view as read-only.

 CLEAN UP Leave InfoPath open if you are continuing to the next section of this chapter. Otherwise, click the Save button to save the XSN file to your computer, and then close InfoPath Designer.

Feel free to publish and test the form that has been created so far. The form can be filled out and submitted. The next time the form is opened, it will switch to the approvals view so that the manager can approve it. The manager approves and submits it, and then the next time the form is opened, the VP approves and submits it. Finally, the next time it is opened, it is on the read-only view because the process is complete.

Workflow Approvers

There is one last item to finish up. The approver names and the emails are still missing. Each time the form is submitted, a workflow needs to send an email to someone so that they know it is their turn to take action. Before the workflow can be created to send emails, you need to define *who* exactly the approvers will be.

For Contoso's reimbursement form project, the requirements are as follows:

- Because the user profiles in the organization are up to date and have accurate manager names for each user, the user profile service will be used to obtain the initiator's manager name.

- The manager will be prompted with a people picker control so that they can pick the name of the VP who needs to approve this request.

The next step will be to build functionality into the form so that the proper user names are obtained. In Chapter 9, you learned about working with the User Profile Service to obtain information about a user. In this reimbursement form, the User Profile Service will be used to get the manager's name of the person submitting the request. One way to get information about the currently logged-on user is by using the userName function. However, this function is limited because it returns only the logon name. You have used this function in a couple of places so far in this chapter. When you want to get any detailed information about a user other than just her user name, the User Profile Service comes in handy.

In the following exercise, you will create a new field for the next approver's name and populate it at each step of the approval process. Throughout the approval process, each time the form is submitted, the name of the next approver needs to be determined. The NextApprover field that was created earlier in this chapter will now be used. The first approver will be the manager.

 SET UP Open **ContosoReimbursementform.xsn** in Design mode, and then switch to the New view.

1. On the ribbon, on the **Data** tab, click the **Form Load** button.

2. Notice that the **New Form** rule is a disabled. Click the drop-down box for this rule, and then select **Enable**.

A data connection has already been created, which receives data about the logged-on user from the User Profile Service web service. This **New Form** rule first queries the User Profile Service and then sets the form's **Manager** field to the name of the logged-on user's manager. Then it sets the requestor's **FullName** field to the current user's full name. When the form is first submitted, because the next approver will be the manager, you will set the **NextApprover** field to that value.

Manage
Rules

3. On the form's **New (default)** view, double-click the **Submit** button, and then click the **Manage Rules** button.

4. Click to select the **Set Fields** rule that you have already created. Click the **Add** button to add another action, and then select **Set a Field's Value**.

5. Set the **NextApprover** field to the value of the **Manager** field, which can be found under the **Requestor Group**. Click **OK** on all three dialog boxes.

Now, the first **Submit** button sets two fields. In a previous exercise, you created the rule that sets the **FormStatus** value to "**Manager Approval**". Now, there is a new rule that sets the **NextApprover** field to **Manager**. This manager field will have a specific person's name in it, and the first email will be sent to that person.

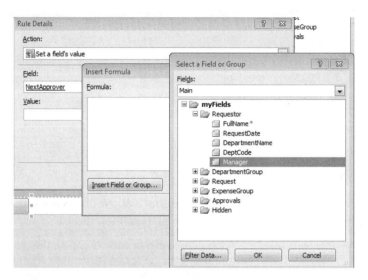

6. The second requirement in this project was to allow the first approver to select the next approver's name from a people picker. Switch back to the **Approvals** view.

7. In the list of fields on the right, expand the **Approvals** section and the **Manager_ Approval** section to see the **PickTheVP** section.

This section will be used as a people picker control. If you don't see the fields on the right, then on the ribbon, click the **Data** tab, and then click **Show Fields** button.

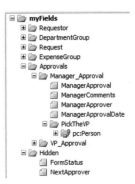

8. Drag **PickTheVP** onto the form, in the space above the **Manager Approval** form's **Submit** button. At the left of this control, type **Pick the VP:**.

Note Whomever is selected in the people picker control will be the next approver, so when the manager clicks **Submit**, that person's logon name appears in the **NextApprover** field.

9. In the **Manager Approval** section, click to select the **Submit** button. In the **Rules** pane, click to select the **Approved** rule that you created in the previous exercise. Click the **Add** button, and then select **Set a field's value**.

10. In the **Field** box, select the **NextApprover** field.

11. For the **Value**, click the **Function** button. Click **Insert Field or Group**, and then inside the **PickTheVP** section, choose the **AccountId** field.

Note The Account ID is the domain\user name of the person who has been selected in the people picker. You want to ensure that when it is time to pick a VP, the manager cannot submit the form with no one selected in the people picker. Typically, a validation rule would be the way to go, but because validation rules cannot be created on people picker controls, another method can be used. You can disable the **Submit** button if the people picker is empty.

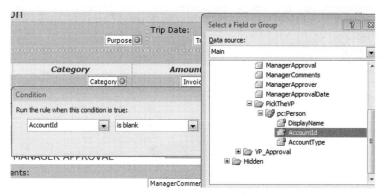

12. In the **Manager Approval** section, select the **Submit** button; in the **Rules** pane, click **New**, and then select **Formatting**.

13. Name this rule Disabled. Set the condition to **AccountId is blank**, and then select **Disable this control**.

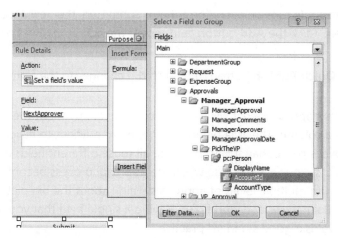

14. The **NextApprover** field needs to be cleared out if the form is rejected. Click to select the **Rejected** rule that you already created. Click the **Add** button, and then select **Set a Field's value**. Set the **NextApprover** field to a value of nothing (empty), and then click **OK**.

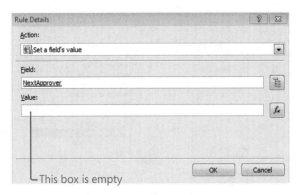

This box is empty

The **NextApprover** field also needs to be cleared out after the form is finished, because whether or not it is rejected at the end, there is no **NextApprover**.

15. In the **VP Approval** section, click to select the **Submit** button. In the **Rules** pane, select the **Set Approver Info** rule.

    Because this rule runs on every form that is submitted, the new action can be added here. Click the **Add** button, and repeat the action that was performed in step 14.

16. Click the **Quick Publish** button to publish the changes to the form.

Now that the next approver field will have the correct values in it at the correct time, it can be used as a column. The idea being that it is more efficient to have one field with the next approver's name than it is to promote all those different fields up to SharePoint as columns. This is especially the case when the approval process becomes longer and more complex with multiple levels of approvals. Think about the big picture when it comes to SharePoint views and workflows. Having a single field that you always use for the next approver is a good standard practice.

 CLEAN UP Click the Save button to save the XSN file to your computer, and then close InfoPath Designer.

This NextApprover field can also contain the name of a SharePoint group. For example, if another level of approval needs to be added—such as to send the form to the Accounting department—a SharePoint group can be created called "Accounting Team." The action on submit would then be to set the value of the NextApprover field to "Accounting Team."

Workflow for Emails

Much of the workflow for this reimbursement form has been done inside the form itself. Because of this, the SharePoint Designer workflow that will be created will be very simple. We want to make it easy for the approver to simply click the hyperlink so that he can activate the workflow. The FormStatus and NextApprover fields will be used in a workflow that will have a very simple structure, as follows:

- If the FormStatus is not Rejected or Completed, send an email to NextApprover. This email will let the next approver know that there is a form ready for approval.

- If the FormStatus is Rejected, send an email to the person who created the form, informing him that it has been rejected.

- If the FormStatus is Completed, send an email to the person who created the form, informing him that it was approved at all levels.

That's it! Extremely simple. Let's get started.

Tip If the workflow that you are creating is going to be specific to only a single list or library, a reusable workflow is not necessary and a list workflow can be created instead.

In the following exercise, you will create a workflow in SharePoint Designer 2010. The goal is to create a standard workflow that can be used with not only this reimbursement form but with any other forms in the organization. When much of the logic is accomplished inside the form itself, the workflow does not need to be complex. Because the FormStatus and NextApprover fields were created as site columns, they can be used in multiple forms, and they can also be used in a reusable workflow. After a reusable workflow is created, it can be associated with any library.

SET UP Open SharePoint Designer 2010, and then open the site where the form has been published. Click Workflows on the left side. Also open the reimbursement form library in the browser.

Reusable
Workflow

1. On the ribbon, click the **Reusable Workflow** button.

2. Name the workflow **Form Approvals**, change the content type to **Form**, and then click **OK**.

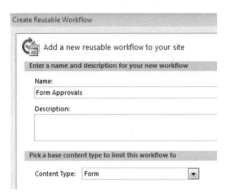

Action

3. Because you will need to insert a hyperlink in each email, to directly open the form that is being approved, you will create this hyperlink in a workflow variable so that it can be reused. Use the **Action** button to add a **Set Workflow Variable** action.

4. Click **workflow variable**, and then choose **Create a new variable**.

Set <u>workflow variable</u> to <u>value</u>

5. Name the variable **FormLink**, as a string, and then click **OK**.

6. Click **value**, click the ellipsis (**...**) button, and then open the string builder.

The following URL depicts the necessary format. It will need to be built here as a hyperlink: ***CurrentSite***/_layouts/FormServer.aspx?XmlLocation=***CurrentItem***& Source=***CurrentSite***&DefaultItemOpen=1

Add or Change Lookup

7. Each instance of bold text is a lookup to be added by using the **Add or Change Lookup** button. For each of the three references, pick **Workflow Context** as the data source, and then choose either **Current Site URL** or **Current Item URL** for the field, as appropriate. Click **OK**.

Note The workflow context data source is especially useful because this URL will work with any form in SharePoint, and there is nothing absolutely related to any one library.

8. After all of the references have been added, use the following screenshot as a guideline to ensure that the URL is a clickable hyperlink. At the bottom of the **String Builder** dialog box, click **OK**.

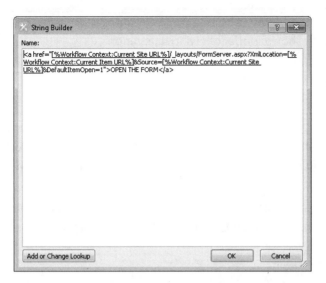

This first step in the workflow will appear as shown in the following illustration:

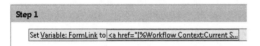

9. Because this workflow will use site columns, click the **Association Columns** button. Use the **Select Site Column** button to add both the **FormStatus** and the **NextApprover** columns, and then click **OK**.

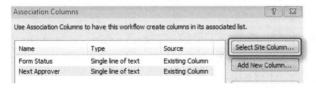

10. Add the first condition to the workflow. With the cursor below the **Set variable** action, use the **Condition** button to add two conditions called **If current item field equals value**.

You want the conditions to be that the form status is not equal to **Rejected** or **Completed**, as shown in the following illustration.

> If <u>Form Status</u> <u>not equals</u> <u>Rejected</u>
>
> <u>and</u> <u>Form Status</u> <u>not equals</u> <u>Completed</u>
>
>   (Start typing or use the Insert group in the Ribbon.)

Else-If Branch **11.** Click the **Else-If Branch** button to add another branch. Put the cursor under the word **Else**, and then add another **If current item field equals value**. Repeat this again, adding a third else-if branch and a third condition.

The second else-if statement should be that the form status equals **Completed**, and the third else-if should be if the form status equals **Rejected**.

> If <u>Form Status</u> <u>not equals</u> <u>Rejected</u>
>
> <u>and</u> <u>Form Status</u> <u>not equals</u> <u>Completed</u>
>
>   (Start typing or use the Insert group in the Ribbon.)
>
> Else if <u>Form Status</u> <u>equals</u> <u>Completed</u>
>
>   (Start typing or use the Insert group in the Ribbon.)
>
> Else if <u>Form Status</u> <u>equals</u> <u>Rejected</u>
>
>   (Start typing or use the Insert group in the Ribbon.)

Now it's time to create the actions. The first condition's action should be to send an email to the next approver.

12. With the cursor in the first area labeled **(Start typing or use the Insert group in the Ribbon)**, on the ribbon, click the **Action** button, and then add the **Send an email** action. Click **these users** to configure the email.

13. In the **To** box, use **Workflow Lookup for a User** to select the **Next Approver** field, and then click **OK**.

14. For the subject, type **Please approve this form**. In the email body, type **A form is ready for your approval**.

15. Also in the email body, click the **Add or Change Lookup** button to add the workflow variable called **FormLink**, and then click **OK**.

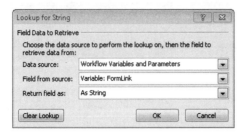

16. The simple email notification is complete. Click **OK**.

17. After each of the other two conditions in the workflow, use the **Send an email** action. The following table outlines the settings for the other two conditions. Also insert the **FormLink** variable in each email.

Condition	To	Subject	Body
Form status equals completed	User who created current item	Form has been approved	Your form has been approved at all levels.
Form status equals rejected	User who created current item	Form has been rejected	Your form has been rejected.

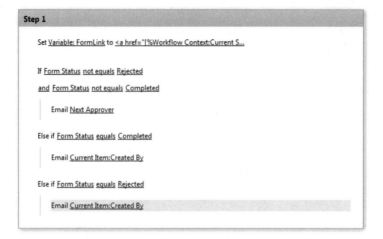

18. On the ribbon, click the **Publish** button to publish the workflow to SharePoint.

> **Tip** If the reusable workflow is created at the top level of the site collection, the **Publish Globally** button can be used to publish the workflow for use in any form library in the whole site collection.

Now it's time to associate the reusable workflow with the reimbursement form library.

19. In the library in the browser, on the ribbon, click the **Library** tab, and then click **Workflow Settings**.

20. In the **All** drop-down box, select **Form**, and then click **Add a workflow**.

21. Select **Form Approvals**, which is the workflow you just created, and then type the name **Form Approvals** in the name field. Clear the check box to allow the workflow to be manually started; select the check boxes to start the workflow when an item is created and when one is changed. Click **OK**.

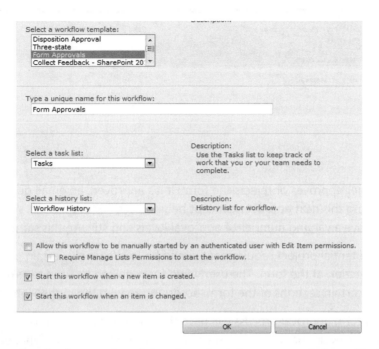

Now that the form and workflow have both been created, they will all work together in conjunction with one another.

 CLEAN UP Close SharePoint Designer, and then close the browser.

To run through the solution that has been created in this chapter, go to the Reimbursement form library, and then click the Add Document button to fill out a new form. Take a look at the Next Approver column in the library to see the account name of the manager who will receive the first email.

Type	Name	Created	Created By	Form Status	Trip Date	Total Amount	Next Approver	Form Approvals
	Charlotte Weiss-2011-07-24T11_45_14 ☐ NEW	7/24/2011 11:45 AM	Charlotte Weiss	Manager Approval	9/1/2011	90	contoso\cj	Completed

➕ Add document

The manager receives the following email and clicks the link, which takes her directly to the form.

From:	Conotoso Forms <sharepoint@contoso.com>		Sent:	Sun 7/24/2011 11:46 AM
To:	cj@contoso.com			
Cc:				
Subject:	Please approve this form			

A form is ready for your approval.

OPEN THE FORM

The manager approves or rejects the form; if it's approved, an email goes to the next approver. Using this next approver concept behind each Submit button, your approval process can have a varying number of approval levels and still use this same workflow.

Another potential project requirement would be to allow only certain people to see the approval section of the form. The userName function can be used to take certain actions and show certain sections of the form, according to who the logged-on user is.

Not every form approval process will have the same requirements. There will be different approval levels and an endless set of possible combinations of what each approver needs to do. There will also be different possibilities as to what takes place when a form is rejected. In this form, the workflow is over when it is rejected, and the initiator would need to start over with a new one if she wanted to change any of the original fields. Sometimes it is a requirement that the initiator should be able to open the form, make changes, and resubmit for approval.

With three different types of rules, many different actions, and endless possibilities, with InfoPath, you can get creative with how each form will turn out and what the user's experience will be. Using the skills you've developed in this chapter, with conditions that use logic, you can build in more functionality by just thinking through the form's process logically.

Note To learn more about SharePoint Designer workflows, we recommend Penelope Coventry's excellent book, "Microsoft SharePoint Designer 2010 Step by Step," (2010, Microsoft Press; ISBN: 978-0-7356-2733-8).

Key Points

- While approval processes are commonly requested, requirements can vary greatly from form to form.

- Each InfoPath form can have its own workflow inside the form, using logic and conditions. SharePoint Designer workflows can also be used in conjunction with an InfoPath form.

- Multiple form views can be used to represent each phase of a form's workflow.

- Fields can be created for workflow use, and they do not need to be displayed on the form.

- A calculated value can be inserted to display multiple fields concatenated into one phrase.

- InfoPath form fields can be promoted to SharePoint by using existing site columns.

- Form load rules that switch views are a great way to tightly control what is seen in the form at each stage, instead of letting users manually switch between views.

- Many formatting rules can be created in each approval section, to control what can be done at each stage of approval.

- The user name and today functions can be used to store information about the current user and date.

- A SharePoint Designer workflow can be used to look at the values in the form's columns and send emails accordingly.

Chapter at a Glance

Understand InfoPath Forms Services in SharePoint Central Admin, **page 336**

Learn how to use the Fiddler to monitor browser forms, **page 342**

Analyze the effects of attachments on form performance, **page 346**

12 Managing and Monitoring InfoPath Forms Services

In this chapter, you will learn how to:

- ✔ Work with the InfoPath settings in SharePoint Central Administration
- ✔ Analyze and monitor browser forms for potential performance concerns
- ✔ Minimize postbacks for browser forms

Because this book is focused primarily on Microsoft InfoPath plus Microsoft SharePoint 2010 scenarios, it is imperative that we include a chapter on more advanced topics related to InfoPath Form Services (IPFS). Until now, you've received a fairly rudimentary introduction to IPFS. This chapter will dive into the more technical aspects of how IPFS works, how you can ensure the best performance, and how to manage an IPFS environment.

At the most basic level, IPFS seems like a simple idea: allow form templates that have been created in InfoPath to be published to a SharePoint site and then rendered in a browser on the client system, rather than in the InfoPath client. Despite the conceptual simplicity of IPFS, a great deal of behind-the-scenes technology is required to deliver this level of form parity for browser clients. While we certainly do not have the space in this book to cover every technical detail of IPFS, you will learn the requisite minimum technical knowledge to become a competent steward of the browser-based forms in your environment.

IPFS integrates with the core SharePoint Server platform, which includes several server products and components that are built on the SharePoint 2010 platform. Assuming you have a properly designed SharePoint farm, IPFS does not really require much in the way of care and feeding. This is the good news. However, because IPFS is a SharePoint server-based technology, you might want to understand some of its administrative tools and techniques, even if you're not the primary SharePoint administrator. This chapter's exercises will help to familiarize you with some of the most important IPFS administration tools.

> **Practice Files** No practice files are required to complete the exercises in this chapter.

IPFS Settings in SharePoint Central Administration

In the SharePoint Central Administration console, in the General Application Settings area, you will find important settings that control various facets of IPFS across the entire SharePoint farm. Unless you are managing a very large SharePoint environment (or a multi-tenant hosting service), these are not settings that you will need to adjust very often, but it is important to know what modifications are possible at the SharePoint farm level.

Tip If you are charged with administering a SharePoint environment, you will probably find it useful to become proficient with Windows PowerShell scripting. IPFS offers a rich set of PowerShell commands that can help to automate and improve efficiency of most administrative tasks. Most of the GUI-based administrative tasks that we discuss in the upcoming exercise have companion commands available in PowerShell, as well. A full reference is available on TechNet at *http://technet.microsoft.com/en-us/library/ee906553.aspx*.

To ensure that you have a basic understanding of the IPFS administrative options for your SharePoint environment, the following exercise walks you through the primary IPFS configuration settings in SharePoint Central Administration.

 SET UP This exercise assumes you have an appropriate level of administrative access to a SharePoint server.

1. From the **Start** menu, in the **Microsoft SharePoint 2010 Products** folder, open **SharePoint 2010 Central Administration**.

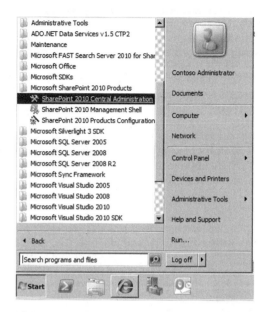

Tip You can find the SharePoint program folder on the **Start** menu of any server installed in the SharePoint farm. You can also access SharePoint Central Administration by going to a URL from a browser on a system than has access to your SharePoint environment. The URL begins with http://, followed by *your server name*, followed by a colon, and then the port number that was assigned to Central Administration when SharePoint was installed—for example, http://yoursharepointserver:1234.

2. In SharePoint Central Administration, click **General Application Settings**.

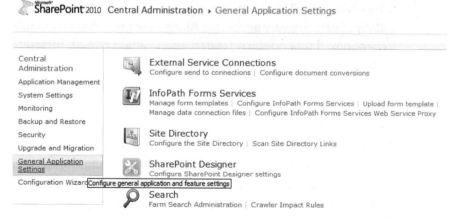

3. In the **InfoPath Forms Services** section, click the **Manage form templates** link. This is used for uploading administrator-approved form templates that potentially need to be available across the entire farm. (Administrator-approved templates were covered in Chapter 6, "Publishing and Submitting Form Data," if you need a refresher.)

Tip Uploading the administrator-approved template is only the first step; you will also need to activate the template to the appropriate site collection(s). You can do this on the **Manage Form Templates page**, on the **Site Collection Features** page, or via PowerShell.

4. Click the drop-down selector on any of the templates you've uploaded; you'll see that some have useful options for activating, deactivating, quiescing, or removing the template.

Note To quiesce a template basically means to instruct SharePoint that you want to exclude the availability of a form for *new* instances, removing it from service only *after* all users have finished using it. **Remove form**, on the other hand, removes the form from service instantly whether or not anyone is using it.

5. Click back to **General Application Settings**, and then click **Configure InfoPath Forms Services**.

On the **Configure InfoPath Forms Services** page, you will find a variety of settings with which you can tweak performance and security settings for IPFS across the entire SharePoint farm. In most cases, the default settings are best. However, always select the very important **Allow users to browser-enable form templates** check box. If that option is cleared, users cannot publish browser-based templates anywhere on your SharePoint farm.

In the **Thresholds** area, notice that the maximum number of postbacks on any given form session is 75. Later in this chapter, you'll learn how to analyze a form to understand when, where, and why your form is generating postbacks. Average sized, well-designed, browser-based forms should have only a handful of postbacks.

Thresholds	
Specify the thresholds at which to end user sessions and log error messages.	Number of postbacks per session: 75
	Number of actions per postback: 200

Below the **Thresholds** area, in the **User Sessions** section, there are two important settings. The first setting defines the maximum amount of time that a single user IPFS session can stay "alive" on the SharePoint farm: 1,440 minutes. Although that seems like a lot, keep in mind that SharePoint will terminate any browser sessions that do not post back to the server for 60 minutes. So even though a user could theoretically continue to fill out a browser-based form for an entire 24-hour period, he would need to be actively working on the form at least once per hour. The other setting here is a critical one: the maximum size of any form instance. Normally, this isn't a problem, but in the case where you've added file/picture attachment controls on your form, the user could add very large files. Without this control in place, you could have a real mess on your hands. The default of 4 MB should be sufficient in most cases.

User Sessions	
Specify time and data limits for user sessions. User session data is stored by the Microsoft SharePoint Server State Service.	Active sessions should be terminated after: 1440 minutes
	Maximum size of user session data: 4096 kilobytes

Tip Remember, the **User Session** settings are *farm-wide* settings. This means raising or lowering any of the default values impacts every site collection in your SharePoint environment. Use caution before making any changes to the defaults. If you are unsure about any of the settings on this page, it's best to just leave them set at their default values. They have been configured for optimum performance and maximum security.

6. Go back to **General Application Settings**.

The following are brief descriptions of the available links here:

○ The **Upload form template** link takes you to the same page you can get to from the **Manage form templates** link. If your primary task is to upload a new template, rather than manage an existing template, this is a handy shortcut.

○ **Manage data connection files** is a place to upload cross-domain data connection files that you want to make available to the entire farm. These are the same type of DCL connections that you saw in Chapter 7, "Receiving Data from SharePoint Lists and Business Connectivity Services," except that this is a way to upload them to a central location for use anywhere in the farm.

Tip To use centrally managed cross-domain connections, you must enable them in the **Configure InfoPath Forms Services** page of Central Administration.

Cross-Domain Access for User Form Templates	
Form templates can contain data connections that access data from other domains. Select this check box to allow user form templates to access data from another domain.	☐ Allow cross-domain data access for user form templates that use connection settings in a data connection file

○ The last link on the IPFS section of the **General Application Settings** screen is **Configure InfoPath Forms Services Web Service Proxy**. Clicking this link opens the **Web Service Proxy** page.

One of the most common challenges with browser-based forms (aside from performance) is related to the security and authentication process. Sometimes, form designers are surprised when their forms work just fine in the InfoPath client but fail anytime someone attempts to use the same form in the browser. This often happens because (unlike the InfoPath client) a browser form communicates with the server via the XMLHTTP protocol, which is **stateless**. In other words, the browser form cannot pass on the user credentials to remote data sources the same way a regular InfoPath client form can (via NT LAN Manager [NTLM]). This more complex submission process can introduce authentication problems in scenarios for which the data connections are in different domains (other servers). This is generally referred to as a *double-hop problem*, and it is a very common challenge for IPFS administrators.

Occasionally, you will have scenarios in which you want to connect a browser-based form to a web services data source that resides outside the domain of your SharePoint environment. In these cases, user authentication can become very complex because the browser-based forms do not have the ability to forward the user credentials to the remote server. Conveniently though, SharePoint provides the web proxy service for IPFS, which will essentially act as a proxy between the form and the third-tier data source. The web proxy service provides a facility for SharePoint to pass on the user's authentication credentials to the remote web service, ensuring that the user can fill out the form and retrieve data from the web service, as expected. Notice in the following screenshot that you are given the option to enable the web proxy for user forms. This option controls whether or not the web service proxy is available to forms uploaded by users. If the **Enable** check box is left cleared, only forms uploaded by administrators can use the web service proxy.

Tip To take advantage of the web service proxy, the data connections will need to be defined in a UDC file, as was discussed in Chapter 7.

 CLEAN UP When you are done exploring Central Administration, close your browser.

IPFS Performance Factors

We are all familiar with the frustrating experience of using slow websites on the Internet. Because IPFS is an HTTP-based system, you can encounter some of the same performance challenges as slow Internet sites—*if* you don't have a solid plan in place to mitigate the potential issues. Aside from a poorly designed SharePoint environment (a discussion of which is beyond the scope of this book), several conditions can negatively impact the performance of browser-enabled forms. The following are the most common factors that you are likely to encounter:

- **HTML**   Some forms grow to a size that requires large amounts of HTML to be transferred between the server and the browser. This can reduce the responsiveness of a browser-based form.

- **XML**   Similar to the HTML problem, some complex forms can cause performance issues. Because IPFS processes the form XML on the server, forms with large amounts of complex XML create additional server overhead. Large amounts of XML can also slow form rendering in the browser.

- **Postbacks**   Some form controls, actions, and certain features require the browser to communicate with the server during the form-filling session (above and beyond the initial load of the form). This interchange of data is called a *postback*.

- **Slow network**   In the case of browser-based forms, the user's perception of performance is heavily determined by the speed of the network connection between their client system and the SharePoint server farm. If the network connection is slow, it won't matter how well-designed your forms are, they will still feel slow to the users.

- **SharePoint servers not scaled properly for concurrent form users**   Many people filling out a browser-based form at the same time can potentially place a heavy stress on the server, which can decrease performance while causing an increase in latency.

Many of these potential performance inhibitors can be easily eliminated by making one or more design changes within your browser form. The challenge when chasing down an IPFS performance issue is to narrow down the potential candidate pool of problems; that can be a difficult task without sufficient information. Therefore, a deeper understanding of how IPFS actually communicates with a SharePoint server and obtaining a snapshot of the underlying web traffic that your form is generating is sometimes a necessary task.

To facilitate this information gathering, you need to install one additional software utility on your system. This free tool is called Fiddler, and its primary purpose is to log all HTTP activity between your computer and a website (in this case, the server hosting the browser form). Even if you've never done any network traffic analysis, Fiddler makes it very easy to see all the details of what your form is doing at load and submission time.

In the following three exercises, you will use Fiddler to help you understand how to do basic performance analysis of IPFS forms.

Installing Fiddler and Monitoring the IPFS Form Load Process

 SET UP Open a browser on your system, and navigate to *http://www.fiddler2.com/fiddler2/*.

1. Download and install the Fiddler tool per the instructions on the Fiddler website.

   Tip Be sure to install Fiddler on the system where you will be opening and using the browser-based forms during the exercise.

2. Find the final version of the **products.xsn** template that you created in Chapter 1, "Introducing Microsoft InfoPath 2010," (or download it from the Chapter01 practice files folder on the companion website). Open **products.xsn** in Design mode in InfoPath Designer.

3. Publish the **products.xsn** template as a browser form to a form library on your SharePoint server.

4. Go to the SharePoint library where the products form is published, and leave your browser window open as shown in the following screenshot.

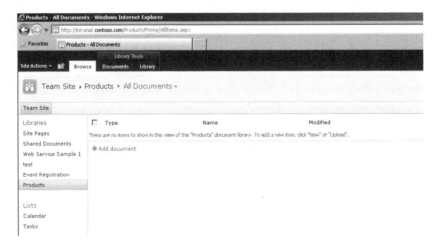

5. Open Fiddler on your system. You can find it in the **Start** menu.

   Note A full tutorial of Fiddler is beyond the scope of this book, but you will find it to be an easy, intuitive tool. The Fiddler interface consists of two main parts, the **Web Sessions** pane on the left and the details area where you can view the statistics, raw text, images, XML, and so forth that are actually part of the HTTP traffic.

6. On the top of the right pane, click the **Inspectors** tab, the **Headers** tab on the **Request Headers** pane, and the **TextView** tab for the details pane.

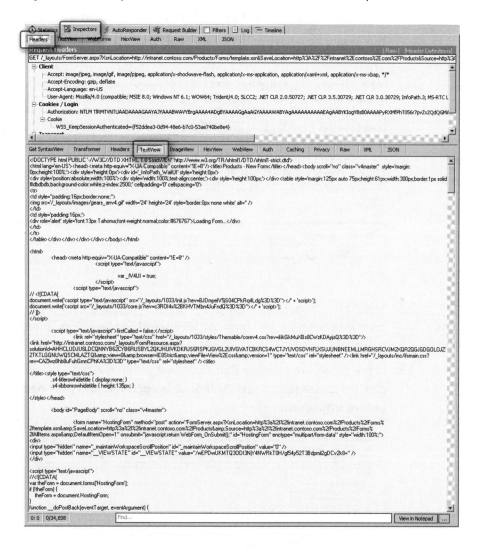

7. In Fiddler, press **F12** to stop capturing traffic.

8. In the **Edit** menu in Fiddler, choose **Select All**, and then press the **Delete** key to remove all the entries.

9. Press **F12** again to start capturing only the web traffic related to the products form.

10. Return to your browser, and then click the **Add document** link to create a new instance of the products form.

11. Go back to Fiddler. Press **F12** one more time to stop the capture.

    You should now have an entry in Fiddler that appears as shown in the following screenshot.

    Note The primary entry that you are concerned with is the one in blue (the second entry in the screenshot that follows), which is a 200 HTTP HTML event. This particular capture row represents the actual contents of the products form that have been pushed down to your browser from IPFS. As you will see, this includes all the HTML, JavaScript, and data from external sources such as the **products.xml** file that is attached to the form as a resource file. Perhaps the most useful piece of information on this particular pane is the **Body** column, which represents the size of the form that is pushed from the IPFS server to the browser on your client system. In this case, it is 10,797 bytes. (Your result might vary a little.)

12. Select the primary 200 HTTP event (blue) by clicking it. In the **Request Headers** pane, you will now see some of the detailed header information from this particular event.

13. In the details area, ensure that **TextView** is still selected. You will likely need to click the message that says **Response is encoded and may need to be decoded before inspection**.

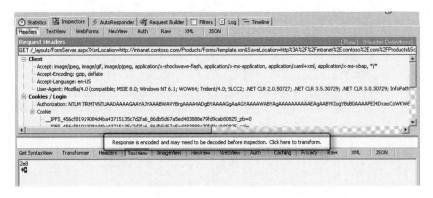

Note After you have transformed the text, Fiddler gives you a view into the raw HTML so that you can see the details. Even if you're not familiar with HTML, these details can still help you see exactly what's going on in your form. If you want to analyze a form's contents to figure out what is happening when IPFS creates a new instance of the form, you now have all the data necessary to do so. Even the XML resource file that you created and attached to the form template is available here.

14. In the bottom of the details pane, use the **Find** box to search for data from the XML file you attached to the form back in Chapter 1. Type **widget** in the search box, and you will see Fiddler has captured everything. Notice that the prices are also embedded in the HTML.

Tip The fact all the product data is downloaded to the user's browser when the form is loaded illustrates a very important point for troubleshooting performance. When a user loads an instance of an IPFS form, the size of the initial package of HTML that is pushed down with the form is dependent on the size of the form, number of controls, XML resource files, images, and so on. It doesn't take much imagination to realize what would happen if the products file had several thousand items in it. That's why a much better strategy for a large data set would be a filtered data connection where the data resides on a server rather than an embedded XML resource file.

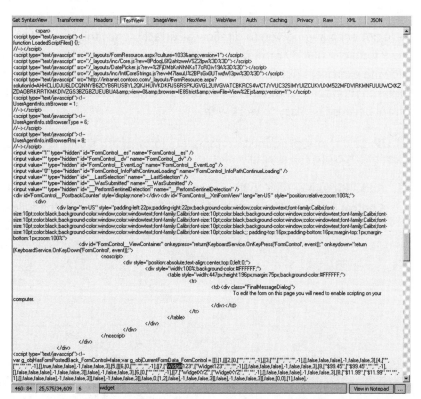

You can see from the preceding exercise that monitoring the details of IPFS HTTP traffic is easy to do with a web analysis program such as Fiddler and that such a program can be an invaluable addition to your toolkit when troubleshooting performance problems.

 CLEAN UP Close Fiddler if you do not intend to move on to the next exercise.

Monitoring the Products Form with a Picture Control

As mentioned earlier in the chapter, there are many possible reasons why your IPFS forms are not performing as well as you'd like. One of the most obvious is a form that generates a lot of traffic because of the size of the HTML that the form is generating. Among the many ways that you can end up with large, unwieldy forms, one of the most common is giving users the ability to add attachments. When a user embeds a file or picture in a browser-based form, the attachments must be saved with the form to the SharePoint form library.

We're not encouraging you to disallow all attachments; this is merely one example of how a form can quickly grow into a performance challenge. Therefore, the point of the following exercise is not to pick on any certain controls but to illustrate how to use Fiddler to monitor a form that has an attachment. In the exercise, you'll use the picture control because it's easy to work with.

 SET UP Open your products.xsn template in InfoPath Designer. You can also download it from the practice files location.

1. Add a **Picture** control to the products.xsn template, and then in the **Insert Picture Control** dialog, select **Included in the form**, as shown in the following screenshot.

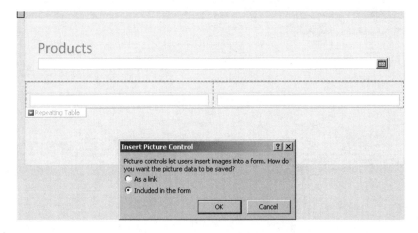

2. Right-click the **Picture** control, and then select the **Specify a default picture** option. Browse to find a picture on your computer to attach to your form.

It doesn't really matter what image you pick for the purposes of the exercise; look for something around a megabyte or two in size.

3. After you have added a picture, republish the products form to the same form library that you used in the previous exercise (or a new library if you didn't do the previous exercise). You can republish the form by using the **Quick Publish** button on the InfoPath Quick Access Toolbar.

4. Repeat steps 5–13 from the previous exercise.

To summarize, open Fiddler, clean out any web sessions that you captured, and then capture the web traffic for the new instance of the products form, now that you've attached a picture to it.

The primary thing you should notice is that Fiddler now has a second entry when your form instantiates. Your original form is still a nice compact 10 KB, but the overall IPFS traffic has grown dramatically due to the image embedded in the form.

As shown in the screenshot that follows, it has added over 131 KB. This might not seem like much, but imagine a production system with several forms and lots of users, each of them generating extra traffic on the SharePoint server. Images are used here in the exercise as an easy way to illustrate how to monitor a form for size problems, but in the real world, a form can become unwieldy in numerous ways. Fiddler can help diagnose a variety of problems.

5. To see the actual image you added to the form, highlight the new entry in Fiddler, and then in the details pane, click **ImageView**. Again, the power of a tool like Fiddler becomes evident when the time comes to troubleshoot an IPFS performance issue.

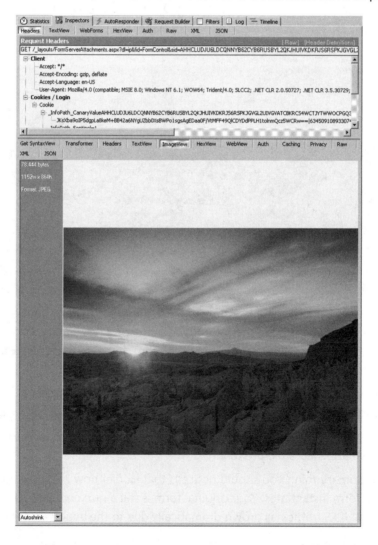

CLEAN UP Close out of InfoPath Designer and Fiddler if you do not intend to continue on to the next exercise.

Maximizing Performance by Minimizing Postbacks

Aside from the overall size of the HTML generated for a form (which we looked at in the previous two exercises), probably the most common of all the potential factors that might affect IPFS performance are postbacks. Some form controls, actions, and features require a user's browser to communicate with the server while in the process of a form-filling session. The interchange of data during a session is called a postback, and it usually occurs when a form needs to send data from the user's browser back to the server for processing and then has to wait for a response to update and re-render the form. This can make postbacks a particularly expensive performance problem because they can quickly increase the required network traffic for a form each time a postback occurs.

Note Postbacks are relevant only for browser forms because of the stateless nature of HTTP communication. No postback concerns arise when using the InfoPath Filler client because the InfoPath Windows client requires much less communication with a server than an identical IPFS form. The InfoPath client does much of the processing that IPFS forms require a server to do, thus network communication is reduced.

Because IPFS forms are so reliant on the server, postbacks will sometimes be unavoidably necessary. Fortunately, the challenges that postbacks pose can be mitigated by a forms designer who has the knowledge and techniques to minimize them. Sometimes the difference between creating a poor performing form and a good one is not to eliminate postbacks but rather to minimize them by giving thought to the problems postbacks can cause if the form user interface is built without appropriate consideration of performance. When designing a browser form, most controls have an option on the control properties for forcing postbacks (see the following illustration). This would be a rare exception though; generally, best practice is to leave this option at the default setting.

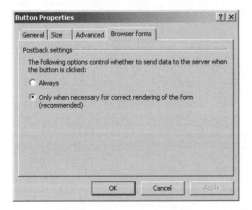

Armed with the proper knowledge of postbacks—why they occur and how to monitor your forms to identify potential problems—you can design a form to minimize the situations that cause them, usually without losing important functionality.

A few of the most common scenarios that cause postbacks are as follows:

- **Data connections**   The function of a data connection is to make a query connection to an external data source—such as an XML file, a database, a SharePoint list, or a web service—so that a form can receive and be updated with some data from the data source. When a data connection is activated by an event in a form, such as a button click rule, the form is required to communicate with the server to fetch the data, creating a postback situation.

- **Calculations**   A calculation can cause a postback because quite often the calculation requires processing by the server.

- **Switching views**   Using multiple views is often considered a best practice to improve the usability and performance of InfoPath forms. By careful grouping of related items and limiting the number of controls in each view, you can improve the form-loading performance rather than placing everything in a single view. So while best practice principles dictate that views are useful, you, as the designer, should be aware that each time the view is switched, a postback is required to send the user's information to the server, retrieve the new view, and then reload it in the browser.

  Tip If you'd like to monitor a view-switching postback, you can publish the Blue Yonder Records Management Request form from Chapter 5, "Adding Logic and Rules to Forms," to a form library as a browser form. Use Fiddler to monitor the form-load process, and then watch what happens when you switch views in the form. Notice that each view switch is an HTTP event that is essentially equivalent to reloading the entire form.

- **Multiple binding events**   Events such as insertion or removal of repeating tables and repeating or optional sections also cause postbacks.

  Tip For an example of an optional section postback type, you can publish the Flight Delay Form from Chapter 3, "Form Design Basics: Working with InfoPath Layout, Controls, and Views," to a form library as a browser form. After you have published it, make sure that you are capturing traffic with Fiddler. Open a new form instance, and then in the Choice Section, switch from a hyperlink to a file attachment, as shown in the following illustration.

If you watch activity in Fiddler while making the selection indicated above in the Flight Delay form, you'll see a postback event that looks similar to the following illustration, triggered by the selection of a different option in the choice group.

Monitoring a Data Connection Postback with Fiddler

In the following exercise, you will use Fiddler to monitor a form-load process and then capture a postback event during the form-filling experience. The form is one you're already familiar with if you completed the exercises in Chapter 9, "Working with the SharePoint User Profile Web Service."

 SET UP Browse to the form library where you published the **Event Registration** form in Chapter 9. Alternatively, if you did not complete the exercises in Chapter 9, for the purposes of this exercise, any form with a data connection that loads as a result of a rule on a button will work.

1. Start Fiddler.

2. In the form library, add a new instance of the form by clicking the **Add Document** link.

   You should see an event in Fiddler that represents the initial form load, similar to the screenshot below.

#	Result	Protocol	Host	URL	Body
3	200	HTTP	intranet.contoso.com	/_layouts/FormServer.aspx?XsnLocation=http://intranet.contos...	16,851

3. After you have loaded the form, enter a user's name in the people picker control, and then click the **Load User Data** button.

4. Switch back to Fiddler, and you will see a postback event that was generated because the button click made the call to the User Profile web service data connection.

#	Result	Protocol	Host	URL	Body
4	200	HTTP	intranet.contoso.com	/_layouts/Postback.FormServer.aspx	10,039

The event generated by the preceding exercise did not cause a large amount of network traffic. However, in a real world scenario, where the button is connected to a larger data source such as a database, the postback events could become very unwieldy. Some designers will set the data to load when the form is first loaded. This strategy can be problematic because the initial form load has a great deal of impact on users' perception of overall performance of the form. In some circumstances, a better approach is to give users a button in the interface that loads data (similar to the Event Registration form). This approach sets the expectation that a delay will occur so that users are not surprised when the form takes a few seconds to fetch data.

CLEAN UP Close out of InfoPath Designer and Fiddler.

Now you know how to monitor a form and watch for postbacks. This is a useful skill for any IPFS forms designer. Postbacks are a necessary evil with browser forms; it is simply the nature of the way any HTTP-based form application must work. So the goal isn't to eliminate them—that's not really possible. However, now that you know when, where, and why they occur, you can design your forms to minimize the impact on performance and usability that postbacks will cause for your users.

Key Points

- SharePoint Central Administration has a rich set of GUI administration tools for IPFS.
- Fiddler is a free web traffic analysis tool by which every IPFS administrator and form designer can benefit.
- IPFS performance is heavily dependent on well-designed forms.
- Large attachments can diminish performance of an IPFS form, especially in high volume scenarios.
- Form designers should try to minimize the impact of postbacks whenever possible.

Chapter at a Glance

Work with custom views, **page 364**

Learn to apply conditional formatting to views, **page 380**

Add buttons to SharePoint pages for creating new forms, **page 383**

Utilize the Content Query Web Part to surface information, **page 390**

Add Key Performance Indicators that report metrics from your forms, **page 396**

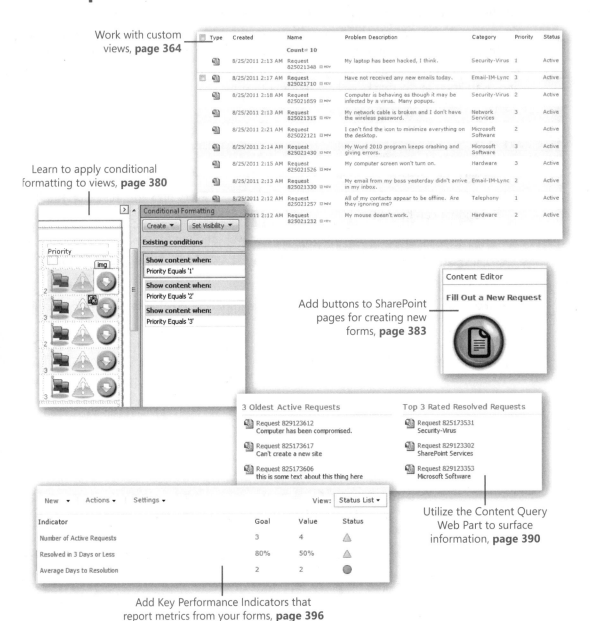

13 SharePoint Views and Dashboards

In this chapter, you will learn how to:

- ✔ Plan the site's interface with views and Web Parts
- ✔ Display only pertinent forms to the currently logged-on user
- ✔ Create views for form administrators
- ✔ Report from the data collected in forms

So far in this book, you have learned all about creating forms and filling out forms. Views in forms can control what fields are displayed at any given time, and rules and logic can be used to hide or format specific data. Everything that you have learned so far, though, has been applicable only within the Microsoft InfoPath form.

For each new form project that you take on, one of the phases of the requirements gathering process is to discuss the user interface on the Microsoft SharePoint site. What do end users first see when they get to the SharePoint site? Where do they click to fill out a new form? Do they see a list of outstanding forms pending action? Do they see a list of forms that they have submitted, with each form's status? For form administrators who need to see all forms, where do they click to get to their administrator view? Can users see only their own forms? It is easy to use views and filtering to show only pertinent data to each logged-on user.

SharePoint offers several different methods to create a "report" of data. In this chapter, you will learn about ways to create professional-looking dashboards that generate reports from any information in SharePoint lists and libraries.

> **Practice Files** Before you can complete the exercises in this chapter, you need to copy the book's practice files to your computer. The practice files you'll use to complete the exercises in this chapter are in the Chapter 13 practice file folder. A complete list of practice files is provided in "Downloading the Practice Files and eBook," on page xxvi.

The Help Desk Request

The business process that will be created in this chapter is a Help Desk application for Contoso. An InfoPath form is needed so that employees can quickly fill out requests. The Help Desk staff needs to be able to quickly process and route the requests. The employees who are requesting technical support and the Help Desk personnel will need to see high-level views of the forms that have been submitted. Reports and Key Performance Indicators (KPIs) will be needed.

As you build this system and learn about the SharePoint Web Parts, start thinking about ways in which these concepts can be used. This is not just a Help Desk system; the methods that you are learning are applicable in any line of business. Some examples of other business processes are travel requests, patient admittance, expense reports, case management, project management, referral tracking, change management, and much more. Web Parts and views are the tools that you can use to build any type of business process automation that is needed in your organization. No programming knowledge is needed.

At Contoso, the tracking and reporting of Help Desk calls is necessary, so you have created an InfoPath Help Desk Request form. When the form is published to SharePoint, several columns are promoted so that they can be used to obtain metrics.

In the following exercise, a SharePoint site will be created just for the Help Desk request system.

➡ **SET UP** Open your SharePoint site in the browser.

More Options...
Create other types of pages, lists, libraries, and sites.

1. Click **Site Actions**, and then click **More Options**.

2. In the **Filter By** field on the left, select **Site**. Click to select the **Blank Site** template.

   Tip It is very important that the Blank Site template is used in this step. All of the exercises in this chapter are dependent on the site having this template.

Blank Site

3. On the right, type **Help Desk System** as the name of the site, and type **helpsite** as the URL. Click **Create**.

4. Click **Site Actions**, and then click **Site Settings**. Click **Manage Site Features**.

5. Next to **SharePoint Server Enterprise Site features**, click the **Activate** button.

6. Next to **SharePoint Server Publishing**, click the **Activate** button.

   When activating the SharePoint Server Publishing feature, the following notification might be displayed: **The feature being activated is a site scoped feature which has a dependency on a site collection scoped feature which has not been activated.**

CLEAN UP Leave the browser open if you are continuing to the next section of this chapter. Otherwise, close the browser.

If you receive this message, it means that the publishing feature needs to be activated at the site collection level. This feature is needed later in this chapter when the Content Query Web Part is used. This change will affect all of the sites in the site collection.

 SET UP If you have received the above error message, the following steps need to be taken. If this feature is not enabled, it will only affect your ability to do the exercise in this chapter regarding Content Query Web Parts.

1. Use the folder icon at the upper-left corner of the site, and then click the very top level of the tree. Your upper-level site will not have the same name as the following screenshot.

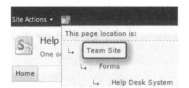

2. Click **Site Actions**, and then click **Site Settings**.

3. Under **Site Collection Administration**, click **Site collection features**.

4. Next to **SharePoint Server Publishing Infrastructure**, click the **Activate** button.

5. Navigate back to the Help Desk System site that was created in step 3. Click **Site Actions**, and then click **Site Settings**. Click **Manage Site Features**.

6. Next to **SharePoint Server Publishing**, click the **Activate** button.

This site is a great blank slate to work with, and it is ready for the InfoPath form to be published. The Help Desk System site will be used in all of the exercises in the rest of the chapter.

 CLEAN UP Leave the browser open if you are continuing to the next section of this chapter. Otherwise, close the browser.

In Chapter 6, "Publishing and Submitting Form Data," you learned the details behind the process of publishing forms to SharePoint. The sample form will be published to your new blank SharePoint site so that all of the views and web parts can be created.

In the following exercise, you will publish the example Help Desk form to your new Help Desk System site and then configure the data connections.

SET UP Open Helpdesk **Requests.xsn** in Design mode. Open your Help Desk System site in the browser.

1. On the ribbon, click the **File** tab, and then click **Publish**. Click the **SharePoint Server** button.

2. When prompted, save a copy of the file to the folder **C:\InfoPath Files**. If this folder does not exist, create it first.

3. For the location of your SharePoint site, enter the URL of the test site that you have been using in this book's exercises. Click **Next**. (In this Contoso example, the site is called http://forms.contoso.com.)

Publishing Wizard

Enter the location of your SharePoint or InfoPath Forms Services site:

http://forms.contoso.com/helpsite

Example: http://www.example.com

4. On the next wizard page, select the default options, and then click **Next**.

   The form is now browser enabled and published to a form library.

5. Select **Create a new form library**, and then click **Next**.

6. For the new library name, type **Helpdesk**, and for the description, type **This is the help desk request form**. Click **Next**.

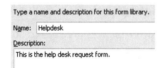

Type a name and description for this form library.

Name: Helpdesk

Description:

This is the help desk request form.

7. For the promoted columns, verify that the following columns are in the list: **Category**, **Problem Description**, **Contact Number**, **Status**, **Request ID**, **Priority**, **Resolution Type**, **Resolution**, **Resolved By**, **Product**, **Opened Date**, **Resolved Date**. Click **Next**.

8. If the **Adjust data connections to the new location** check box appears, select the check box, click **Publish**, and then skip to step 18. Otherwise, click **Publish** and go on to step 9.

   Tip For a detailed explanation of this message, refer to the sidebar "Adjusting Data Connections," on page 299, in Chapter 11, "Building an Approval Process."

9. On the **Data** tab, click the **Data Connections** button.

10. Select the **Main submit** connection, and then click the **Modify** button.

11. In the **Document library** text box, enter the URL of your own site before the **/Helpdesk**. The Helpdesk is the library that you just created. Click **Next**.

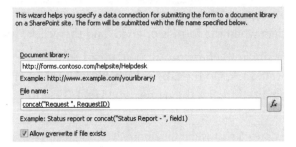

This wizard helps you specify a data connection for submitting the form to a document library on a SharePoint site. The form will be submitted with the file name specified below.

Document library:

http://forms.contoso.com/helpsite/Helpdesk

Example: http://www.example.com/yourlibrary/

File name:

concat("Request ", RequestID)   *fx*

Example: Status report or concat("Status Report - ", field1)

☑ Allow overwrite if file exists

12. Clear the **Set as the default submit connection** check box, and then click **Finish**.

13. On the **Data Connections** screen, select the **Helpdesk Requests Query**, and then click the **Modify** button.

Data Connections

Data connections for the form template:

Helpdesk Requests Query
Main submit

Add...

Modify...

Remove

Convert to Connection File...

Convert to Previous Version

14. Enter the URL of your own SharePoint site, and then click **Next**.

15. Select the library called **Helpdesk**, and then click **Next**.

16. Select the check boxes next to the following fields: **Status**, **Product**, **Category**, **Priority**, and **Created By**. Click **Next**.

The SharePoint list has the following fields that you can select from.

Select fields:

☑ Product
☐ Opened_Date (Opened Date)
☐ Resolved_Date (Resolved Date)
☑ Category
☑ Priority
☑ ID
☐ Created
☑ Created_By (Created By)
☐ Modified
☐ Modified_By (Modified By)
☐ Copy_Source (Copy Source)
☐ Checked_Out_To (Checked Out To)
☐ Version

☐ Include data for the active form only

Sort by: ID

Sort order: ◉ Ascending
             ◯ Descending

< Back   Next >   Cancel

Library Settings

17. Click **Next**. On the last page of the wizard, be sure to clear the check box to automatically retrieve data when the form is opened, and then click **Finish**.

18. On your SharePoint site in the browser, in the **Quick Launch** pane on the left side of the page, click **Helpdesk**. On the **Library** tab, click **Library Settings**. Click **Title, description and navigation**. For the name, type **Help Desk Requests**, and then click **Save**.

> **Tip** You might have noticed that when the library was originally created, it was named "Helpdesk" with no spaces. In this step, we have changed the library to a more descriptive name. This is a nice trick that avoids URLs containing the characters %20 in place of spaces in the original list or library name.

Add document

19. On your SharePoint site, on the ribbon, in the **Quick Launch** pane, click **Help Desk Requests**. Click **Add Document** to fill out a new form.

Create several forms using a variety of categories and priorities. Use the following table as a guide to create some test forms.

> **Note** The Problem Description field is required, so get creative with these and make up your own Help Desk issues. Feel free to explore the form as you go.

Category	Priority
Hardware	Medium
Hardware	Low
Telephony	High
Network Services	Low
Email/IM/Lync	Medium
Email/IM/Lync	Low
Security/Virus	High
Security/Virus	Medium
Microsoft Software	Low
Microsoft Software	Medium

✖ **CLEAN UP** Leave InfoPath Designer and the browser open if you are continuing to the next section of this chapter. Otherwise, click the Save button to save the XSN file to your computer, and then close InfoPath Designer. Close the browser.

Views

In SharePoint, the concept of a view is similar to that in InfoPath. It is a different way of looking at the same set of information. When an InfoPath form has been published to SharePoint, all of the column information can be used for sorting, filtering, and displaying the data in as many different views as are necessary. What does a view consist of? Here are the major components:

- **Columns**   Select the columns to be displayed, and choose the number order in which to display them from left to right.

- **Sorting**   Select column names to sort by, and choose ascending or descending order.

- **Filtering**   Select a column name, and type a value to filter by.

- **Grouping**   Groups allow drill-down functionality. You can select up to two grouping levels, and choose whether to automatically collapse or expand the groups. Groups are a great alternative to folders. Instead of a folder structure, simply create views to organize the information in a multitude of ways.

Note For more documentation and details about views in SharePoint, go to *http://office. microsoft.com/en-us/sharepoint-foundation-help/create-modify-or-delete-a-view-HA010377693. aspx?CTT=3.*

It is useful to be able to see this same list of requests in different ways so that you can quickly assess the list of specific requests. Instead of scrolling through a long list, which could be many pages in length, views are your way of creating custom sets of highlighted information, which is just an easy way of reporting on this data. To begin the reporting exercises, you will create the following views:

- **My Requests**   Requests that the currently logged-on user submitted

- **My Active Requests**   Requests that the currently logged-on user has submitted, which have not been resolved yet

- **High Priority by Category**   Only high priority requests, grouped by category

- **Active Requests by Requestor**   Requests that were submitted as high priority, grouped by the name of the person making the request

- **Recently Resolved Requests**   Requests that have been resolved in the past month

- **6 Month by Category**   Requests that have been worked on in the last 6 months, grouped by category

In the following exercise, you will create several views in the Help Desk Requests library. The first two views will be created in detailed steps, and then after that, simple tables will depict the proper settings to use for each view.

 SET UP Open your Help Desk System site in the browser. To open the form library, in the Quick Launch, click the Help Desk Requests link.

1. On the ribbon, click the name of the **All Documents** view (which is a drop-down box), and then select the **My Documents** view.

   The **My Documents** view already exists in form libraries by default, so we're modifying it first. This view provides a list of forms that were filled out by the currently logged-on user.

   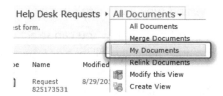

2. On the **My Documents** view, click the view drop-down box, and then click **Modify this View**.

   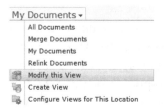

3. Change the **View Name** to **My Requests** (instead of **My Documents**).

4. Select the check boxes next to the following columns, with ordering numbered according to the following table.

Column Name	Position from Left
Type	1
Created	2
Name (linked to document with edit menu)	3
Problem Description	4
Category	5
Priority	6
Status	7

5. In the **Sort** section, under **First sort by the column**, select **Modified**, and then select **Show items in descending order**.

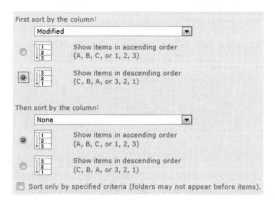

Notice that the **Filter** section is set up so that **Created By** is equal to [**Me**]. Leave that setting as it is.

6. Expand the **Totals** section. In the drop-down box next to the **Name** field, select **Count**.

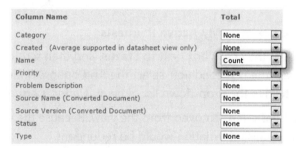

7. In the **Style** section, select **Shaded**, and then click **OK**.

When the shaded style is used, it makes the list more visually appealing and more distinctly differentiates the rows.

Type	Created	Name	Problem Description	Category	Priority	Status
		Count= 10				
	8/25/2011 2:13 AM	Request 825021348 □ NEW	My laptop has been hacked, I think.	Security-Virus	1	Active
	8/25/2011 2:17 AM	Request 825021710 □ NEW	Have not received any new emails today.	Email-IM-Lync	3	Active
	8/25/2011 2:18 AM	Request 825021859 □ NEW	Computer is behaving as though it may be infected by a virus. Many popups.	Security-Virus	2	Active
	8/25/2011 2:13 AM	Request 825021315 □ NEW	My network cable is broken and I don't have the wireless password.	Network Services	3	Active
	8/25/2011 2:21 AM	Request 825022121 □ NEW	I can't find the icon to minimize everything on the desktop.	Microsoft Software	2	Active
	8/25/2011 2:14 AM	Request 825021430 □ NEW	My Word 2010 program keeps crashing and giving errors.	Microsoft Software	3	Active
	8/25/2011 2:15 AM	Request 825021526 □ NEW	My computer screen won't turn on.	Hardware	3	Active
	8/25/2011 2:13 AM	Request 825021330 □ NEW	My email from my boss yesterday didn't arrive in my inbox.	Email-IM-Lync	2	Active
	8/25/2011 2:12 AM	Request 825021257 □ NEW	All of my contacts appear to be offline. Are they ignoring me?	Telephony	1	Active
	8/25/2011 2:12 AM	Request 825021232 □ NEW	My mouse doesn't work.	Hardware	2	Active

✚ Add document

8. Create a new view called **My Active Requests**. On the ribbon, click the **Library** tab, and then click the **Create View** button.

9. In the **Start from an existing view** section, click the **My Requests** view.

10. In the **View Name** box, type **My Active Requests**.

11. In the columns, clear the check box next to **Status**, and then scroll down to the **Filter** section. Under the first condition, select the **And** option. Under **When column**, select the **Status** field in the drop-down list of fields. Under **is equal to**, type **Active**.

The status column has been removed from the view. Because the view contains only active requests, this information would be redundant.

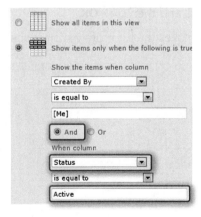

12. Scroll down to the bottom of the page, and then click **OK**. Currently, because none of the Help Desk requests have been resolved, this view's items look the same as **My Requests**.

13. Click the name of the first request in the list, using the hyperlink in the **Name** column.

> **Note** Your requests will not have the same names as those shown in the following screenshot, because these numbers are generated by using the date that the request was created.

14. At the upper-right of the form, click the **Resolve** button.

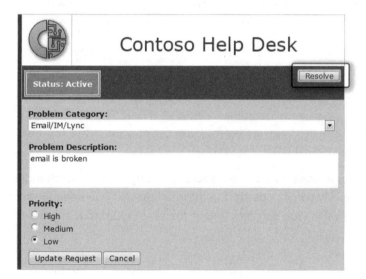

15. Fill in some text about the solution to the problem, and then at the bottom of the form, click the **Update Request** button.

16. Repeat steps 13–15, resolving one more request.

17. Notice that the list of active requests now has two less items in it. On the **Library** tab, click **Create View**, and then select **Standard View**.

The next four views will be created according to the following chart.

View Name	High Priority by Category	Active Requests by Requestor	Recently Resolved Requests	6 Month by Category
Columns	Type, Name (linked to document with edit menu), Created, Created By, Problem Description, Modified, Modified By	Type, Name (linked to document with edit menu), Created, Problem Description, Category	Type, Name (linked to document with edit menu), Created, Category, Resolution Type, Resolved By, Resolved Date	Type, Name (linked to document with edit menu), Created, Created By, Modified, Priority, Status
Sort	Created - descending	Priority - ascending, then Created - ascending	Modified - descending	Created By - descending
Filter	Priority is equal to 1 AND Status is equal to Active	Status is equal to Active	Status is equal to Resolved AND Modified is greater than [Today]-30	Created is greater than [Today]-180
Group By	Category	Created By, then Priority	None	Category

 CLEAN UP Leave the browser open if you are continuing to the next section of this chapter. Otherwise, close the browser.

Now that several views have been created, you can see how much more useful the data is and how quickly you can get to the information that you need. Besides being able to quickly create views, you can click any of the view columns at any time, to sort and filter on the fly.

Ratings

Newly introduced in SharePoint 2010, ratings allow users to quickly rate items with a rank of 1 to 5 stars. The stars are displayed as a column in the list or library views. When an item has been rated by one or more people, the stars next to it display its average rating.

Ratings are a great way for help desk personnel to get feedback from their peers as to how they did with their problem resolutions in the system. On this site, it will not be necessary for non-Help Desk personnel to see the ratings, because they pertain only to help desk employees learning how to do their job well.

In the following exercise, you will turn on ratings and rate some forms.

SET UP Open your Help Desk System site in the browser. To open the form library, in the Quick Launch, click the Help Desk Requests link.

Library
Settings

1. On the ribbon, click the **Library** tab, and then click **Library Settings**.

2. Under **General Settings**, click **Rating Settings**.

3. Under **Allow items in this list to be rated**, select **Yes**, and then click **OK**.

   Notice that there is text on this page that describes exactly what the rating settings are.

4. In the breadcrumb trail at the top of the page, click the **Help Desk Requests** link.

   Notice that the rating field has been automatically added to the default view of the list. All of the stars are white because nothing has been rated yet.

5. Go down the list of items. Click a star on each one to quickly give each item a rating, with varying numbers of stars.

   When you are finished, the column will show yellow stars indicating the ratings that you have given.

Rating (0-5)

These ratings will be used in later exercises, as a part of metrics and KPIs.

Tip On the SharePoint server, a timer job runs every hour, compiling all the ratings into averages and displaying them as blue stars. After you have rated each of these items, the next time you refresh the page, it will appear as though all the stars have disappeared. After the "User Profile Service Application - Social Rating Synchronization Job" has run, the stars will be blue.

Alerts Based on Views

In all lists and libraries in SharePoint, individuals can create email alerts so that they will be notified of changes to a list, library, or specific item. There is also a way that alerts can be created based on information in specific views. This works only with views that have a filter set up. When a view-based alert is set up, the user receives email notifications only when something is changed that falls under the filter criteria of that view.

People with full control permissions are able to create alerts for other people or groups, but everyone else can create alerts only for themselves.

In the following exercise, you will create an alert based on a filtered view. In the previous exercise, you created a view called High Priority by Category. The filter on this view is Priority is equal to 1 and Status is equal to Active. In this example, you want only to receive emails regarding the active, high-priority Help Desk requests.

 SET UP Open your Help Desk System site in the browser. To open the form library, click the Help Desk Requests link.

   1. On the **Library** tab, click the **Alert Me** button, and then select **Set alert on this library**.

Important If your SharePoint server administrator has not set up SharePoint to send outgoing emails, this setting will not be enabled.

2. In the **Alert Title** field, type **Help Desk High Priority**.

3. Scroll down to the **Send Alerts for These Changes** section.

4. Select **Someone changes an item that appears in the following view**. In the drop-down box, select **High Priority by Category**, and then click **OK**.

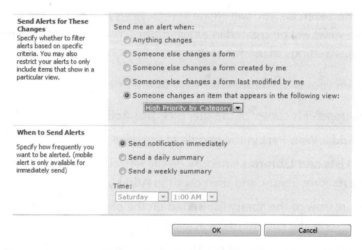

After you've completed the preceding steps, you will receive a notification email when the alert is first set up. Each alert that you receive will show you all of the information about the request, and who added or changed it.

Alerts are a great way to stay informed about changes or additions in SharePoint. This can be done with no code and no workflows. When your project requirements reach a complexity level that cannot be achieved with regular alerts, workflows are the next level to accomplish what you need.

Library Web Parts

To get to each list and library on the site, end users must click the links in the Quick Launch on the left side of your SharePoint site. They must click again to see the desired view of a list or library. The Views drop-down box must then be used to select a view. In SharePoint, for information that is of immediate relevance, Web Parts can be used to display that information on the home page of your site or on other site pages or Web Part pages. In this chapter's Help Desk example, all of the demonstrated Web Parts will be placed on the home page of the site.

Tip As a best practice, instead of overloading a home page with Web Parts and long lists, try to present information that is relevant and concise. Generally, site visitors would prefer not to scroll down the page.

In the following exercise, you will create several views in the Help Desk Requests library. The first two views will be created in detailed steps. Following that, simple tables will depict the proper settings to use for each view.

 SET UP Open your Help Desk System site in the browser.

1. At the upper-left corner of the site, click **Site Actions**, and then click **Edit Page**.

2. Click **Add a Web Part** in the middle of the page.

3. In the **Lists and Libraries** category on the left, click the name of the **Help Desk Requests** form library, and then click the **Add** button.

   A default view of the library is inserted on the page. You will need to modify this view, to show the current user's active requests.

4. At the upper-right corner of the **Help Desk Requests** Web Part, click the black drop-down box, and then click **Edit Web Part**.

You can change the view by using the properties of the **Help Desk Requests** Web Part, which are located in the right panel of the page.

5. In the **Selected View** drop-down box, select **My Active Requests**.

   A message pops up, alerting you about switching to a different view. Click **OK**.

6. Use the following table to configure settings in the Web Part tool pane, and then click **OK** at the bottom.

Field Name	Setting
Toolbar Type	No Toolbar
Title	My Active Requests
AJAX Options	Show Manual Refresh Button

Each logged-on user will now see a list of their active requests in the middle of the page. A refresh button will be displayed in the upper-right corner of the Web Part. The user can click this button to see the most recent set of relevant data.

Now, when people visit the site, they will immediately be greeted with their own list of requests.

 CLEAN UP Leave the browser open if you are continuing to the next section of this chapter. Otherwise, close the browser.

Filter Web Parts

The Enterprise version of SharePoint includes an extremely useful set of Web Parts, called filter Web Parts. These are used to filter the data in other Web Parts. To function correctly, filter Web Parts need to be connected to other Web Parts, which send filter information or parameter data. The Web Part that is sending the filter data is called the provider, and the Web Part that receives the filter is called the consumer Web Part.

When Help Desk employees visit the site, they want to quickly see a list of their most recently resolved requests. They frequently refer to these items when users call them to ask more questions, or if similar problems occur. You might have noticed that when a request is resolved, the Resolved By column contains the logon name of the person who resolved the ticket. This information is automatically captured in the form when the Resolve button is clicked.

In other views, we have used the Created By field to filter views. The [me] variable can be used in filters when the column is a Person or Group column. Unfortunately, one of the limitations of InfoPath is that columns that are promoted from within the form cannot be promoted to become a Person or Group field. However, there is a trick that you can use to get around this.

In the following exercise, you will create a SharePoint group that contains all the Help Desk employees. You will add a new Web Part to the home page that displays a list of recently resolved requests to the logged-on Help Desk employee. Finally, you will configure the Web Part so that only Help Desk personnel can see it.

SET UP Open your Help Desk System site in the browser.

1. Click **Site Actions**, and then click **Site Settings**.

2. In the **Users and Permissions** section, click **People and groups**.

3. In the Quick Launch pane, click **Groups**.

4. Click the **New** button, and then name the group **Help Desk Staff**. Leave all the rest of the fields as default values, and then click **Create**.

5. In the breadcrumb trail at the top of the page, click **Help Desk System** to navigate back to the home page. Click **Site Actions**, and then click **Edit Page**.

6. On the right side of the page, click **Add a Web Part**. In the **Lists and Libraries** category, select **Help Desk Requests**, and then click the **Add** button.

7. Click the drop-down box at the upper-right of the **Help Desk Requests** Web Part, and then select **Edit Web Part**. Click **Edit the current view**.

8. Use the following table to configure the view settings, and then click **OK** at the bottom of the settings page.

Section Name	Setting
Columns	Name (linked to document with edit menu), Problem Description, Resolution
Sort	Resolved Date - descending
Filter	Status is equal to Resolved
Tabular View	Unchecked
Group By	Category - ascending, then Created By - ascending
Style	Newsletter
Item Limit	15 - Limit the total number of items returned to the specified amount

Open the Web Part tool pane again. Configure the following Web Part settings, and then click **OK**.

Field Name	Setting
Toolbar Type	No Toolbar
Title	My Recently Resolved
Target Audiences (In the **Advanced** section)	Help Desk Staff

With the target audience set this way, only people in the Help Desk Staff SharePoint group can see this Web Part.

9. Click **Site Actions**, and then choose **Edit Page**. On the right side of the page, click **Add a Web Part** again. In the **Filters** category, select **Current User Filter**, and then click the **Add** button.

10. On the **Current User Filter** Web Part, click the black arrow in the upper-right corner, and then select **Edit Web Part**.

11. In the **SharePoint profile value for current user** drop-down box, select **User name**, and then click **OK**.

    Note The **User name** property stores the NT login of the current user. This is the same syntax that is used in the **Resolved By** column.

12. Click the arrow at the upper-right corner of the **Current User Filter**, and then click **Connections | Send Filter Values To | My Recently Resolved**.

13. In the **Connection Type** field, select **Get Filter Values From**, and then click **Configure**.

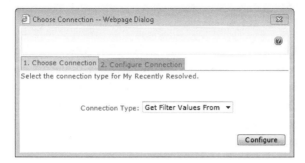

14. In the **Consumer Field Name** field, select **Resolved By**, and then click **Finish**.

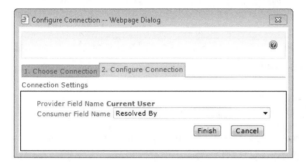

15. On the ribbon, on the **Page** tab, click **Stop Editing**.

16. Open a few more Help Desk requests, and then click the **Resolve** button to include more data in this Web Part.

Now that the Web Part has been completed, it is relatively compact and displays the most recent items that are commonly needed for reference.

XSLT List View Web Part

SharePoint Designer 2010 can be used to customize views when the regular list settings just aren't enough. One example of a quick way to create visually appealing views is to create conditional formatting rules. You might be familiar with the concept of conditional formatting from working with other products such as Microsoft Excel. This means that you can create rules, and based on conditions that you define, the data is displayed or formatted in a different way.

Notice that in the My Active Requests view, the priority column is simply displayed as a number. But what if you want to give site visitors a better visual indication of the status of their requests?

In the following exercise, you will use SharePoint Designer to customize the way the priority column displays on the home page.

Exercise Caution When Using SharePoint Designer

When using SharePoint Designer to edit pages, it is recommended that you do so with care. When editing XSLT list views, especially on a site's home page, it is not necessary or advisable to click the Advanced Mode button. You can click the Split button at the bottom to see the page's code, but some parts are locked down. If you want to see the code for a particular field inside the SharePoint list or library, on the Design tab, click Customize XSLT. This is a great way to dig in and see what code is behind the scenes, without using the Advanced Mode button.

 SET UP Open your Help Desk System site in SharePoint Designer 2010, and open the same site in the browser.

1. In SharePoint Designer, click **Edit site home page**.

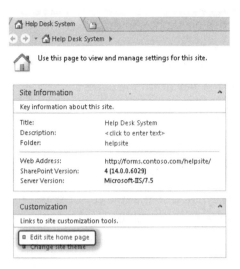

2. Position the cursor in the priority cell next to the priority number of the first request.

   You are going to insert three different images, which will be used as priority icons, and conditional formatting rules will be applied to each.

3. On the ribbon, click the **Insert** tab, and then click **Clip Art**.

4. In the clip art search box, type **red flag**, and then click **Go**. Click to select the flag and insert it into the Web Part.

5. In the **Accessibility Properties** dialog box, in the **Alternate text** box, type **High Priority**, and then click **OK**.

   This flag will now be displayed in your table, next to the priority number, and it will appear in the priority cell all the way down the page.

6. Click the right arrow on the keyboard so that the cursor is next to the image. Two more images need to be inserted next to this one.

   Note Keep in mind that any images can be used; they do not need to be the images used in this exercise.

   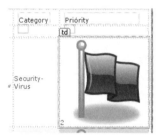

7. In the clip art search box, type **yellow exclamation**, and then click **Go**. Select the first image.

   Again, clicking the image automatically inserts it in the page. Type the alternate text **Medium Priority**. Use the right arrow on the keyboard to move the cursor to the right again.

8. In the clip art search box, type **down arrow**, and then click **Go**. Select the first image. Type the alternate text **Low Priority**.

9. Double-click the red flag. On the **Appearance** tab, select the **Specify size** check box. Specify a width and height of **30 pixels**, and then click **OK**. Repeat this step for the yellow and green images.

10. Click **Save**. At the prompt to save embedded files, click **OK**.

11. On the ribbon, on the **Options** tab, click **Conditional Formatting**. Select **Show Taskpane**.

    The conditional formatting task pane appears next to the clip art task pane. Click the **X** at the upper-right corner of the clip art task pane to close it.

12. Click to select the red flag image. In the **Conditional Formatting** task pane, click **Create**, and then select **Show content**.

13. In the **Condition Criteria** dialog box, select **Priority** for the field name, and then type the number **1** for the value (even though it's not in the drop-down box). Click **OK**.

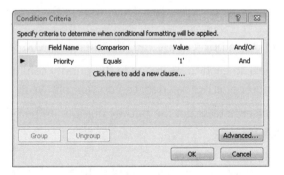

14. Click to select the yellow exclamation image. Click to create a new rule to show content. For the condition, the criterion is that the priority field is equal to 2. For the green arrow, the condition is that the priority is equal to 3.

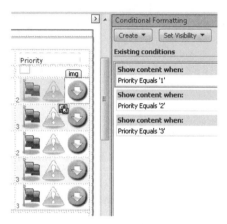

15. Click to select the value in the **Category** field in the first row of data. In the **Conditional Formatting** pane, click **Create**, and then select **Apply formatting**. The condition is that the category equals **'Security-Virus'**. Click **Set Style**.

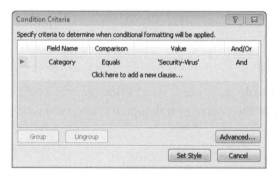

16. Select the **color** drop-down box, choose **red**, and then click **OK**. Save the page.

Notice the numeral next to each row's image in the priority column in the screen-shot in step 14. This number is not needed, so you can remove it.

17. In SharePoint Designer, click to select the priority number in the priority column, and then press **Delete**.

When you have completed the preceding steps, go back to the Help Desk System home page in the browser and refresh the page. Notice that the icons that are displayed in the priority column correctly match the priority numbers that you used in the conditional formatting rules.

CLEAN UP Save the page and close SharePoint Designer. Leave the browser open if you are continuing to the next section of this chapter. Otherwise, close the browser.

Now that the conditional formatting has livened up the site, it is easy for you to quickly view your active requests. Click the heading of any column to sort or filter information to find what you need.

The New Form Button

On the help desk site, one of the most common activities will be for employees at Contoso to fill out new help desk requests. This activity needs to be something that is easy and intuitive.

It's important to understand the structure of InfoPath URLs. In Chapter 11, you learned how to use the URL of an existing form in a workflow email hyperlink. Each time you fill out a new InfoPath browser-based form, InfoPath uses a certain hyperlink. The following is an example of a new form hyperlink. Let's examine the following URL example. A question mark (?) appears before the first parameter in the URL, and ampersands (&) appear before each parameter thereafter:

Note Chapter 8, "Using the InfoPath Form Web Part," has a section dedicated to URL query strings and parameters.

http://forms.contoso.com/_layouts/FormServer.aspx?XsnLocation=http://forms.contoso.
com/helpsite/HelpDesk/Forms/template.xsn&SaveLocation=http%3A%2F%2Fforms%2E
contoso%2Ecom%2FHelpsite%2FHelpDesk&ClientInstalled=true&Source=http%3A%2F%
2Fforms%2Econtoso%2Ecom%2FHelpsite%2FHelpDesk%2FForms%2FAllItems%2Easpx&
DefaultItemOpen=1

The elements that make up the preceding hyperlink are described here:

- **http://*mysiteurl*/_layouts/FormServer.aspx**   This is a part of the URL because InfoPath Forms Services is being used for this browser-based form.

- **XsnLocation=http://*mysiteurl*/*LibraryName*/Forms/template.xsn**   The location of the form's template.

- **SaveLocation=http://*mysiteurl*/*LibraryName***   This is needed only for forms that use the Save buttons in the form toolbar. This is not required if users are utilizing submit functionality only. See Chapter 6, for more detailed information about submitting versus saving.

- **ClientInstalled=true**   Not required.

- **Source=http://*mysitehomepage***   The part of the URL that instructs the form where to redirect the user after he has filled out the form. A best practice is to use the URL of your home page so that the user never needs to navigate to the form library if you do not want them to.

- **DefaultItemOpen=1**   An important part of the URL that ensures that the form will be opened in the browser and not InfoPath Filler.

In the following exercise, you will create a button on the home page called "Fill Out a New Request." An image will be uploaded to SharePoint to be used as the button.

SET UP Open your Help Desk System site in the browser. Place the **NewFormButton.png** resource file in the folder called C:\InfoPath Files.

1. Click **Site Actions**, and then click **Edit Page**.

2. Click **Add a Web Part** in the middle of the page.

3. In the **Media and Content** category, select the **Content Editor** Web Part, and then click the **Add** button.

4. Click **Click here to add new content**.

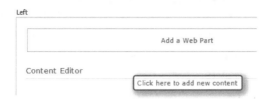

Picture

5. Type **Fill Out a New Request**, and then on the **Insert** tab, click the **Picture** button.

6. In the **Select Picture** dialog box, click the **Browse** button. Browse to **C:\InfoPath Files**, and then double-click **NewFormButton.png**. Back in the **Select Picture** dialog box, click **OK**.

   Note The Site Assets library was automatically created during the preceding exercise when the images were placed in the XSLT list view Web Part. This is the same library where this new form button is being placed.

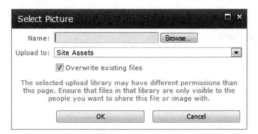

7. Click the **Save** button, and then on the **Page** tab, click **Stop Editing**.

New
Document ▾

8. In the **Quick Launch** pane, click the **Help Desk Requests** link. On the ribbon, on the **Documents** tab, click **New Document**.

9. In the address bar at the top of the browser, select the URL, and then press **Ctrl+C** to copy it to the clipboard.

10. Paste the URL in Microsoft Word or Notepad (or any text editor) so that you can take a look at it to gain a better understanding of the components.

After taking out the parts that are not needed, using the syntax explained earlier, the URL now looks like this: http://forms.contoso.com/_layouts/FormServer. aspx?XsnLocation=http://forms.contoso.com/helpsite/HelpDesk/Forms/template. xsn&Source=http://forms.contoso.com/helpsite&DefaultItemOpen=1.

11. Copy this new URL to the clipboard.

12. In the browser, click the **Back** button, to go back to the **Help Desk System** home page. Click **Site Actions**, and then click **Edit Page**.

13. In the **Content Editor** Web Part, click to select the image that was inserted in step 6. On the **Insert** tab, click **Link**.

14. Paste the hyperlink in the **Address** text box, and then click **OK**.

 15. On the ribbon, on the **Format Text** tab, click the **HTML** button, and then select **Edit HTML Source**. Type **border="0"** in the IMG tag, and then click **OK**.

Note When the hyperlink was created on the image, this caused a blue square border to appear around the new form button. This is undesirable, so we have used code to remove the border.

16. At the upper-right of the **Content Editor** Web Part, click the black drop-down arrow and then select **Edit Web Part**.

17. Expand the **Appearance** section, and change the **Chrome Type** value to **None**. Click **OK**. This removes the chrome so that the name of the Web Part will not be displayed, because it is not needed for this new form button.

Tip When the term "chrome" is used, it is referring to the frame of the web part—the box around it. The Chrome Type is a setting in the properties of every SharePoint web part.

On the **Page** tab, click **Stop Editing**.

The Web Part is complete. Now, when people visit this site, it will be clear how to do what they need. Users can click a button to fill out a new form, or they can open one of their existing forms.

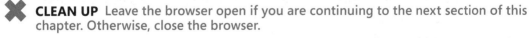 **CLEAN UP** Leave the browser open if you are continuing to the next section of this chapter. Otherwise, close the browser.

> ### Wireframes
>
> Your own sites will be created according to the requirements of each individual project. A best practice is to draw out or diagram the wireframes of a site. Wireframes are a simplistic way of sketching out the basics for the way information will be presented on a page, with no regard to colors or branding. When you talk to the business about each new form and process, use what you learned in Chapter 2, "Form Requirements: Using a Decision Matrix," to gather requirements about the data and form fields. Then use what you learned in this chapter to gather requirements pertaining to the user interface of the SharePoint site. Talk through and wireframe all of the Web Parts, pages, and views to ensure that everyone is in agreement and to eliminate multiple iterations of the solution. There are even software products available whose sole purpose is mockups and wireframing.

Dashboards Based on Form Libraries

Now that you have seen how to put together a Help Desk site with a robust form and several custom views, the last step is to utilize the power of SharePoint to create a dashboard for some basic reporting on the information in the forms. Too often, form designers become so focused on the forms that they forget about the power of SharePoint to aggregate the promoted properties of the form and to build KPIs and other types of reports on it. SharePoint has many Web Parts that can be used to increase the value of the data collected in your forms, and certainly you don't want to overlook KPIs and the Content Query Web Part.

In the next two exercises, you will learn how to use the SharePoint KPI Web Part and the Content Query Web Part to build a dashboard for Help Desk managers to monitor the performance and service levels of the Help Desk. The requirements you have been tasked with for the dashboard page are as follows:

- A KPI that reports the average number of days to resolve a request
- A KPI that indicates how many of the high-priority requests are resolved in three days or less
- A KPI that displays the total number of active requests
- A Web Part that shows the top three rated Help Desk requests that are status = resolved
- A Web Part that shows the oldest three requests that remain in active status

Dashboard Pages and Content Query Web Parts

 SET UP Open your Help Desk SharePoint site in the browser.

 New Page
Create a page you can
customize.

1. On the **Site Actions** menu, choose **New Page**, and then name it **Help Desk Dashboard**. Click **Create**.

   Tip In step 2 of the first exercise in this chapter, this site was created by using the Blank Site template. If you did not use this template, your experience on the site will be much different, and it will be difficult to follow the instructions in this exercise.

2. On the ribbon, on the **Page** tab, from the **Page Layout** drop-down box, select **Blank Web Part page**. Scroll down to the zone labeled **Top Left**, and then click **Add a Web part**.

3. In the Web Part **Categories** section, select **Content Rollup**. Select **Content Query** as the Web Part to add on the page, and then click the **Add** button.

4. Click the **open the tool pane** link to configure the Content Query Web Part.

   The goal with this first Content Query part is to display the three oldest Help Desk requests from the forms library.

5. In the tool pane, expand the **Query** section of the Web Part.

6. Select the **Show items from the following list** option, browse to the **Help Desk Request** form library, and then select it.

7. Set the **Additional filters** values so that the **Status** field is equal to **Active**.

   This ensures that the Web Part returns only Help Desk requests that are still being resolved.

8. Expand the **Presentation** section of the tool pane.

9. In the **Sort items by** drop-down box, select **Opened Date**. Change the **Limit the number of items to display** option to **3**.

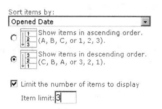

10. While still in the **Presentation** section of the tool pane, use the item style drop-down box to change the style to **Title, description and document icon**. Find the **Description** field in the **Fields to Display** section. Enter **Problem Description;** in the **Description** field. This adds the problem description text from the form to the data that the **Content Query** Web Part returns.

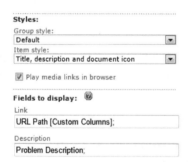

11. Expand the **Appearance** section of the tool pane, and change the **Title** field to **3 Oldest Active Requests**.

12. At the bottom of the tool pane, click **Apply**, and then click **OK**.

13. The dashboard page is still in edit mode, but it should now look similar to the following screenshot.

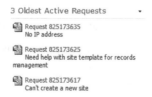

Note The possibilities are unlimited for the types of content queries you could display on a dashboard. Let these examples spur your imagination for what's most applicable in your business.

14. Add another **Content Query** Web Part to display the top three rated resolved requests so that you can monitor which Help Desk employees are doing great work. In the **Top Right** zone, add another **Content Query** Web Part on the page.

The steps to configure this one are very similar to the first with a few small changes. First, your query must include a filter to return only forms where the Status = Resolved, which you set in the **Additional Filters** section beneath **Query**.

Additional Filters:
Show items when:

| Status |
| is equal to |
| Resolved |

15. In the **Presentation** section, in the **Sort items by** drop-down box, select **Rating (0-5)**, change the **Item Limit** value to **3**, and then add **Category** as the data you want to pull into the **Description** field.

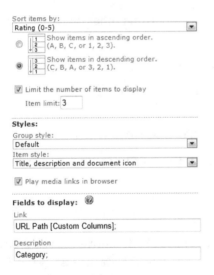

16. In the **Appearance** section, rename the **Title** to **Top 3 Rated Resolved Requests**. Click **Apply**, and then click **OK**.

17. On the ribbon, on the **Publish** tab, click **Publish**, and then click **Continue**. Your page should now look like the following screenshot:

3 Oldest Active Requests

📄 Request 829123612
Computer has been compromised.

📄 Request 825173617
Can't create a new site

📄 Request 825173606
this is some text about this thing here

Top 3 Rated Resolved Requests

📄 Request 825173531
Security-Virus

📄 Request 829123302
SharePoint Services

📄 Request 829123353
Microsoft Software

Congratulations! You now have a good start on a dashboard page that reports aggregate information from the Help Desk forms library for the management team.

 CLEAN UP Leave the browser open if you are continuing to the next exercise of this chapter. Otherwise, close the browser.

KPI Web Parts

Now you will add the following KPIs to support the other three requirements that have yet to be accomplished:

- A KPI that reports the average number of days to resolve a request
- A KPI that indicates how many of the high-priority requests are resolved in three days or less
- A KPI that displays the total number of active requests

To add KPIs to your Help Desk dashboard, you first need to add a Status List, which is where the following exercise begins.

SET UP Open your Help Desk SharePoint site in the browser.

Status List

1. In the **Site Actions** menu, select **View All Site Content,** click **Create**, and then scroll through the templates until you find the **Status List**. Name it **Help Desk Requests KPI List**, and then click **Create**.

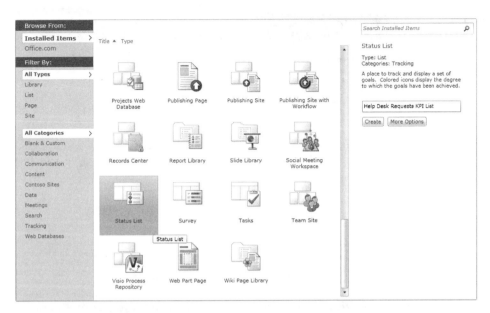

2. To add the indicators, click **New**, and then select **SharePoint List Based Indicator**.

3. Name the indicator **Number of Active Requests**. In the **List URL** field, select the library that holds the Help Desk Request forms.

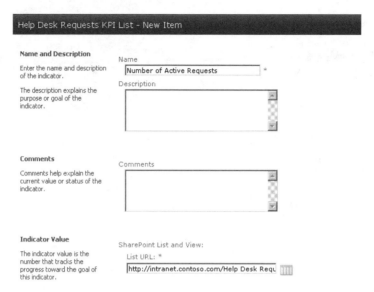

4. In the **View** drop-down box, select **Active Requests by Requestor**.

5. Scroll down to the bottom of the **Indicator** dialog box. Change it so that the **Better values are** field is set to **lower**. Because your Help Desk site is fairly small, you want to keep active requests lower than three, so set the green indicator value at **3**. Set the yellow value at **10** so that the status will be red if there are more than 10 requests.

6. Click **OK**. Your indicator is now added to the list. On your site, you have 4 active requests, so the indicator shows yellow status.

For your next two indicators, you want to display metrics related to the resolution time of requests. But to do that, the indicator needs a view on the form library that displays only the resolved requests. It also needs to have a calculated column that calculates the difference between the open and close dates. That will allow you to build a variety of KPIs related to resolution time.

7. In the **Library Settings** for the Help Desk Requests form library, create a new **calculated column** called **Total Days to Resolution**.

8. Using the **Insert Column** selector, insert the resolved date and opened date columns into the formula dialog, as shown in the following screenshot. Set the data type to **Number** and the number of decimal places to **0**. Clear the **Add to default view** check box.

9. In the **Help Desk** form library, on the ribbon, go to the library settings, and then click the **Create View** button. Select **Standard View**, and then name the view **Days to Resolution**.

10. In the columns section, place a check box next to the new **Total Days to Resolution** column. In the **Filter** section of the view settings, set the filter so that the **Status** column is equal to **Resolved**.

You now have a new calculated column that displays the total days to resolution for resolved help desk requests, in a new view.

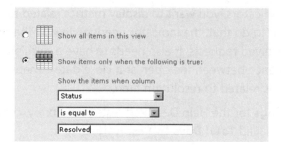

The next KPI you'll add calculates the number of requests that are resolved in 3 days or less.

11. Browse back to the **Help Desk Requests KPI** list. Add a new **SharePoint List Based Status indicator** named **Resolved in 3 days or less**.

12. In the **List URL** dialog, direct it to the **Help Desk Requests** form library. Change the **View** value to the **Days to Resolution** view you created previously in this exercise.

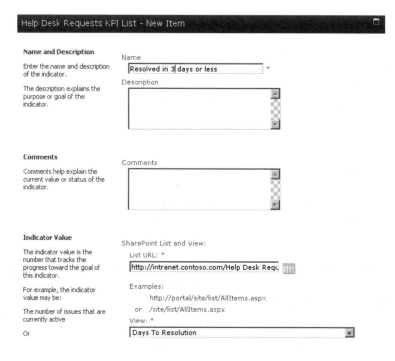

13. In the **Value Calculation** area, select the **Percentage of list items in the view where** option, and then select the **Total Days to Resolution** column. Set the Boolean drop-down to **is less than or equal to**, and then enter **3** in the value field.

14. The goal at the Help Desk is to have 80 percent of requests resolved in three days or less, so set the green indicator under the **Status Icon Rules** section at **80**. Set yellow at **50**, and then click **OK**. You now have a second indicator in your KPI list.

Status Icon Rules:
Better values are [higher ▾]

Display ⬤ when value has met or exceeded goal [80] *

Display ⚠ when value has met or exceeded warning [50] *

Display ◆ otherwise

15. Add another indicator in your KPI list using the settings in the following table, and then click **OK**.

Setting	Value
Name	Average Days to Resolution
List URL	Pick the Help Desk Requests library
View	Days to Resolution
Value Calculation	Calculation using all list items in the view.
	Average of Total Days to Resolution
Better values are	Lower
Display green	2
Display yellow	4

16. You should now have three indicators in your list, similar to the following screen-shot. Browse back to the **Help Desk Dashboard** page, and then click the **Edit** button to place the page in edit mode.

17. Add the Status List Web Part to the dashboard page that you created in the previous exercise by scrolling down to find the Web Part zone called **Header**, which is above the two other Web Parts on the page. Click **Add a Web Part**, select **Status List** from the **Business Data** category, and then click the **Add** button.

18. Open the **Status List** tool pane, and then in the **Indicator List** field, select the **Help Desk Requests KPI list**. Select the **Hide the Toolbar** check box. Click **OK** at the bottom of the tool pane.

19. On the ribbon, on the **Publish** tab, click the **Publish** button, and then click **Continue**.

You now have a useful Help Desk dashboard page that managers can use to quickly gather information about the performance of the Help Desk. In the preceding exercise, we've only scratched the surface of what's possible with the Content Query Web Part and KPIs. Experiment by adding your own performance metrics and queries.

![X] **CLEAN UP** That concludes the exercises for this chapter. Close your browser when finished with the exercise.

Key Points

- Multiple views can be created so that information can be sliced and diced in many different ways. This is a very simple method of reporting in SharePoint.

- Ratings can be used to allow other users to provide quick feedback about how useful a particular item is to them.

- Alerts can be created based on filtered views so that you can be notified about only a specific set of items that have been added or changed.

- Library Web Parts are also called list view Web Parts, and they can be placed on any Web Part page. Each Web Part can be configured with its own view settings.

- The current user filter Web Part can be used to filter columns that have a name value but that are not Person or Group fields.

- When the view settings that can be configured in the browser are not sufficient for what you are trying to accomplish, SharePoint Designer can be used to modify Web Parts and views.

- Create a new form button on your home page so that site visitors have a quick way to fill out a new InfoPath form. If your site has multiple InfoPath forms, you can create a button for each.

- Several useful Web Parts exist in SharePoint for presenting metrics and aggregated information from InfoPath form libraries.

- KPI Indicators are a great way to show the executives a concise snapshot of relevant information in a form library or a list.

Chapter at a Glance

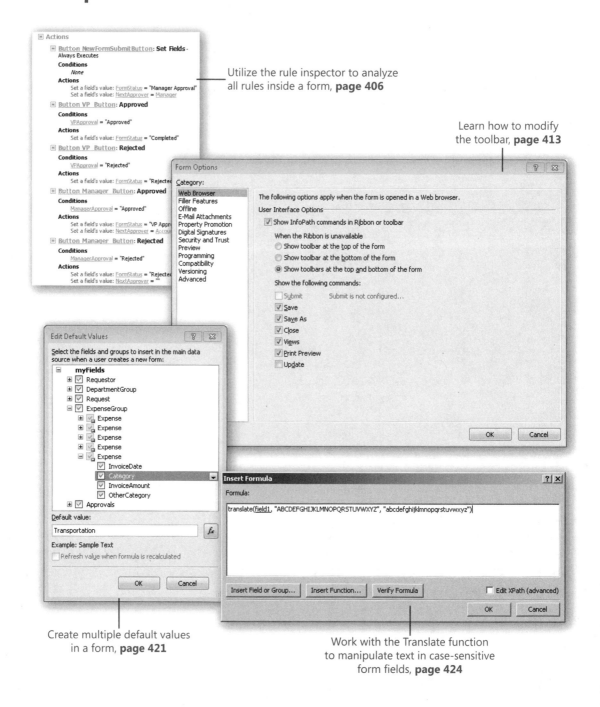

Utilize the rule inspector to analyze all rules inside a form, **page 406**

Learn how to modify the toolbar, **page 413**

Create multiple default values in a form, **page 421**

Work with the Translate function to manipulate text in case-sensitive form fields, **page 424**

14 Advanced Options

In this chapter, you will learn how to:

✔ Inspect and document a form's logic

✔ Merge data from multiple forms

✔ Relink XML forms to their XSN template file

✔ Set default values of items in a repeating table

✔ Weigh the options for filling out forms offline

In this book, we have tried to cover the major scenarios in which you can benefit from the use of Microsoft InfoPath with Microsoft SharePoint 2010. However, some topics either didn't fit neatly elsewhere or might have been covered too lightly and deserve a closer look. Therefore, this chapter is designed to help advance your understanding of a number of key InfoPath topics about which our real-world experience has taught us are valuable for InfoPath forms designers to be aware. So although this chapter is a collection of topics which might seem somewhat unrelated to one another, we believe they are important enough that they needed to be included in the book.

> **Practice Files** Before you can complete the exercises in this chapter, you need to copy the book's practice files to your computer. The practice files you'll use to complete the exercises in this chapter are in the Chapter 14 practice file folder. A complete list of practice files is provided in "Downloading the Practice Files and eBook," on page xxvi.

The InfoPath Rule Inspector

In Chapter 5, "Adding Logic and Rules to Forms," you learned all about form rules. You might have deduced that when rules have been created on controls and as form load rules, forms can become a bit complex with various rules affecting different fields in the form. This is where the InfoPath Rule Inspector can help.

The Rule Inspector is a tool that can be used to analyze all of a form's rules. Not only can you view the big picture, as a list of all rules in the form, but any specific field can be targeted. To access the Rule Inspector, on the ribbon, on the Data tab, simply click the Rule Inspector button. You can click any of the orange hyperlinks if you want to see more details about a given field or rule. Alternatively, in the Fields pane on the right side of the screen, right-click any field name, and then click Rule Inspector.

The Rule Inspector is a great troubleshooting tool that can also be used for documentation. The tool provides a print button, so if all of the logic behind the form needs to be saved with a project's documentation or inspected further, you can print out a hardcopy.

Tip Office 2010 has built-in functionality for sending a file to Microsoft OneNote instead of to an actual printer. When you click the Print button and choose Send To OneNote 2010, you are prompted to pick which notebook to save to. If you are using OneNote to take notes regarding each of your InfoPath projects, you can quickly save the rules as part of your documentation.

The Rule Inspector has four sections, with the rule information automatically categorized for you:

- Validation
- Calculated Default Values
- Actions
- Programming

The panel on the right has four sections that are specific to a selected field or group:

- Rules that depend on this field or group
- Rules that are triggered by a change in this field or group
- Rules that may change this field or group

At Contoso, a new InfoPath form specialist has been hired and is tasked with troubleshooting an InfoPath form. Somewhere hidden in the form's logic, its status field is being set to a value of "VP Approval", but it is not apparent how and where that is happening.

In the following exercise, you will open an existing form and use the Rule Inspector to examine some of the logic in the form. The Contoso Reimbursement form was built in Chapter 11, "Building an Approval Process," and has many different logic rules built in. You will explore the Rule Inspector and then pinpoint the place in the form where the FormStatus is being set to "VP Approval".

SET UP Open **ContosoReimbursementFinal.xsn** in Design mode, and then switch to the New view. This is done on the Page Design tab by clicking the View drop-down box and then selecting the New (default) view.

1. On the **Data** tab, click **Rule Inspector**.

2. Scroll through the list of rules to see all the rule information. Click any orange link to see more information about that item, which will appear in a new pane on the right.

3. Close the **Rule Inspector** dialog.

4. In the **Fields** pane on the right side in InfoPath, expand the **Hidden** section, right-click the **FormStatus** field, and then click **Rule Inspector**.

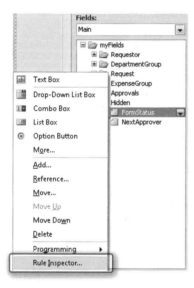

5. In the right pane of the **Rule Inspector** dialog, scroll down to the section **Rules that may change this field or group**.

   For troubleshooting, assume that you are trying to figure out when and why the **FormStatus** field is being changed to **"VP Approval"**. You can find the action where the form status is set to this value, and you know that it happens when a button is clicked, but because the buttons do not have appropriate labels, you have no way to know which button it is. It's time to fix the button labels so that they are more useful.

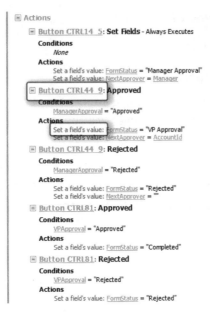

6. Close the **Rule Inspector** dialog again. In InfoPath Designer, double-click to select the **Submit** button.

7. On the **Properties** tab, click the **Control Properties** button.

   Tip You can also press Alt+Enter to open a control's properties.

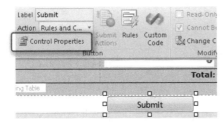

8. In the **ID** box, type **NewFormSubmitButton**, and then click **OK**.

9. On the **Page Design** tab, use the **View** drop-down box to switch the current view to **Approvals**.

10. In the **Manager Approval** section, select the **Submit** button, and then press **Alt+Enter** to open the control's properties.

11. In the **ID** box, type **Manager_Button**, and then click **OK**.

12. Repeat steps 10 and 11 for the **Submit** button in the **VP Approval** section. In the **ID** box, type **VP_Button**.

    Now that all of the form's buttons have been given more descriptive IDs, the rules in the **Rule Inspector** will make more sense.

13. Right-click the **FormStatus** field again, and then select **Rule Inspector**.

14. In the **Rules that may change this field or group** section, take a look at the **Actions** section again.

    You are searching for the place in the form where the FormStatus is changed to **"VP Approval"**. The value that you are looking for can be found in the rules, and now that all of the buttons have been labeled correctly, notice that the **Manager_ Button** is the one that is being clicked and that the rule is called **Approved**. The rule name is depicted in bold black text next to the name of the button.

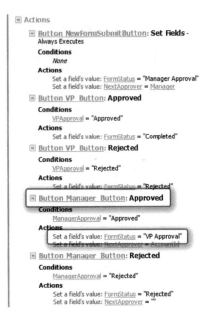

15. Close the **Rule Inspector** dialog box.

16. In the **Manager Approval** section, double-click the **Submit** button, and then on the ribbon, click **Manage Rules**.

17. In the **Rules** pane on the right, click to select the **Approved** rule.

    Problem solved! There is the action that sets the **FormStatus** field to **"VP Approval"**.

CLEAN UP Click the Save button to save the XSN file to your computer, and then close InfoPath Designer.

In the preceding exercise, you learned how to document and troubleshoot form logic. This example form is relatively simple, but you can imagine how useful this skill will be as the complexity of the form increases.

Merging Forms

Merging InfoPath forms is a way to look at several forms that have been submitted to SharePoint, merged together as a single form. This is most useful when many different items exist in a form's repeating control, which need to be viewed in a single list.

By default, each form library in SharePoint has a view called Merge Documents. This view consists of all forms in the library, with a check box next to each form name. Multiple forms can be selected, and the Merge button on the ribbon is used to merge the selected forms together. An example of this default view is displayed in the following screenshot:

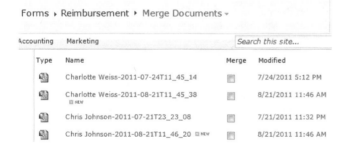

When any check boxes in the Merge column are selected, the contextual ribbon in SharePoint switches to the Documents tab. After all of the desired documents are selected, you can use the Merge button to generate a form that contains all of the forms combined together.

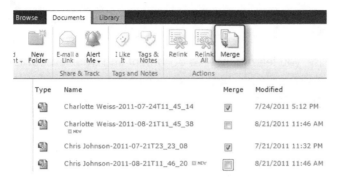

Important Before you can merge forms, the InfoPath client software must be installed on your computer.

Each control in your InfoPath form has an Advanced tab that contains merge settings, which allow the value in that field to be merged when form merging is done. For example, the following illustration shows the Control Properties screen for a repeating table. The Merge Settings button is in the middle of the screen.

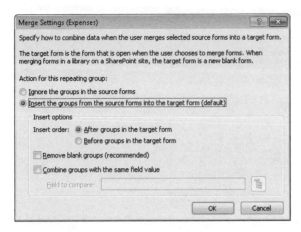

The preceding screenshot demonstrates that when the Merge Settings button is clicked, the following configuration actions can be performed:

- **Ignore the groups in the source forms**   Choose this setting to prevent a field or group from being merged. All of the other options on this screen are disabled if this is selected. The **Insert the groups from the source forms into the target form** option is the default and is the opposite of this setting.

- **Insert order**   By default, when multiple forms are selected to be merged, they are merged in the order in which they are seen in the Merge Documents view. With this setting, you can select the order in which the merged information is added to the form.

- **Remove blank groups**   If there are empty rows in the repeating table, you can use this option to skip them when the merge executes.

- **Combine groups with the same field value**   If multiple items in the merged forms contain the same value for the field that you select here, they will be treated as a single item when the forms are merged.

When dealing with controls that are not repeating, the default settings are a bit different. A text box has default merge settings that appear (see the following screenshot).

Note that text boxes are not set up to merge by default. For each control that is not a repeating one, if the value in this control needs to be merged, this setting should be changed to Combine The Value In The Target Form With The Values From The Source Forms.

The following settings can be further configured:

- **Ignore blank fields**   Choose this setting to skip data from forms that do not have a value in this field.

- **Separate each item with**   Use this drop-down box to select a separator character such as a space or a comma.

- **Prefix each item with**   Pick a field to be used as a prefix for the data that is displayed in the field when it is merged with other forms. A useful field to select might be a field that contains the name of the person who filled out the form.

In addition to the preceding field level settings is a merge setting that applies to the form as a whole. Click File, choose Form Options, and then in the Advanced section, you can clear the Enable Form Merging check box if you would not like this to be an option for users.

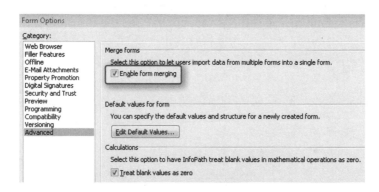

There is another way that forms can be merged; however, it requires that the InfoPath client software is being used. In the InfoPath Filler software, open any form, click File, and then click Save & Send. In the Import & Link section, click Merge Forms, and then click the Merge Forms button on the right.

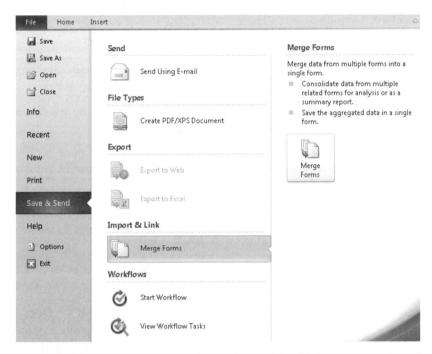

You will now be prompted to select a form with which to merge the current one. This part could be a bit tricky for end users, because they need the ability to browse to the form library by using its URL. Locate the existing form (XML file) with which to merge, and then click the Merge button.

Relinking Forms

As you learned in Chapter 1, "Introducing Microsoft InfoPath 2010," each form that has been filled out is an XML file. The form template on which the files are based is the XSN file. This XSN file is created by the form designer and published to SharePoint. Each time an existing form (XML file) is opened, there is a reference to the form's template, which is its XSN file. When a form template has been published to a form library, all the XML forms in that library are linked to the template. An example of the location of a library template would be the following URL:

http://SiteName/FormLibraryName/Forms/template.xsn

What does it mean to relink forms, and why would you need to do it? We'll go over how to relink forms, but first, here are two examples of situations in which forms need to be relinked:

- The SharePoint site URL has changed because the site has been moved or upgraded to a new location.
- The XML files have been physically moved to a new library.

If either situation occurs, the XML files are no longer linked to their XSN template and will need to be relinked to the correct XSN file location.

Follow these steps to relink forms:

1. Open the form library in the browser, and then on the ribbon, click the **Library** tab.

2. In the **Current View** drop-down box, select **Relink Documents**. Notice the descriptive text at the top of the page, which presents more information about relinking documents.

> Conotoso Forms › Reimbursement › Relink Documents ⌄
>
> Use this page to relink documents that are not correctly linked to their content type's document template. To relink all documents in this library, click Relink All Documents. To relink specific documents, select the Relink check box for each document you want to relink, and then click Relink Selected Documents. Before using this page, ensure that the "New" button works for each content type, and that each document is assigned to the correct content type, otherwise this page will link the documents incorrectly.

3. Select the **Relink** check box next to a document. Notice that the **Documents** tab on the ribbon displays two buttons: the **Relink** button for individual files that are selected or the **Relink All** button to relink all items in the library.

When the forms have been relinked to the correct XSN file, no problems or errors should occur when opening them.

Browser and Filler Buttons

A few default buttons exist in the toolbar of forms that are filled out in the filler and in the browser. You can also configure the settings in the Form Options dialog box to specify which buttons are shown or disabled.

The following illustration shows the Web Browser settings for the default screen for a new browser-based form.

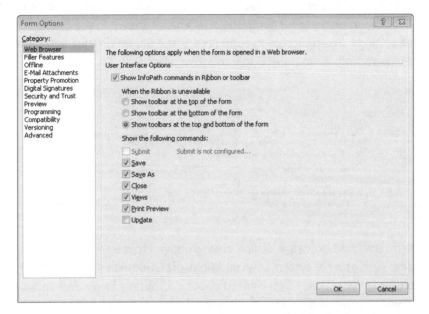

When a browser-based form is filled out, a toolbar is displayed at the top and bottom of the form. You can remove the toolbar or choose to display it only at the top or only at the bottom of the form. The form also displays a set of buttons, such as Save and Views, which can be individually added or removed. A Submit button will not exist until the first submit data connection has been created. If the form's compatibility level is not that of a browser-based form, this section will not exist in Form Options.

The Filler Features section of the Form Options screen appears as follows.

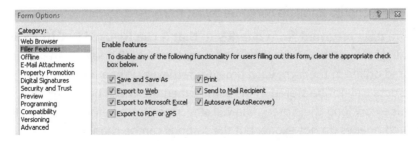

The options here are a bit different than the browser buttons. When using InfoPath Filler, the end user has several choices for exporting the form to other programs. You can disable any of these options by clearing the check box adjacent to it. If the Save and Save As option is not selected in this dialog box, the Save and Save As buttons in the Web Browser tab will be disabled.

Offline Forms

Several different methods are available in the Form Options dialog box for filling out InfoPath forms while the client computer is offline, as shown in the following screenshot. The same settings are applicable to form library and SharePoint list InfoPath forms. None of the offline settings or features apply to forms when they are filled out in the browser.

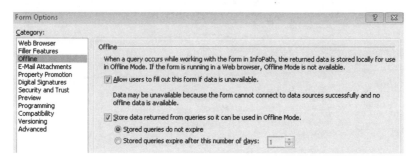

When forms are filled out while offline, they are saved to a temporary location other than SharePoint, such as a file system or even Microsoft Outlook. In Chapter 6, "Publishing and Submitting Form Data," you learned about submitting forms and about the difference between saving and submitting. When a form needs to be filled in offline, the form does need to have the Save and Save As features enabled in the Filler Features settings.

The offline settings are as follows:

- **Allow users to fill out this form if data is unavailable**   This setting refers to data connections that receive information. If this check box is left clear, if the form has data connections that receive data, and if that data is not stored in the form offline, users will receive an error when they try to fill out the form while offline. The error states that "One or more data sources required to fill out this form cannot be reached. Should InfoPath continue trying to connect to data sources for this form?"

- **Store data returned from queries so that it can be used in Offline Mode**   This setting refers to data connections that receive data. By default, the retrieved data is stored offline in the form each time it is retrieved. When this check box is left clear, the data will not be stored in the form. When the check box is selected, you can decide how long the stored data will stay in the form before it expires. By default, stored queries do not expire, but the settings can be changed to specify a certain number of days before the data expires and must be retrieved again. With this setting, before going offline, each user would have had to fill out this form by using InfoPath Filler. This would guarantee that the data is stored in the form.

- **Store a copy of the data in the form template**   The Data Connection Wizard presents a page that asks about storing a copy of the data in the form template. If you would like the data to be stored in the form template, select this check box. The data will be available in the form, whether or not the user filling out the form has a connection to the retrieved data. This setting is different from the previous bullet point because it is *not* necessary for each user to have filled out the form in InfoPath Filler to retrieve the data while online. The data is already stored in the form.

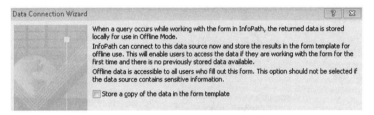

How does a user fill out a form if she can't get to SharePoint? If an end user has previously filled out a form by using InfoPath Filler, it is easy. The next time InfoPath Filler is opened, the program will remember recently used form templates; these templates will be available under the File menu when New is selected.

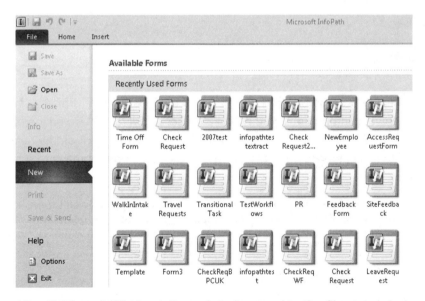

After the form is filled out, it needs to be saved to the file system instead of being submitted. When the user is back on the network again, the form's XML file can be opened and then submitted to SharePoint.

Offline Forms in Outlook

Outlook is another tool to use for filling out offline forms, and it even has some built-in InfoPath integration. InfoPath folders can be created in the Outlook client software, and Forms can be filled out from within Outlook without ever having to go to SharePoint. Be aware, however, that the InfoPath client software is required for using this functionality. From the Home tab, click the New Items button, select More Items, and then click Choose InfoPath Form.

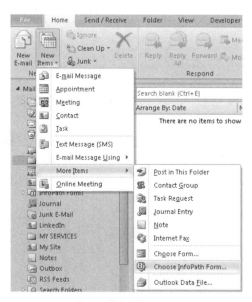

You are then be prompted to pick from a list of the most recent forms that you have filled out on your computer using the InfoPath Filler software. When working offline, you use the form's Save button to save a copy to Outlook. When back on the network, you need to remember to open that form and click the Submit button to submit it to SharePoint.

Important In Form Options, in the E-Mail Attachments section, by default there is a check box next to **Enable InfoPath e-mail form functionality for this form template**. If this box is check box is cleared, users will not have the ability to fill out this form from within Outlook.

Offline SharePoint List Forms

When working with SharePoint lists, the offline capabilities are a bit different. To work with SharePoint list forms and data offline, SharePoint Workspace 2010 is required. This software is a part of the Microsoft Office 2010 suite of products.

Sync to SharePoint
Workspace

Go to any SharePoint list whose form has been customized by using InfoPath. On the ribbon, on the List tab, click **Sync To SharePoint Workspace**.

Tip This button will be disabled if the SharePoint Workspace software has not been installed on your computer.

When viewing a SharePoint list inside of SharePoint Workspace, you can use the New button at the upper-left to create a new item in the list, whether you are currently online or offline.

A major difference between offline items in SharePoint Workspace and any other type of offline InfoPath form is that the next time your computer is online, your new or modified forms will automatically synchronize with the server according to the sync settings. With the other offline methods, the end user must remember to open the saved local copy of the form and then click the Submit button to submit to SharePoint; this is not done automatically.

Email Attachments

You can create a type of data connection that allows an email to be sent directly to someone from within InfoPath. Depending on the form's security settings, the form can be sent in the body of the email, and even filled out inside of the email. When working with InfoPath and SharePoint, the InfoPath email attachment functionality is inferior compared to sending an email via a SharePoint Designer workflow. The following table compares the email attachment data connection with sending an email by using a workflow.

Email Data Connection	Email Via Workflow
Email body consists of dynamic text only. There is no ability to insert form fields.	You can use form fields inside of a completely dynamic and customizable interface.
When the email is sent from within the form in the client software, the user is prompted with an extra dialog box that requires him to click a Send button.	As long as the workflow has been set up to run automatically when an item is created or changed, the email be sent without requiring any action on the user's part.

Tip Chapter 10, "InfoPath Integration with SharePoint Designer Workflows," and Chapter 11, "Building an Approval Process," provide information about how to create SharePoint Designer workflows.

When email attachment data connections are used, there are settings in the Form Options dialog box about which you should be aware. The following are the attachment options:

- **Always send the current view and the following attachments**   Select whether an attachment should be included in the email.

  - ○ **Form data**   The XML file is attached.

  - ○ **Form data and the form template**   The XML and the XSN template are attached.

  - ○ **None**   There are no attachments. Only a snapshot of the current view will be sent in the body of the email.

- **Enable InfoPath e-mail form functionality for this form template**   With this check box selected, users can fill out forms from within Outlook, as was described in the Offline Forms section, earlier in this chapter.

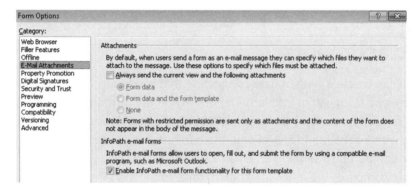

Tip One useful way to use email attachments is to send the form in the body of an email to a person to whom you do not want to give access to the SharePoint form library. This would be a case where the recipient is viewing read-only information.

Form Preview

In several of this book's exercises, forms have been previewed to see what they look like before being published. Previewing a form is a quick way to evaluate its appearance when it is being filled out, or to test rules and logic.

The Preview button is on the Home tab, and a smaller version of it is in the Quick Access Toolbar.

There are some extra settings for previewing forms that can be especially useful when troubleshooting. Take a look at the Preview section in the Form Options dialog box.

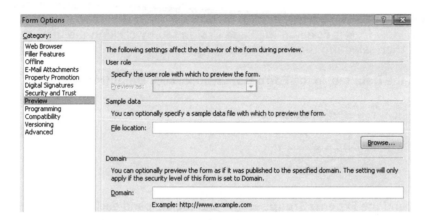

The following settings on the Form Options screen can be uniquely useful:

- **User Role**   User roles are available for non–browser-based forms only. For filler forms, when user roles have been created in the form, select the name of a role in the Preview As drop-down box. The next time you click the form's Preview button, you will be viewing it as if you were a member of that specific role.

- **File location**   This setting is great for troubleshooting. Browse to select the URL to one specific form that has been filled out (XML file), or simply paste the URL in the box. The next time you use the Preview button, the form is displayed as that specific form. An example of a use for this setting is when a user informs you that her form is giving an error or that she doesn't see a field that is supposed to be there. Use this feature to preview that specific form to dig deeper into the problem. As opposed to opening the form in the same way the end user would open it in the browser or filler, in InfoPath Designer you can put fields on the form or switch to different views that the end user might not have the ability to see. The syntax for the URL is http://YourSharePointSite/YourFormLibrary/OneSpecificFile.xml.

Default Values

In the following exercise, you will create default values for rows in a reimbursement request and test the functionality by previewing the form. Before getting started with the steps, click the Preview button to take a look at the list of expenses on the form. Notice that the list of expenses comprises two rows by default. More rows can be added by clicking Insert Another Expense. Close the preview. The goal of this exercise is to supply several default rows in this table, with each row having a common type of expense selected.

SET UP Open **ContosoReimbursementform.xsn** in Design mode, and then switch to the New view. This is done on the Page Design tab by clicking the View drop-down box and then selecting the New (default) view.

1. On the **Data** tab, in the **Form Data** section, click **Default Values**.

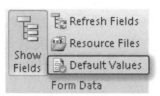

2. Expand the **ExpenseGroup** section, and then expand each **Expense** node. The blue icon next to each **Expense** section indicates that it is part of a repeating control.

3. In the first **Expense** section, click the **Category**. In the **Default value** box, type **Meals**.

4. Click the preview button in InfoPath to see the resulting behavior. The first row in the list of expenses has a default value now in the **Category** field.

Close
Preview

5. Close the preview.

6. On the **Data** tab, click **Default Values** again. A row will be added for each type of expense, which will give people a bit of a head start when filling in this reimbursement form.

7. In the second **Expense** section, click the drop-down box, and then click **Add another Expense below**.

8. Repeat step 7 twice, adding a fourth and fifth expense section.

9. Use the values in the following table to fill in the categories of all five expense sections under **ExpenseGroup**. This is a repeat of step 2.

Expense Section	Category Default Value
1	Meals
2	Airfare
3	Lodging
4	Parking
5	Transportation

10. Each of the five category fields now has default values. Click **OK**.

11. Preview the form again.

The end result is that the form has five rows in the list of expenses by default, and a different category is already selected for each row. More rows can also be added by clicking Insert Another Expense.

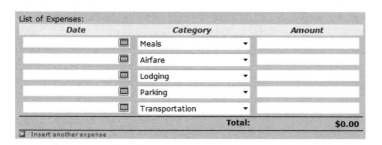

Anytime a repeating control is required to have a pre-existing number of rows, this method can be used to add more rows and optionally add default values to them.

 CLEAN UP Click the Save button to save the XSN file to your computer, and then close InfoPath Designer.

The Other Category

During the exercise in which you learned about default values, you might have noticed an extra text box in the Design view of the form. This text box is used in situations where the Other category is selected. When Other is selected from the drop-down box, users can type in the name of any category that is not already listed. Take a look at the rules behind the controls in the category column, as a bonus, to learn how this functionality was accomplished.

Advanced Functions

In Chapter 5, you were introduced to InfoPath functions when we introduced the concepts of functions and then used the *concat* and *now* functions in an exercise. While most of the functions in InfoPath are self-explanatory, there is one common question that form designers have that concerns use-cases for which the requirement dictates the necessity to have an automatic conversion of some text from uppercase to lowercase or vice versa. Your forms might need this for any number of reasons—for example, to compare two fields for which case sensitivity matters. Another example is ensuring that a field that must be all uppercase or lowercase in fact is—even if the user didn't enter it properly.

The InfoPath function that supports this requirement is called *Translate*. This function has three arguments that will return a converted text string. The first argument defines what the text string is, the second argument states which characters to change in the string, and the last argument specifies what to change the characters to. The characters in the second argument are converted to the characters in the third argument's matching position. Because the characters in the second position are converted to match the third argument, *Translate* is also a useful function for stripping unwanted characters out of a string by providing a null value in the third argument.

The following exercise will help you to understand how to use *Translate* to convert the case from whatever the user entered to all lowercase.

SET UP Open InfoPath Designer, and then create a new Blank form.

1. Add two **Text Box** controls to the form.

2. Right-click the second **Text Box** control to open the properties dialog box.

3. Click **Default Value**, and then click the **Insert Formula** button.

4. Select **Insert Function**, and then in the **Text** category, select **Translate**.

5. In the **Insert Formula** dialog box, double-click the first **insert field** link, and then select the first text box control you added to your form (probably named **Field1**).

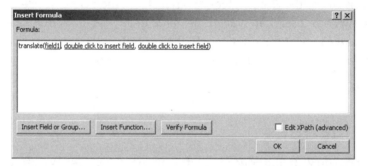

6. Replace the other two **double click to insert field** items with the following text: **"ABCDEFGHIJKLMNOPQRSTUVWXYZ"**, **"abcdefghijklmnopqrstuvwxyz"**. This must be typed exactly as shown.

   Note Remember, the **Translate** function takes the second argument and converts it to the third. So what you're doing here is telling the formula to convert anything in the first text control that is typed in uppercase to lowercase. You could also do the opposite direction.

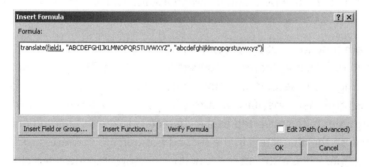

7. Click **OK** twice to go back to the form, and then preview it.

8. Enter some combination of uppercase and lowercase characters in the first text box, and press **Tab**.

   You should see the characters appear in the second text field as a default value, but all have been converted to lowercase.

| JOHNDOE@ acmeCorp.com |
| johndoe@ acmecorp.com |

 CLEAN UP Click the Save button to save the XSN file to your computer if you want to keep it, and then close InfoPath Designer.

If you'd like to see another, more sophisticated example of how to use the handy *Translate* function, open the Help Desk template from Chapter 13, "SharePoint Views and Dashboards." In this form, the Create New Request button has a submit rule on it. The first Action on the Submit rule is to set the RequestID field value.

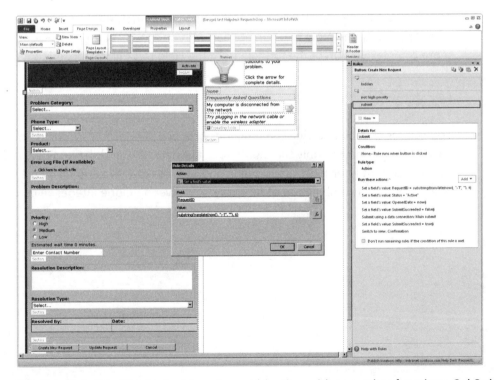

The *Translate* function is used here in combination with two other functions, *SubString* and *Now*.

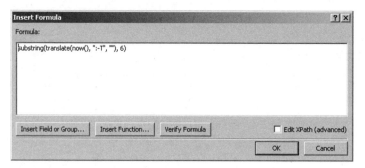

The goal here is to create a Request ID that is generated from the *Now* function but to strip off several unwanted characters and start returning values at the sixth position. So the *Translate* function takes the Now value as its first argument. The second argument shows what text you want to be replaced. Any text that is :, or –, or T will be replaced by the third argument, which is just a null value in quotes. In other words, get rid of anything that equals :, or –, or T.

To further illustrate and clarify, in the following screenshot, the first field is a standard text control with the Now function applied with no modification. The second has the more complex version of the formula from the Help Desk form applied to it.

You can see that by applying the functions properly, the form is stripping out unwanted characters and leaving only the month (08), the date (26), and the numbers that represent the current hour (06), minutes (46), and seconds (52). We end up with a very effective way to use a combination of functions to deliver a unique integer value for the ID field of the form.

Key Points

- The Rule Inspector can be used for troubleshooting and documentation of rules.

- Forms can be merged when repeating control information needs to be displayed in one form all together, using data from multiple forms.

- Relinking forms reestablishes the connection between an XML file and its lost XSN template.

- You can choose the toolbar buttons that are displayed in the browser and InfoPath filler.

- There are several different methods by which users can fill out forms when they are not on the network, with several different settings for the form designer to understand.

- SharePoint Designer workflow emails are preferable to sending a form via the email data connection.

- Specific forms can be previewed, which can be used as a troubleshooting method.

- Default values can be set up for repeating controls, which is applicable when there is a set of static choices.

- The *Translate* function is a useful and powerful mechanism for manipulating text, especially when combined with other functions.

Index

D

G

H

I

X

Y

About the Authors

Darvish Shadravan is employed at Microsoft where he has spent nearly 15 years in a variety of technical positions. He currently holds the title of Senior Technical Specialist. For the past six years he has been focused on the SharePoint and Office products, helping enterprise customers understand how to most effectively deploy and leverage the Microsoft collaboration platform. Along the way, he has spoken at several SharePoint events worldwide, often representing the InfoPath Product Group. You can contact Darvish via Twitter @dshadravan or find him on LinkedIn.

Laura Rogers is a Senior SharePoint Consultant at SharePoint911, and a Microsoft MVP. She has seven years of experience in SharePoint implementation, training, customization and administration. Her focus is on making the most of SharePoint's out-of-the-box capabilities. She works extensively with SharePoint Designer workflows, InfoPath and Data View Web Parts. Laura's previous books are *Beginning SharePoint 2010: Building Business Solutions with SharePoint*, and *Professional SharePoint 2010 Administration* (both published by Wrox). Her blog is *http://www.sharepoint911.com/blogs/laura*, and she is *@WonderLaura* on Twitter.

How To Download Your eBook

To download your eBook, go to

http://go.microsoft.com/FWLink/?Linkid=224345

and follow the instructions.

Please note: You will be asked to create a free online account and enter the access code below.

Your access code:

BXBVDHL

[Using Microsoft® InfoPath® 2010 with Microsoft® SharePoint® 2010 Step by Step]

Your PDF eBook allows you to:

- Search the full text
- Print
- Copy and paste

Best yet, you will be notified about free updates to your eBook.

If you ever lose your eBook file, you can download it again just by logging in to your account.

Need help? Please contact: **mspinput@microsoft.com**

Now that you've read the book...

Tell us what you think!

Was it useful?
Did it teach you what you wanted to learn?
Was there room for improvement?

Let us know at http://aka.ms/tellpress

Your feedback goes directly to the staff at Microsoft Press,
and we read every one of your responses. Thanks in advance!